LOVE ROCK REVOLUTION

K RECORDS and the Rise of INDEPENDENT MUSIC

MARK BAUMGARTEN

Foreword by Stella Marrs

SASQUATCH BOOKS
SEATTLE

Printed in the United States of America

Published by Sasquatch Books
17 16 15 14 13 12   9 8 7 6 5 4 3 2 1

Cover design: Anna Goldstein
Interior design and composition: Anna Goldstein
Interior photographs: Beat Happening concert in Olympia at the North Shore Surf Club, courtesy of K Records (page 1); Beat Happening performing in Chicago, March 1991, by Marty Perez (page 139); The Hive Dwellers performing at Northern in Olympia, June 1, 2009, by Judith Baumann (page 223)

Lyrics and logo reprinted with the permission of K Records.

Library of Congress Cataloging-in-Publication Data
Baumgarten, Mark.
  Love rock revolution : K Records and the rise of independent music / Mark Baumgarten.
        p. cm.
Includes index.
ISBN 978-1-57061-822-2
1. K Records (Firm) 2. Sound recording industry—Washington (State)—Olympia. 3. Punk rock music—Washington (State)—Olympia—History and criticism. I. Title.
ML3792.K2B38 2012
781.6609797'79--dc23

                      2012001170

Sasquatch Books
1904 Third Avenue, Suite 710
Seattle, WA 98101
(206) 467-4300
www.sasquatchbooks.com
custserv@sasquatchbooks.com

SUSTAINABLE FORESTRY INITIATIVE
Label applies to the text stock

Certified Sourcing
www.sfiprogram.org
SFI-00341

CONTENTS

WHAT I LEARNED IN OLYMPIA:

A FOREWORD BY STELLA MARRS

THE OLYMPIA I REMEMBER had a culture of a commons. The commons as the party, or show space, or access to tools, or information like mailing lists and touring contacts. Continual sharing of resources was the only way production could happen. There were always chances to play publicly through small house shows and spaces that came and went. Languages developed, and bands evolved from the inspiration of last week's shows. It was a culture full of examples of "making" that allowed us to model for each other "how to do it."

I have a memory from the early '80s of John Foster performing his epically long song "The Kennedy Saga." Against a musical backdrop of physical endurance and repetition, John was rocking back and forth, singing an inventory of the mythic hardships for our dead American hero. The preening cock-rock god of the dominant music culture had been replaced by a new face of virility that was not afraid to cry. I also remember teenaged Calvin Johnson on his knees, surrounded by cardboard boxes, in the living room of a house without insulation that he and I shared on Legion Way. Day and night, day after day, he alphabetized and cataloged a collection of 16,000 records that were being warehoused. It set a new bar for me, witnessing these models of intensity and focus.

Once I came back from a trip and there was a buzz of a new development. There would be an alley show! It was a new way to have a party: an out-of-the-way piece of pavement, a candle, and a guitar. Why not play when the stakes are that low?

Living in a small college town, making experimental work was an isolated activity. You also had to provide a structure for the work to live within. So these early venues for music, writing, and art emerged in order to extend our work locally and beyond. The originators: Mr. Brown, *OP Magazine*, Sub Pop, Girl City, and K Records. Then later waves: Kill Rock Stars, Punk in My Vitamins, Cha Cha Cabaret, and so many, many more.

But really, how did any of it happen? Circulating beneath this story is a current of desire. It was the underlying engine for everything that happened. A creative culture of individuals surviving by sharing space and tools, and aiming at a series of frenzied public deadlines? Late night waffle parties and shared beds, all that borrowing, arguing, and scraping it together? *Totally fun!*

INTRODUCTION

LET ME SAY FIRST that this is not my story.

I was born in 1978, just months after the hero of this book received his broadcasting license from the FCC and started playing records at his local college radio station. I grew up in a small farm town in Wisconsin, far from the sleepy, green capital city where this story primarily takes place. Prior to my college years, I had heard of a few of the bands that appear in these pages, but knew the music of only one artist who had released a full-length album on K Records: Beck.

Even if curiosity had led me from Beck's breakout major-label debut, *Mellow Gold*, to the relatively obscure album he released on K Records just a few months later, I probably wouldn't have thought anything of it.

I wasn't lazy or stupid. I just didn't understand that something like K Records could exist. I loved music, but as a kid growing up in a small farm town, there were few places I could discover it. I found it on my parents' record shelf, where LPs by Roger Miller and John Denver leaned up against *The Dukes of Hazzard* soundtrack and "Disco Duck." I also found it on Z93, a radio station fifty miles away that played the Kenny Loggins theme from *Footloose* so often that, despite having never seen the movie, I biked to the local Pamida department store and bought the soundtrack—a cassette, my first. I played the tape incessantly. When Cyndi Lauper performed on the American Music

Awards in 1985, I held my small Panasonic tape recorder up to the television and pressed "record."

Never did I imagine meeting Kenny Loggins or Cyndi Lauper. They were more ideas than real people, voices on the radio as distant from me as the astronauts I hoped to someday join in space.

My cousin Kurt provided the gateway to a different type of music. Kurt was eight years older than me and the coolest guy I knew. I remember walking into his room and quickly past a frightening Iron Maiden plaque to stare at a giant poster of Eddie Van Halen holding a ruby red guitar gloriously festooned with haphazard white stripes. A few years later, Kurt went off to study engineering at the University of Wisconsin.

One day he came home from school and brought my older brother Eric a cassette tape with two dozen songs recorded on it. I don't remember them all, but I do know that there was no Van Halen. Instead I heard all of this wonderful, strange music: "Don Henley Must Die" by Mojo Nixon, "Holiday in Cambodia" by the Dead Kennedys, and my favorite, "Punk Rock Girl" by the Dead Milkmen.

My brother and I listened to the tape constantly, we fought over it, and when we heard that the Dead Milkmen would be playing in that big town fifty miles away, we went. There, in a little, dark all-ages club, we saw a band play live, close enough to touch. We screamed and we danced and then we went home, exhausted but exhilarated.

This isn't a book about the Dead Milkmen. What happened that night of my first concert, though, is what this book is all about. At that moment, dancing wildly to my favorite band playing my favorite song, music changed for me. It was no longer about listening; it became about joining in. When I moved to Minneapolis, I started writing about music, putting on all-ages shows on Sunday afternoons at a bar near campus, guest DJing at my campus radio station, and playing music with friends in drafty lofts and practice spaces. Eventually I moved to the Pacific Northwest to focus on writing and to be part of the flourishing independent music scene in Portland, Olympia, and Seattle. I soon discovered that the things I had been doing in Minneapolis were of the same sort that served as the foundation for the culture of independence that sustained the Northwest's wealth of fearlessly inventive artists. As I dug deeper into the history of the Northwest artists I loved—Elliott Smith, Built to Spill, Modest Mouse, Sleater-Kinney, Nirvana—I discovered a common root: K Records. As I explored K Records, I discovered new favorites— Beat Happening, Heavenly, and, most of all, the Halo Benders. What I didn't discover was much of a coherent narrative about how all of this amazing music came from the same place. More puzzling to me was how K could be responsible for so much and still be so obscure. There must be a story here, I thought.

As I began uncovering the story of K Records, I found that the most compelling part was not how the label had grown from its meager beginnings as a cassette label in 1982, but how little it had changed. Currently operating out of an old synagogue near downtown Olympia, the label maintains its underground bona fides in both business practice and, in many cases, sonic fidelity. Music from its bands is now available in CD, LP, and digital formats, but the songs maintain the lo-fi aesthetic that was established with early cassette releases recorded straight to a boom box. K has a history of its bands going on to bigger and better things, but Calvin Johnson still believes in the handshake deal and the same generous terms that he gave for his first release thirty years ago: the label and the talent split all profits down the middle. Independent labels around the world might accept the idea that corporate cash—in the form of an ownership stake or licensing deals—is now an inevitable part of doing business, but K stands by its long-held credo, which greets anyone visiting the label's website: "The K revolution is exploding the teenage underground into passionate revolt against the corporate ogre."

To create this story, I spent hour upon hour conducting interviews and paging through books, zines, and volume upon volume of the Pacific Northwest's late, and great, music monthly *The Rocket*. I blindly typed names into search engines in the hope that a personal story, interview, or, miraculously, a video might surface to breathe life into another part of an expansive story that has touched so many lives. I sent queries through my social network, hoping that the hive mind could help bring the dots I was connecting closer together. Oftentimes I was lucky and those broad queries resulted in long phone calls or in-person interviews with characters I had not yet been able to track down. In a couple cases, sources that weren't interested in speaking contacted me after a question that they could answer appeared on their computer screens.

I know I've captured only part of the story here, and I am sure that I have gotten a few points wrong, but everything that I have set down in this book I believe to be true. I couldn't say such a thing with such confidence if I lived in a time when other people's stories and songs weren't so readily available, where people weren't so free to speak their minds.

An earlier version of that democratization of information is the linchpin of the K story. Without Xerox machines to create zines, cheap recording technology to create cassettes, and all-ages spaces to help foster speech (and song) for all to hear, the revolution would have remained just an idea trapped in someone's journal. What that revolution, the love rock revolution, has accomplished is profound. With apologies to Marshall McLuhan, the purpose of a revolution can be found in the manner its messages have been shared. In the case of K, the sharing was done in the spirit of honest and brave experimentation, the root of all wonderful and inspiring art. That idea of sharing without fear is at the heart of K's revolutionary act. Rock was how these artists chose to share. Love is what came from their fearlessness in doing so.

Unfortunately we live in a culture obsessed with winners. The dominant narratives of our time are told by them. The problem with the story of K is that the label has never been a winner in the marketplace. The stories of other record labels have been told with writers filling in the gaps between hit records. With K, there are no hit records. Its story has largely remained a mystery. But if you just hear the stories of the "winners" in our world, you aren't getting the whole story. You aren't hearing some of the best parts.

There are people who became winners in this book, those who went on to fame and fortune. But this is not a story about them. When I first sat with Calvin Johnson to talk about his record label, he told me that most of the journalists who have wanted to talk to him have only been interested in the famous people who have crossed his path. He was happy, he said, to just tell the story of what happened. Most of the other people I interviewed were happy to do the same—to tell the story of feeding culture even if it never, really, fed their bank accounts.

I found myself profoundly inspired by the stories I was told in the course of researching this book, by the music I heard, and by the great quantity of love, hope, and heartbreak that this story contains. I hope, for you, that I have managed to share even a sliver of that inspiration. I only wish I could share the pleasure of having the chorus to "Teenage Caveman" stuck in your head, constantly, for six months straight.

PART I

YOUTH

I know the secret: rock 'n' roll is a teenage sport, meant to be played by teenagers of all ages—they could be 15, 25, or 35. It all boils down to whether they've got the love in their hearts, that beautiful teenage spirit.

—Calvin Johnson, 17, in a letter to the *New York Rocker* (1979)

THE FIRST SONG that Calvin Johnson ever loved was "Little Green Apples." A country ballad written by Bobby Russell, the song was made popular by R & B singer O. C. Smith in 1968, when Calvin was six years old, living with his parents and his older brother and sister in Baltimore.

Music was elusive for Calvin. His family wasn't especially musical, so he gleaned pop music knowledge on his own. Like most kids in the late '60s, he spent his Saturday mornings watching *The Monkees* on television. "The Monkees were cool because they were funny," Calvin recalls. "But I didn't know any of their songs." He also discovered the Beatles through the band's weekly animated series, but the thick accents and strange art turned Calvin off. As a young man, he wrote off the greatest band of the century as boring, paying little mind to their music.

Music popped up elsewhere in his life. He heard it on the car radio while going to school or running errands with his mom. But it was at the local YWCA, where his mom worked, that Calvin discovered "Little Green Apples."

"They had a jukebox that cost a nickel, but it always gave the nickel back," Calvin says.

There, Calvin would sit and listen to "Little Green Apples" for free, feeding that same nickel in again and again. "There's no such thing as Dr. Seuss," Smith sang, "or Disneyland and Mother Goose, no nursery rhyme . . ."

In 1970 Calvin's family moved across the country to a small town on Washington State's Olympic Peninsula. A more monumental shift occurred a few months later, when Calvin's older brother, Streator, bought a small AM radio. Isolated by geography and youth, Calvin listened religiously to the Top 40 radio stations picked up by the small radio. At the time, the charts were dominated by British men, including the first post-Beatles output from John Lennon ("Imagine") and George Harrison ("My Sweet Lord") and definitive songs by Rod Stewart ("Maggie May") and the Rolling Stones ("Brown Sugar"). For Calvin, though, the era was defined by the music of American women.

Three songs teased Calvin's curious mind: "Rose Garden" by Lynn Anderson, Joan Baez's cover of the Band song "The Night They Drove Old Dixie Down," and Janis Joplin's "Mercedes Benz." "Rose Garden" was a verified crossover hit. Charting high on Billboard's country and pop charts, it was surely burned into Calvin's brain by repetition. The other two are oddities, which is what made them so appealing to Calvin.

"'The Night They Drove Old Dixie Down' really struck me because it was a song that told a story, but not really," he says. "It was a series of images that I couldn't really connect up, and I couldn't figure out what they were talking about. 'Mercedes Benz' was so weird because it was stark a cappella, and the imagery was so wrong and weird. But I really liked it. I liked how naked it was."

Two years after moving to the West Coast, the Johnsons were on the move again, this time to Ellensburg, a small high-desert town in the middle of Washington. There, Calvin attended an experimental elementary school staffed by teaching students from Central Washington University, where Calvin's father, who had served as press secretary for Washington State Governor Albert D. Rosellini from 1957 to 1965, was head of the journalism department. "All the weirdos in town were going there," he recalls. "Or they were sending their kids there."

In the fifth grade, Calvin's new friends reintroduced him to the Beatles. While listening to the band with his friends, Calvin had a revelation. "This is music," he thought. "This is exciting." Now with jobs and disposable income, Streator and his sister Wendes began to bring music home. Soon the Johnson house was filled with the latest hit records by Bachman-Turner Overdrive, the Carpenters, Grand Funk Railroad, Deep Purple, and the Rolling Stones. Calvin soaked it up, but he also found himself digging deeper.

"I was pretty into BTO, and the Rolling Stones seemed cool," Calvin says. "But Streator was buying the contemporary Rolling Stones records. I went to this garage sale and they had these earlier records, these Decca albums. And they were selling for a quarter each, so I bought two of those, *Aftermath* and *12x5*, and just listened to those over and over again. I could not get enough of those records. Eventually I had to hide those records because I was so sick of listening to them—I was addicted to them."

Aftermath, released in 1966, was a huge achievement for the Stones; it was the first full-length album consisting of all original songs penned by Mick Jagger and Keith Richards. *12x5*, on the other hand, featured the band doing what made them famous: covering rhythm and blues by great American artists including Chuck Berry ("Around and Around"), Bobby Womack ("It's All Over Now"), Wilson Pickett ("If You Need Me"), and Dale Hawkins ("Susie-Q"). The Stones weren't the only band to graduate from cover material to originals; most early rock 'n' roll musicians or bands relied on the music of others to propel their own fledgling careers, the way that Elvis Presley, Bob Dylan, and the Beatles did.

Calvin discovered early Beatles records while on family trips to Seattle. There, in the dollar bin of Horizon Books on Capitol Hill, he found the band's first two U.S. releases: *Introducing . . . the Beatles* and *Meet the Beatles!* While his friends were obsessing over

Abbey Road, Calvin preferred the band's recordings from ten years earlier, with songs written in the heyday of rock 'n' roll.

"*Introducing . . . the Beatles* was, like, half covers," Calvin remembers. "That was really exciting to look at them and realize, 'Hey, they didn't write this song. Who wrote this song?' That's how I found out about the Shirelles and Carl Perkins and Chuck Berry and Arthur Alexander and the Cookies. And it was just like, 'Oh! I've got to hear these original versions.'"

Calvin's love for early rock 'n' roll was apparent enough that for his eleventh birthday he received the soundtrack to *American Graffiti*. Calvin had never seen the George Lucas–directed film, which had been released earlier that year, but that didn't matter. The soundtrack featured forty-one of the biggest doo-wop and rock 'n' roll hits of the '50s and early '60s. Those songs by Chuck Berry, Buddy Holly, and other early luminaries made it onto a personal playlist that included contemporary favorites like BTO and Steppenwolf but increasingly moved to the era of sock hops and drag races depicted in *American Graffiti*. Soon after his birthday, Calvin bought the screenplay for the movie. He would read it three times before actually seeing the film.

Soon after that birthday, Calvin's father died of a sudden heart attack. A year later, as the sole provider for four children, Calvin's mother moved the family to Olympia, where she started working for the Washington Federation of State Workers.

In Olympia, Calvin continued to explore new sounds, though he maintained a fascination with the Beatles that went beyond their music. One day he checked out a library book that recounted the band's early days playing the union halls and coffee shops of Liverpool. He read about the fans in the city who would watch the band play long before it had a record to its name. As far as Calvin knew, there was no such thing in Ellensburg. The bands that he loved lived only on the records he bought, the radio, television, or, at best, across a crowded coliseum, as was the case when he would later attend a Steve Miller Band concert at the age of fourteen.

"It just seemed so much more exciting to me that you would go to a show with a hundred people and see the band right there than a show with thirty thousand people where you can't even see the band," Calvin recalls. "I wished that I could experience this kind of world where this existed. And it's only been eight years; why can't this still exist. Then, when punk rock came around, I was like, There it is. That's what I've been waiting for. That's the local thing. Local bands playing to local audiences and being a self-sufficient scene."

When Calvin first read about the emergence of this new thing called "punk rock" in his brother's issues of *Rolling Stone* and *Creem* in 1976, he had no way of hearing it. Even in Olympia, punk was nearly nonexistent. The radio stations didn't play it. The record stores didn't sell it. Punk existed only as a news item, largely derided by parents and authorities as a depraved culture threatening the day's youth.

Calvin didn't let that stop him from coveting it.

"I knew I liked the Ramones," he says. "All I had to do was hear them. I knew that these bands, like the New York Dolls and the Stooges, were great, and I was pretty sure I knew what they probably sounded like. It just made a lot of sense that they would be good."

In December of 1976, Calvin was finally able to hear the music he had known he would love. *Weekend*, an NBC news magazine that ran on one Saturday night each month when the *Saturday Night Live* cast was given a week off, aired a program on the punk rock culture that had just recently jumped from the clubs to the charts. The three-part story opened with footage of a band called the Damned performing the song "Fan Club" as an audience of young fans pogoed and slam danced with complete abandon.

After the first verse, host Lloyd Dobyns introduced his audience to punk, alluding first to the fashion.

"There are those in England who wish straightjackets were still the fashion," he said. "Punk rock groups usually play in private clubs or rented halls. And they tend to act out the theme of the lyrics: violence and destruction. The punk rock movement first got British attention when a girl was blinded in one eye by a flying glass at a punk rock performance. The proper punk philosophy is not that society must be changed, but that it must be destroyed. Whether they believe that is questionable, but they have convinced people they mean it, and punk rockers have an earned reputation for destruction and violence."

The rest of the program featured much hand-wringing over self-mutilation and Nazi symbolism, as well as footage of the Sex Pistols performing their first single, "Anarchy in the U.K.," and—most importantly to Calvin—footage of teenagers dressed in strange clothes bouncing into each other and dancing in ways he had never seen before.

"I saw this thing and I was just like, 'Oh yeah, this is cool,'" Calvin recalls. "Because England was so different than America. It actually was a teenage music in England. Punk rockers in England were teenagers, whereas in America teenagers didn't care about it, they didn't even know. They had never heard of punk rock. If they had, they didn't want anything to do with it. It just seemed stupid. Which it was, in the best possible way."

It was clear to Calvin that he had to get his hands on some punk records from the U.K. However, none of those records were being widely distributed in the U.S. Punk records from American bands like the Ramones or Blondie were available from small independent record labels, and Calvin might have been able to go to his local record store, Rainy Day Records, and place a special order, but he didn't know that. And anyway, he wanted the punk rock that was coming from across the Atlantic.

Fortunately his German teacher at Olympia High School was planning the school's annual monthlong student trip to Europe. The final stop on the itinerary: England. With his mom's permission, Calvin withdrew money from his college fund to pay for the trip. That summer, he flew over the Atlantic Ocean and set foot on European soil for the first time. While his teacher and his fellow students were intent on absorbing the cultures of Germany, France, and Holland, all Calvin could talk about was going to England and buying punk records.

"The other students, they didn't know what I was talking about," Calvin says. "They'd ask me what punk rock was and I'd say, 'Oh, punk rock. It's like . . . punk rockers. They wear, like, leather jackets and beat up little old ladies and squirrels and stuff like that.'"

Punk had become so popular in Europe that Calvin was able to hear a few punk songs on the radio during his travels. He took note of the songs he liked and saved them for his much-anticipated record-shopping spree in England.

But Calvin didn't realize what he was walking into. It was the summer of 1977, and England was burning. While the nation's royalty and its attendant culture celebrated the twenty-fifth anniversary of the Queen's coronation, punk was actively in opposition. Calvin was not there for royalty: he was there for punk. Appropriately, the number one song he searched for was the Sex Pistols' latest, "God Save the Queen." The song, which had been released that May, opens with Johnny Rotten snarling, "God save the Queen. She ain't no human being."

On the day his class arrived in London, Calvin went hunting for a place to buy records. He found one in a Woolworths department store. He approached the middle-aged cashier and asked her if they had the Sex Pistols' infamous latest release. She looked at him coldly before responding with passion, "We don't sell that garbage."

Two days later the class traveled to its final stop, Edinburgh. There, while walking around, Calvin discovered one of the many little punk record stores that had popped up in the storefronts of the Scottish burg. The store was sold out of "God Save the Queen" 45s, but the clerk recommended "Pretty Vacant," another Sex Pistols hit. Then, the fifteen-year-old Calvin—standing in a Scottish record store opposite a very hip clerk—asked if any of the punk songs he had heard during his trip were in stock. Since the songs were all broadcast in languages he didn't understand, Calvin wasn't able to provide titles or even band names. Instead, he sang the songs the best he could. At the end of the day, he walked out of the store with the debut album and a 45 from a band called the Jam, the Sex Pistols single and another by the Stranglers.

"I felt like, okay, the trip's finally paid off," says Calvin. "It was worth the whole trip, touring through France and Holland and all these places."

The records Calvin carried out of that record store held the frenetic essence of rock 'n' roll that he had gleaned from the recordings he loved as a child and the stories he had read about the Liverpool scene. It was a world away from the massive machine that rock 'n' roll had become. He knew that for a fact. On July 17, days before embarking on his European adventures, Calvin had driven with friends to the Kingdome in Seattle. There, he watched Led Zeppelin—then arguably the biggest band in the world—play to fifty thousand people.

"If there was anything to ever convince me that punk rock was the answer, it was seeing that show," he says. "I loved Led Zeppelin, and it was just horrible. So self-indulgent. There was no looking back from there. That's it. I'm done with stadium rock."

A BRIEF HISTORY OF THE JAM

Although Calvin was searching for a very singular idea of punk rock from the 1976 episode of *Weekend*, the records that were safely stowed in his carry-on when he flew back to the United States were not all by bands with the same mission as those he saw on the television show. The Sex Pistols were at the vanguard of a movement that threatened to erase the past while promising "no future"; the Stranglers, however, were part of that past, holdovers from the U.K.'s dying pub-rock scene who would go on to become art rockers. And while the Jam was often lumped into the first wave of punk along with the movement's big three bands—the Damned, the Clash, and the Sex Pistols—the band was something very different.

Paul Weller started the Jam in 1972, three years before the angry punks in those other bands would turn their discontent into music. Sex Pistols singer Johnny Rotten told reporters that he had no musical heroes—and his band's primitive and unwieldy sound certainly came off like a bastard child of the pop era. Weller and his bandmates came up, like the Beatles and the Stones before them, playing the music of their heroes, covering songs by Chuck Berry and Little Richard. Not only did the Jam album that Calvin carried out of the store, *In the City*, feature a cover of a song by American R & B songwriter Larry Williams, it also included a faithful, if grittier, version of the theme song from the *Batman* television series. Such playful antics that honored pop culture rather than skewering it would have been viewed as gauche in the dominant punk rock milieu.

The Jam also performed in sharp, tailored suits, a hat tip to the mod culture of '60s London and another of the band's primary influences, the Who. Unlike the garbage bags, ripped T-shirts, and bondage gear of the popular punk movement, the Jam would have been welcome at any high tea. Fashion wasn't the only thing that the band borrowed: while its music was fast and brutalizing compared to its predecessors, the Jam prized melodies and a more dynamic instrumental interplay above all else.

The most striking difference, though, was in Weller's lyrical style. While the Sex Pistols, the Damned, and the Clash sang songs that almost exclusively called for the destruction of the era's dominant political and social culture, Weller focused his lyrics on getting beyond the griping. The lyrics of the single that Calvin heard on European radio and then sang to that Scottish record store clerk were, above all, life affirming: "All around the world I've been looking for new . . . youth explosion," Weller sang, with his bass player Bruce Foxton echoing the sentiment. "A new direction! We want a reaction! Inflate creation! Looking for new!"

IN 1972 DEAN KATZ traveled from the Evergreen State College in Olympia to Seattle to start a radio station. Like every other student at the experimental college, Katz had the option to apply for an Individual Learning Contract. With the sponsorship of a faculty member, a student could designate a long-term project and receive credit upon completion. Some students published their own poetry; others explored the mating habits of the North American gophers. Katz wanted to start a radio station.

Fortunately, in 1972, there was a way for colleges to start their own low-wattage radio stations: in an effort to promote the new and still-unpopular FM band, the Federal Communications Commission accepted applications from educational institutions for a Class D radio license. Those licenses, offered for a limited time, allowed a broadcaster to transmit 10 watts from a station at the left of the dial (from 88 to 92 MHz), which was also known as the "educational band."

This was the opportunity that created a network of college rock stations that would give rise to its own genre: college rock. Schools across the state of Washington were getting in on the action. Central Washington University's KCAT (now KCWU) was the first, starting in 1962; the University of Washington's KCMU (now KEXP) went live in 1972, Western Washington University's KUGS in 1974, the University of Puget Sound's KUPS in 1975, and Washington State University's KZUU in 1979.

Katz was, by comparison, an early adopter when he arrived in Seattle with his application for a station at Evergreen. He and his advisor agreed that the station would carry the call letters KESC (the initials of Evergreen State College), but somewhere between campus and the courthouse, Katz changed his mind. Reportedly a fan of Mel Brooks and Buck Henry's absurd comedic spy show, *Get Smart*, Katz decided to name his college's station after the show's "international organization of evil." On November 28, 1972, station manager Katz welcomed future volunteers and listeners to the station's broadcast facility on the third floor of the College Activities Building, filled with equipment almost entirely salvaged from other radio stations. Its call letters were KAOS. Chaos was a fitting name for what would become one of the most radical radio stations in America.

But KAOS wasn't there yet. Katz was a student volunteer, like the rest of his crew, and couldn't provide the level of attention that a radio station needs. It wasn't until a man by the name of John Foster came to town, after hitchhiking from Connecticut, that the future of KAOS was assured.

Recently out of the Peace Corps, Foster was broke when he arrived in Olympia in the summer of 1975. He applied for a grant through the Comprehensive Employment and Training Act, a federal program that funded full-time jobs at not-for-profit organizations, including state-run universities. With that grant, Foster became the first full-time employee at KAOS. His first job: cataloging the stacks of records that the station had received since its inception.

"In order to catalog everything, I had to listen to everything," Foster has said. "And I discovered some things that I had no idea existed. For example, I had never heard old-timey music. I had never heard Cajun music. I had never heard Japanese koto music. I had never heard anything from anywhere in the world, aside from the United States."

While learning about different styles of music, Foster also educated himself in the economic realities of the music business; namely, that four major corporations controlled 90 percent of the market. KAOS was no exception to the industry rule, playing mostly major-label releases. Foster knew there was a lot more music out there produced and distributed by smaller, independent companies, and he believed, as an educational radio station, it was KAOS's duty to make sure people heard it.

Foster wrote a policy stating that 80 percent of the records played on KAOS would be independent. At one of the station's Monday meetings, where student volunteers voted on the station's actions, Foster presented the proposal. It passed, and the station immediately became a home for the music industry outsider. In order to help the deejays distinguish the major labels from the independents, he instituted the practice of marking all independent releases with a thick green line. Soon after, the station's operating principle was known simply as the "Green Line Policy."

"There were factions of people who thought they should be able to play whatever they wanted," he has said. "The most common thing I heard was, 'The Grateful Dead don't get played on the radio much, so we should be able to play as much Grateful Dead as we want.' And I would point out, 'Yes, you can play up to 20 percent Grateful Dead, but the policy states that the rest of it has to be independent.'"

The Evergreen campus was only seven miles from Olympia, but for Calvin, it might as well have been on the other side of the world. When Calvin returned to Olympia High School for his sophomore year, his distrust of corporate rock had grown considerably—but his pursuit of new music was a lonely one. Even the one person who expressed interest in the punk records Calvin planned to buy in Europe—a friend of his brother's who played music and listened to progressive rock—had turned against it by the time Calvin returned from abroad.

"I came back and I saw this same guy," Calvin says. "I told him that I had got some of those punk records, and he was like, 'You paid money for that shit?' It was like *The Stepford Wives*. So I had four punk records that I listened to by myself."

There were brief flashes of hope that punk would gain acceptance in the larger culture that surrounded Calvin. KISW, the main FM rock station in Seattle, with a signal that extended the sixty miles to Olympia, played a Sex Pistols song—and then, following complaints from listeners, never played it again.

Another potential breakthrough came late in 1977, when the Sex Pistols were scheduled to play the December 17 episode of *Saturday Night Live*, a premier showcase for the era's greatest up-and-coming musical talent. Again, the band was thwarted, this time when the U.S. government denied the band members' visa requests. *Saturday Night Live* booked another British artist to fill the Sex Pistols' slot. Calvin watched anyway and witnessed the American debut of Elvis Costello. Dressed in a powder blue blazer and jeans, and wearing thick-framed spectacles, the twenty-three-year-old looked nothing like the unruly Sex Pistols. Backed by his band, the Attractions, Costello started a performance of his first single, "Less Than Zero." Two lines in, he stopped his band and apologized to the audience. "I'm sorry, ladies and gentlemen," he said. "There's no reason to do this song here." Then he turned to his band, counted off, and started in on another song: "Radio Radio."

"Radio is in the hands of such a lot of fools," Costello sang as his band whirled away. "Tryin' to anesthetize the way that you feel."

When the song was over, Costello unplugged his guitar and stalked off the stage, his band following behind him. Costello, it was later revealed, had been specifically told not to play the song by *SNL*'s producer, Lorne Michaels, because of its unveiled criticism of the sclerotic state of radio. As a result of the performance, Costello was banned from *SNL* for twelve years. Even if the Sex

Pistols hadn't made it into the American mainstream, a vestige of the band's attitude had.

"It was just so raw," Calvin recalls. "Usually when the band gets done, they're bowing and clapping. He just walked off."

While following the currents of punk through whatever channels he could, Calvin continued to explore the roots of rock 'n' roll, particularly the role of black artists who played before the Beatles and the Rolling Stones got their hands on their music.

Calvin wondered, "How did it get from being a black music to being a white music? Why am I not listening to any current black artists?"

Though none of Calvin's friends listened to punk, he did know a couple kids who listened to jazz. And while he didn't like jazz, he was intrigued by it as a black American art form. So, when Calvin found "The History of Black Music" in a catalog filled with Evergreen night courses, he asked one of his jazz-loving friends if he would like to take the course with him. His friend refused, telling Calvin that he was taking a different class, "Radio for Everyone," that took place over one quarter at the college radio station, KAOS. At the end of the quarter, students able to pass the FCC's test for a third-class radio license could host their own show. Calvin immediately signed up and hatched a plan.

"This is great," he thought. "I'll learn how to do radio, and I'll have a radio show to play my punk rock records on. I'll be the only guy in Olympia playing punk rock. It'll be so cool. Then other people will hear punk rock and then they'll know how good it is."

When he started the course in March of 1978, Calvin learned that he had been beaten to the punch. Thanks to the Green Line Policy instituted by John Foster three years prior, KAOS had been playing punk for years.

"When I started the class, I started listening to KAOS," Calvin says. "And they had punk rock shows, along with all kinds of other shows. I started hearing people like Patti Smith, Modern Lovers, Ramones, and all these bands. But more important than that was that I got access to the record library and all of a sudden I could listen to all these bands I'd been reading about."

Calvin didn't just go to the Wednesday evening class; he went to the station every day after school, rifled through the collection, put headphones on, and listened to records he had only read about. The Stooges, the Velvet Underground, Big Star, Roxy Music, the Clash: they were all there, waiting for him.

In the staff and volunteers at KAOS Calvin found kindred spirits: people who not only knew about punk and liked it but who also were kind to him. After one class, the instructors—station manager Dave Rauh and business manager Toni Holm—asked for volunteers for an upcoming fund drive. Calvin jumped at the opportunity. A few days later, he found himself sitting quietly in front of a phone, waiting to take bids for the on-air auction being conducted in the studio by one of the station's deejays, Stephen Rabow.

Sitting across from Calvin was an Evergreen student, ignoring the young volunteer as she read a British music magazine. On the back cover was a photo of three young musicians, resplendent in blazers made from the Union Jack. Calvin saw his opening. "Hey, is that the Jam?" he asked. The Evergreen student was stunned. The band had yet to release an album in the United States; the fact that Calvin—a high school student who had longish hair and a very unpunk wardrobe—knew about them was a shock. The fact that he owned an album and a 45 by the band was remarkable.

The student introduced herself as Alisa Newhouse. The two started talking, and she asked Calvin if he was going to the Patti Smith concert at the Paramount Theatre in Seattle the next weekend. Despite the fact that he had only read about Smith's music before volunteering at KAOS, Calvin said he wanted to but didn't have a car or a ticket.

That Wednesday, Calvin went to the KAOS offices for his weekly class. For the first time, the station's music librarian, a student named George Romansic, was leading the lesson. He walked the students through the immense music library, explaining the rules, purpose, and history of the Green Line Policy before imploring them to explore the wealth of diverse music available at the station. He asked the students to not only search for the music they knew they liked but to dig for the records that influenced the musicians who recorded their favorite albums.

"He was so earnest," Calvin recalls. "I was thinking that what I never wanted to do was disappoint this guy, because it was so important to him. But that's okay, because I wanted to explore all these records anyway."

Romansic then pulled out a box of seven-inch singles. "These are all new artists that I've read about in magazines," he explained. "I write to them and I tell them I do a show at a radio station, and would they please send us a record."

Someone in the class asked, "Has anyone ever not sent you their record?"

"Yeah, well, there was this one band that wrote back and said, 'Hey, I don't give records away; I sell records. If you want to buy it, it's two dollars.'"

"Well, what did you do?"

"I sent him four dollars—one for me and one for the station."

After the lesson, Calvin asked to look through the box of seven-inches. Just then, Alisa walked by. "Oh George," she said, motioning to Calvin. "This is the guy I was telling you about." With that, George reached into his desk drawer, pulled out a single by the Tom Robinson Band titled "2-4-6-8 Motorway," and handed it to Calvin.

"I didn't really like this record," he said. "I'd like to hear what you think about it."

Calvin was floored.

"My high school experience, at this point, was that I wasn't very well socialized," Calvin recalls. "I didn't have a lot of friends. I had a pretty difficult time. And then to go to the station and have people take me seriously blew my mind. Not only were they interested in the same things I was interested in, but they also legitimately felt that my opinion was relevant."

The following Saturday, Calvin went down to the station to hang out with his new friends, only to find them all gone. After a few minutes, the phone rang. The deejay substituting for Stephen Rabow answered the phone and then handed it to Calvin. The voice was unfamiliar.

"Is this Calvin Johnson?"

"Yes."

"Do you want to go to the Patti Smith concert?"

"Yeah, but I don't have a ticket or a ride."

"That's been arranged."

"Well, um, I have to ask my mom."

"All right. I'll call you back."

An hour later, with his mother's permission, fifteen-year-old Calvin was on I-5, headed toward Seattle with a carful of KAOS employees in a Volkswagen Bug driven by Foster. Calvin didn't know anything about Foster, except that he was the guy who called the studio and he owned the car that was transporting Calvin to his first big punk show.

In 1978 Patti Smith was a paradox: a truly punk artist with a rock star career. She had an impeccable background for a punk. She came from a blue-collar family in New Jersey. She was raised with religion, which she rejected as a teenager around the same time she took a factory job on an assembly line. In 1967, she moved to New York to be an artist. She became an uncompromising one, creating powerful statements through her poetry, acting, painting, and songwriting. Her debut album, *Horses*, started with a line that Johnny Rotten might have snarled if Smith hadn't used it first: "Jesus died for somebody's sins, but not mine." But that album was released on Arista, one of the era's Big Four major record labels.

Three weeks before the show at the Paramount Theatre, the Patti Smith Group released "Because the Night," the first single from the artist's third major-label release, *Easter.* The song, a rock ballad penned by Bruce Springsteen, reached No. 13 on the Billboard Hot 100 chart, making it the biggest U.S. hit to emerge from the New York punk scene. And yet she still managed to create "Rock N Roll Nigger," a controversial and caustic poem-song that played on the same side of the *Easter* LP as "Because the Night," bolstering her punk credentials even as she was anointed the genre's breakout star.

The Ramones were a well-known pop culture commodity, but they were a commercial failure, never charting higher than No. 111 on the Billboard album chart. And though Blondie would become the greatest mainstream success to emerge from the New York punk scene of the '70s, the band's time would not come until the release of "Heart of Glass" in 1979. In 1978, Smith was the pinnacle of punk success in the United States. And the staff and volunteers at KAOS loved her.

That was why, instead of just going to the show, the KAOS crew tried to meet their heroine on her first trip to the region.* First they drove to Seattle-Tacoma International Airport to attempt a rendezvous with the artist, arriving just in time to see her waving from the back window of a fleeing car. Undeterred, Foster and his Volkswagen of Olympians headed to Peaches Records in Seattle's University District, where Smith was rumored to be signing records.

---

*Calvin would later learn that Smith played a show in Portland the night before and that, rather than driving the 150-mile journey, she flew. "That seems very strange," Calvin has said.

Calvin had never seen anything like it: a line of people was waiting for the artist's autograph. As Romansic chatted up Smith's guitarist, Lenny Kaye, Calvin wandered over to where Smith was sitting and signing. The scene frustrated the young punk.

"I was just like, Man, that's not cool," he recalls. "Signing autographs, that's what rock stars do."

Filled with youthful bravado and punk idealism, Calvin approached the artist. "Hey, can I autograph your coat?" he asked.

"What? You can't sign my coat," Smith answered. "This is a good coat. You can't sign this coat."

Later, at the Paramount, Calvin and his new friends stood and waited for the show to begin. Instead of an opening band, the sounds of the Ramones filled the theater. The songs were from the band's third album, *Rocket to Russia*, and Calvin watched as a group of Seattle punks danced to "Rockaway Beach," "Sheena Is a Punk Rocker," and "Teenage Lobotomy." Then Smith appeared, opening the show with the soliloquy from "Rock N Roll Nigger."

"It was just so exciting," Calvin remembers. "Such a great show."

After a pit stop at the Pioneer Square loft belonging to comic artist Lynda Barry, where the Talking Heads' album *77* played as Rabow interviewed Smith, the group headed home. On Monday, Calvin returned to his high school life, more sure than ever that he belonged at the radio station. As he continued to train and listen to KAOS, his technical abilities grew along with his appreciation of music outside of punk.

"The other deejays were interested in punk, but that wasn't their main interest," Calvin says. "They were interested in music; they were into soul and funk and reggae. It was real exciting to hear all these different kinds of music and to have them put it in the context of punk rock. There were bands like the Clash that were talking about reggae and the people at KAOS were making the connection. And James Brown was another hero.

I remembered him from TV when I was a kid, seeing him on *The Flip Wilson Show* and thinking, 'Whoa. That's crazy. That guy's dancin' all crazy.' But I never really listened to his music."

In addition to the music history lessons he received, Calvin also managed to learn how to adhere to the rules set forth by the Federal Communications Commission. At the end of the quarter, he traveled to Seattle and took the licensing exam. He passed.

"I went to KAOS and said, 'I got my license! I can do a show!'"

Since it was summer, the station had open spots for programmers. The next day, Calvin was on the air, filling a five-hour afternoon time slot. He could play whatever he wanted, as long as four out of every five songs came from an independent label. Calvin had no complaints.

A BRIEF HISTORY OF COLLEGE ROCK

The Evergreen State College's hippie credentials do not deserve all the credit for its radio station's radical bent.

When John Foster walked into the offices of KAOS, he wasn't only walking into a creative laboratory at a trusting college; he was walking into a nebulous medium in its most nascent form. Foster took advantage of that, and as a result, his views toward independent music helped form his college radio station into an outlet for unheard music. But like all mediums, college radio was well on its way to being institutionalized.

In 1978, *College Music Journal*, a new publication, began to measure, chart, and report on the music that was filling college airwaves. For student programmers working on the new breed of FM stations in the early '80s, *CMJ* became the resource for independent music. A sort of *Billboard* for the indies, the journal was a helpful road map. Throughout the '80s, college radio and independent record labels had a symbiotic relationship that led to uncharted terrain: the labels provided diverse content and the stations provided adventurous listeners.

As the format's impact grew, so did the audience for new music that wasn't test-marketed by major labels. Likewise, as the audience for college radio grew, those major labels started to look to college radio for new artists. For smart A and R men and women, the focus group was no longer in a boardroom but on the college campus—and *CMJ* provided the vital stats. The music that got the most airplay now had a genre: college rock.

A number of college rock bands were cherry-picked by the major labels during the '80s after excelling on *CMJ*'s charts. R.E.M., the Smiths, 10,000 Maniacs, and the Replacements all found homes on major record labels, and while they failed to top the Billboard charts, they did moderately well for their corporate bosses. And even though they now resided on the other side of Foster's Green Line, they managed to dominate the *CMJ* charts, which were otherwise filled with records from tiny independents.

Then the independent music world was turned on its head: Nirvana was signed by Geffen Records partially on the strength of its 1989 Sub Pop Records debut, *Bleach*, on the *CMJ* charts. The band's next record, *Nevermind*, sold millions, becoming the first college rock hit. Except it wasn't college rock anymore: unable to carry the genre into commercial radio for obvious reasons, an alternative genre was needed. And "alternative" was what it was called.

3

IN THE SPRING OF 1979, Calvin finally cut his shaggy hair short, like most of the punks he had been reading about and listening to during his entire junior year of high school. He stopped shopping for clothes at the South Sound Center, where many of his classmates were buying the latest fashions: tree trunk pants and elephant bell–style jeans. Instead, he shopped at the downtown Olympia outlet of Yard Birds, a local general store chain. There, he was relieved to find the nondescript straight-legged Levi's that he would wear throughout his adult life. ("Fag pants," as his classmates called them.)

While many of those classmates celebrated their teenage years by drinking and smoking at parties—which Calvin had done as recently as his trip to Europe—since his return from overseas, the young punk had become a strict teetotaler.

"It was a personal statement," he says. "I had been drinking in high school, at parties and stuff, but when I went to Europe, I just decided this isn't fun; I'm not really into this. But I also started to think about how it made sense politically. Like, why would you drink and smoke; you are just feeding these industries that are oppressing people. A true rebel wouldn't drink or smoke if they were trying to change something. If you want to change something big, you have to change yourself first. That seemed like a big, important step."

Calvin started to discover that he no longer needed to go overseas to find punk music. A few weeks after turning sixteen, he traveled to Seattle to visit his brother, Streator, who had just enrolled in the University of Washington. There, along University Way, Calvin discovered Cellophane Square, one of the few Seattle record stores that recognized and stocked punk records. Inside, Calvin was drawn to a sign he had never seen before. It read, "Support Local Music." Beneath the sign were a few 45s issued by punk bands from Seattle, Vancouver, B.C., and Portland. The records bore names that Calvin was mostly unfamiliar with—like the Enemy, from Seattle, and Vancouver's Subhumans—but there was one recognizable name: the Wipers.

A few months before, the KAOS crew, minus Calvin, had made a trip to Portland to see two new punk bands, the Wipers and the Neo Boys. With two dollars and fifty cents in his pocket, Calvin could only afford one single from Cellophane Square; he chose "Better Off Dead," the first Wipers single, issued the year before by Trap, a small punk label run out of a record store.

"I remember Dave and Toni talking about how the Wipers were really good," Calvin says. "I was like, I know they're good, so I bought that. Turns out, it was good. Well, if I would have bought the Subhumans, that would've been good. Any of those records would have been good. But I'm proud that I bought the Wipers."

Soon Calvin was playing that single on KAOS, where he had worked his way into his own regular weekly radio show on Fridays, scheduled from 10 p.m. to midnight so as not to interfere with his studies. He also had a bunch of new friends who were into the same music he was and who were driving him the sixty miles north to Seattle to see punk shows at an all-ages venue called the Bird, located in the middle of the city's Capitol Hill neighborhood.

"No teenagers went," Calvin recalls. "I was always the youngest person there."

That spring, Calvin's life was turned upside down yet again. His mom was offered a new job heading women's outreach for the

American Federation of State, County, and Municipal Employees—in Washington, D.C. Since she started in April, while both Calvin and his younger sister, Kirstin, were still in school, she allowed the two youngest siblings to stay in Olympia for the remainder of the school year and, if they wanted, the summer before starting high school in Bethesda, Maryland. Kirstin spent the summer at a friend's house. Calvin spent it at his mom's old house.

During his summer in Olympia, Calvin started playing guitar and singing in his first band, a high school trio called the Beachheads. The band practiced all summer and, one week before Calvin left for the East Coast, played its first and only show. Calvin rented out Room 305 in the College Activities Building at Evergreen and posted a flyer advertising that the show was free and started at 7 p.m. The band started promptly and played seven songs—four originals and three covers—to twelve people, including Streator. Stragglers missed the only chance they would have to see the Beachheads.

"I remember these two women showed up and were really excited, and they were like, 'Oh, we saw the poster. This band's got the crazy name. We can't wait to see them,'" Calvin recalls. "We were like, 'We just played,' and they were like, 'What? That's not how you do it.'"

Those women weren't the only ones. Calvin's friends Toni Holm and Dave Rauh from KAOS ran into Room 305 right after the Beachheads' set. They handed Calvin the first issue of *OP Magazine*. "It's finally here!" they exclaimed.

An extension of an anomalous entity called the Lost Music Network that Foster had started soon after instituting the Green Line Policy at KAOS, *OP Magazine* was a sophisticated fanzine published on newsprint and devoted to covering independent music with a stated emphasis on "articles about music written by musicians." In order to thwart the cycle of music as commodity—and after spending maybe a few too many hours in KAOS's alphabet-ized library—Foster also imbued his publication with an unusual constraint: instead of featuring the newest music of the moment, each issue covered artists whose names started with one letter of the alphabet. The issue that Holm and Rauh handed Calvin that night was issue "A." A few days later, Calvin boarded a plane with a stack of *OP Magazines* in hand and headed to his new home.

"Socially, leaving Olympia behind was kind of liberating," Calvin recalls. "It was really nice to go somewhere where I was a stranger."

One week after the Beachheads show, Calvin was in Chevy Chase, Maryland, living with his mom. But before settling in, he took his first train ride ever, heading north to New York City, where his friend Alisa Newhouse, whom he had met a year before at KAOS, was now living in a loft in SoHo. Alisa invited Calvin to the city to take in a week of punk shows. He saw many of those shows at clubs like TR3 and the Mudd Club, where New York punks, including Shrapnel and Fashion, and Boston punks the Liars played. He caught the first-ever show by the latest British punk export, Gang of Four, and saw the Cramps three times.*

"I had heard the Cramps before when I played their single on KAOS," Calvin says, "and I wasn't really impressed. But when I saw them live they just blew my mind. It changed my life. It was just—this is what rock 'n' roll is all about."

KAOS gave Calvin cred and confidence. He approached every musician he could, told them he had a radio show, and handed them a KAOS card, asking them to send any music they could to the station. After his visit, Calvin even wrote a letter to a local music rag, the *New York Rocker*, boasting of his on-air bona fides

---

*The Cramps were notable for their instrumental makeup. The band did not have a bass player. Later, when Calvin was asked how his band Beat Happening could be considered a rock 'n' roll band if it didn't have a bass player, he would refer his questioner to the Cramps.

while informing the East Coast of his developing rock 'n' roll worldview. Calvin wrote:

"Now, I'm not just your average 'I know all the punk bands' kid. After fifteen months at the good radio station (KAOS-FM in Olympia, Washington) playing great teenage music, I feel that I know rock 'n' roll. I mean, I know it. And I know the secret: rock 'n' roll is a teenage sport, meant to be played by teenagers of all ages—they could be 15, 25, or 35. It all boils down to whether they've got the love in their hearts, that beautiful teenage spirit."

After a week spent getting comfortable with the New York punk scene, Calvin headed back to his unexplored home. But D.C. wasn't entirely new to Calvin: when he told John Foster that he was moving there, Foster gave him a copy of the weekly newspaper he subscribed to in order to keep tabs on D.C.'s scene. What Calvin saw in the paper's club listings was a city swarming with opportunities to see live music that he couldn't find in Olympia or even Seattle.

One of the larger clubs in the city was the Warner Theatre, where Calvin saw his first show in D.C.: a double bill with Gang of Four—whom he had just seen in New York—and the Buzzcocks. Despite the fact that he went alone, Calvin loved the show. Leaving the venue, he saw an older man, an old hippie with a long beard, handing out flyers for an upcoming Half Japanese show. Half Japanese was one of the many D.C.-area bands that Calvin had played on his radio show, along with the Nurses, the Slickee Boys, the Razz, and White Boys. But the show—which Calvin wanted to attend—was the night before Calvin's first day at Bethesda–Chevy Chase High School. He knew he couldn't go, but chatted with the man to find out what else he knew. This man became Calvin's first friend in D.C.

His name was Bill Ash. He owned the Record & Tape Exchange in Arlington, Virginia. He knew of KAOS and *OP*

Magazine through his record store and also because he ran his own label, Wasp Records. Focused mostly on the city's emerging new wave scene, Wasp released mostly 45 singles by regional bands Calvin had never heard of, including True Facts, Insect Surfers, and the Beaks.

School started the next week. Things were different; everyone was wearing the same straight-legged jeans as Calvin. Still, he found his own, unique way to stand out.

"I was really into dying my clothes a lot," he says, "and I dyed a lot of things pink. So, everyone had these Izod shirts with the little alligators on them. So, I took one of my pink T-shirts and I drew a little alligator on it. And I was like, okay, I am going to be like everyone else; I've got a little alligator on my shirt. Some people were like, 'Oh, I love that,' but it didn't really register with me."

Calvin made fast friends with classmates Josh and Leslie Arneson, siblings whose older brother David happened to be in Insect Surfers. Calvin spent a lot of time at the Arneson house, listening to records and talking about music. David was into '60s rock and a few contemporary bands, while Josh tended more toward the rockabilly sound that was taking hold of the D.C. scene. Another fast friend, Eric Castle, listened to jazz. Like Calvin's friends back at Olympia High School, every one of them was skeptical of punk.

If Calvin was going to find any punk fans, it would have to be in the clubs of D.C. Compared to the sixty-mile trek from Olympia to Seattle, the commute to the neighborhoods with punk clubs was easy—but it still presented problems. Buses to the outer reaches of the district stopped at midnight. And even if Calvin could get on the bus in time, the district line was one mile from Calvin's home—a distance he would have to walk or bike. The shows Calvin wanted to see usually lasted until past midnight, so catching a ride with one of his friends or from his mom would be required. Even then, he faced obstacles he rarely encountered in the Northwest.

"When I went to see the Buzzcocks, it was at this place that was around the corner from Adams Morgan," Calvin says, recalling a time when the now-gentrified neighborhood was filled with empty, boarded-up houses. "It was great because there were people on the street and it was lively and it was fun. But I'm sitting there waiting for my mom to pick me up and this policeman, who was black, because everybody was black, drove up and asked, 'What are you doing here?' And I'm like, 'Waiting for my mom to pick me up.' And he was like, 'Well, why don't you sit over here,' and he put me closer to the light. He was implying that I was very vulnerable, but I never had a problem with anything like that. I figured out, early on, that if you just acted like you were supposed to be there, no one questions anything. That was always my strategy in D.C., and it was never a problem."

One night, Calvin convinced a couple of friends to drive him to a venue called Madam's Organ in Adams Morgan to see another pioneering D.C. punk band, Bad Brains. They arrived in time to watch the opener, a "hippie band," play an obnoxiously long set. While the next band, a little-known group called Untouchables, was setting up, Calvin's friends told him that it was too late—past midnight—and they had to head home, long before Bad Brains would take the stage. Calvin would end up seeing Bad Brains the next month at the University of Maryland, but the Untouchables would have to wait.

Even when he could get to a venue, Calvin couldn't always get in to the show. Like the Seattle and New York scenes, at the time, D.C. punk was largely a twenty-one-plus affair. While liquor laws in Washington, D.C., were relatively lax compared to the restrictive laws of Washington State—underage fans were allowed to attend shows at bars in the district—most establishments simply didn't want to hassle with teenagers.

"The Cellar Door and the Bayou," Calvin remembers as the bars hosting punk shows. "They were just these horrid clubs that were staffed with assholes. I remember trying to go to shows at those places and they were such dicks; it was just incredible. It just reinforced the idea that I never want to put anyone through this bullshit."

Throughout his senior year in D.C., Calvin was still paying attention to the other side of the country. Even though West Coast punk didn't receive much respect in the music circles he ran in, Calvin kept an ear tuned to the music coming out of those scenes, buying the debut studio albums by a California band, the Germs, and by the Wipers. He also kept in touch with his friends in Olympia. Foster would send him copies of *OP Magazine* as issues "B" and "C" debuted, and Calvin would take his copies to local record shops to sell on consignment.

When it came time for Calvin to choose a college, the crew at KAOS was insistent that he come back. Calvin had applied at the University of Washington in Seattle but was unsure about returning to Olympia, holding on to the idea that a truly adventurous student went away to college. After some cajoling from his friends and some creative reasoning, Calvin decided that—as he was living in Maryland—going to the Evergreen State College *was* going away to college. He finished his high school career knowing that he was heading back to Olympia. But he still had one summer out east.

Calvin got a job at KB Cinema, the eight-hundred-seat movie house in the district.* There, he spent the summer watching films and playing in a band with his fellow employees. During the day, Calvin would bike to Georgetown to buy records and

---

*The logo was a shield with the letters *KB* inside. While numerous sources have claimed that this was the inspiration for the K Records logo Calvin would design three years later, he maintains that the two have no relation.

window-shop the strange new wave fashions at Commander Salamander, a clothing store. At night, he would go to shows whenever he could.

One show he wouldn't miss was the Cramps. Almost a year had passed since he had seen the band for the first, second, and third times during his visit to New York, and though the Cramps had promised to play D.C. throughout the year, mishaps and lineup changes kept them away from the district clubs. Finally, that August, a few weeks before leaving D.C., Calvin was going to see the band again.

The show was at the Warner Theatre, the same spot in the same seedy neighborhood where he had seen Gang of Four and the Buzzcocks the year before. One of the opening acts was the Slickee Boys (a Wasp Records band). The first act on stage that night was the Teen Idles, a band whose name Calvin recognized from posters in Commander Salamander. When they began playing, Calvin witnessed something he hadn't seen since watching that documentary on British punk years earlier: teen punk rockers, all in the pit, dancing to the band. On stage, though, was the true revelation.

"It was teenagers, on stage, playing great music," Calvin recalls, "and I was like, 'Yeah. This is what it's all about.' The Slickee Boys were great and the Cramps were awesome, but this is the first time I really saw teenagers on stage, doing something like that."

Calvin would take one more trip to New York, to see a band from Athens, Georgia, called Pylon and a little-known band called the Soft Boys, led by Robyn Hitchcock, play its first American show. He then headed back to Maryland to prepare for his return to Olympia.

Before he could board the plane, though, Calvin decided to indulge in at least one nonmusical memento. Many of the students at Bethesda–Chevy Chase High School wore T-shirts from the local surf shop called the Sunshine House that featured the phrase "B-Town" running down the right sleeve; Calvin wanted one for himself and one for his sister.

"I went into the surf shop and there was the bass player from the Teen Idles I had seen the week before," Calvin recalls. "I went upstairs and got a couple shirts and coming down the stairs, I ran into the bass player guy who was walking out. I was like, 'You're the guy from the Teen Idles; I saw you play with the Cramps the other night.' And it was Ian MacKaye."

As Calvin recalls, he and MacKaye spoke for a few minutes about the hardcore music coming out of California, a unique interest they shared.

Unlike the more established bands in the D.C. punk scene, which was focused on the newest British music and the garage punk sounds of the past, MacKaye and his band embraced the heavier, angrier sounds coming from the West Coast. The band went to the source of its inspiration via Greyhound and played shows with a number of bands, including the Mentors and Vox Pop, a band that would later become 45 Grave. The band made connections, but not much money, netting fifteen dollars for a show in Los Angeles and eleven dollars for one in San Francisco.

Calvin had never seen the West Coast punk bands play, but, while working at KAOS, he had developed a love for the forward-looking music coming from independent American bands. Much of it was on California labels such as SST Records and Dangerhouse, and he had been playing it on his radio show for the last year.

MacKaye asked if Calvin was in a band. Calvin said yes, telling MacKaye that he had played music with his KB Cinema coworkers over the summer but that he was leaving for Washington State in the morning.

"Well, it's too bad you're going away," MacKaye said, before bidding farewell to Calvin. "We could have been in a band together."

MacKaye doesn't recall that meeting, but he does remember being introduced to Calvin at a New Year's Eve Party six months later. Calvin had returned to Washington, D.C., to visit his mom for the holidays. The Teen Idles had broken up since his departure, but while there, Calvin did attend the Unheard Music Festival, where he witnessed the first performance by MacKaye's new band, Minor Threat, as well as performances by a number of new D.C. bands, including a band fronted by an aggressive punk named Henry Rollins called S.O.A. Later Calvin would write a critical review for *OP Magazine* where he contended that "trying to dance to one of the bands can be like hand-to-hand combat" and noted that "only one band had a female member and when a girl is dancing she gets special abuse."

Still, to see so many young people getting involved in punk rock was inspiring to Calvin. The groups he saw that night were at the vanguard of a new breed of hardcore.

After introducing himself to some of the musicians at the Unheard Music Festival, Calvin was invited to a New Year's Eve party at the house of a friend's parents. At the party MacKaye, his bandmates and friends, and Calvin listened to a single by the then-defunct Teen Idles, the first release on MacKaye's label. They danced, had a snowball fight, and rang in 1981 completely sober. "It was definitely the funnest New Year's Eve party I have ever been to," Calvin says.

It was a memorable night for MacKaye as well, not least because of the stranger from Washington State who has hanging out.

"In California we'd met a lot of the street punk kids and the beach punks," MacKaye recalls. "And there was a fashion at the time where you'd put bandanas around your boots. Or chains, you know, you adorned your boots with stuff. And I remember Calvin being at this party with blue jeans and a pink bandana tied around his ankle, just wearing sneakers. And I thought, 'This guy's a kook.' That's about it. I'm like, 'That guy's crazy.'"

A BRIEF HISTORY OF HARDCORE

When Calvin tried to turn his Washington, D.C., friends on to California bands like the Germs and Black Flag, a common reply was: "They are just trying to sound like the Sex Pistols." Nothing could have been further from the truth.

Dismayed by the course of excess that the punk movement of the mid-'70s had taken—the bands coupling with the same corporations, drugs, drink, and loud fashion as the pop bands they were supposedly railing against—the bands that appealed to Calvin and influenced Ian MacKaye's Teen Idles were faster, heavier, and as experimental with their music as they were disciplined in their business ethics.

Black Flag, a band from Hermosa Beach, California, is credited with starting the hardcore movement in 1977 (when they were called Panic). Fellow California groups the Germs, Fear, and the Circle Jerks joined in lockstep. SST Records, the label started by Black Flag lyricist and guitarist Greg Ginn, is acknowledged as the first hardcore record label. Many more independent, musician-run hardcore labels cropped up soon after. The Germs' debut, *(GI)*, is widely regarded as the first hardcore album ever released.

Musically, hardcore placed more emphasis on rhythm than it did on melody, discarding the verse-chorus-verse pop formula in favor of loose structures that made room for instrumental and vocal digressions. The uniform was simple: jeans, T-shirts, and crew cuts. Hardcore was noted for its sonic and visual uniformity, which often turned punk rock bills that had once been diverse into a series of carbon-copy acts. Many discovered hardcore through Penelope Spheeris' documentary *The Decline of Western Civilization*, which was first shown in Olympia at the Evergreen State College in 1982.

Washington, D.C., was the first city on the East Coast to have a legitimate hardcore scene, which started when the all-black group Bad Brains released its first single, "Pay to Cum," in 1980. It was the influence of that band, its speed and precision, that helped transform the Teen Idles' sound into Minor Threat, but MacKaye's newest band was doing something more that would establish a new precedent for the emergent art form.

Featured on the band's debut EP, which was released on MacKaye's own Dischord record label in June of 1981, Minor Threat's song "Straight Edge" served as a manifesto for the most uncorrupted of artists. "I've got better things to do than sit around and fuck my head," MacKaye sings. "I've got the straight edge."

BEFORE CALVIN HAD LEFT for Washington, D.C., he had seen evidence of only a few Olympia bands, including a poster for Larry and the Mondellos that hung in the KAOS offices. The band's reference to the golden era of television (its name was based on Beaver Cleaver's chubby, dim-witted classmate, Larry Mondello) and new wave aesthetic piqued Calvin's interest, but Larry and the Mondellos played bars like the 4th Avenue Tavern, where Calvin couldn't go. There was also No Toy Boys, a group of jazz-fusion Deadheads who held no appeal for a young punk rocker. Streator took him to see Strange, a group of locals heavily influenced by the folk music coming out of the Bay Area that had released its own full-length record, but the band left Calvin cold.

When Calvin returned from steeping himself in East Coast punk culture, he found a very different landscape. His friends in Olympia had continued to push the boundaries of their own burgeoning scene. Before, there was only KAOS and *OP Magazine*. A year later, there were the makings of a local music community with actual bands that had taken Calvin and the Beachheads' lead, setting up shows on campus and anyplace else they could book them.

Foster and his Lost Music Network cohorts not only continued to publish *OP Magazine*, which had gained a modest national following after only its first three issues, but they started a record label called Mr. Brown Records & Tapes. In 1980 the label released three new wave singles: one by the Westside Lockers and two by the Beakers, a band featuring former KAOS librarian George Romansic. Using its available resources, the Lost Music Network advertised these singles in the pages of *OP Magazine*, providing the bands with an unusually large potential audience.

What appealed most to this audience was "Snake Attack," a 45 single that was originally released under the auspices of Flat Records, then adopted by the new, more powerful Mr. Brown label. The single was performed by Anonymous—the project of a KAOS engineer named Steve Fisk—and it was weird. Over a bed of modulating synthesizer tones, Fisk recited lines in an eerie speak-sing: "In the dead of night they find you . . . the snake attack." Three minutes in, the music briefly gives way to a department store announcement—"customer service, aisle nine"—and then the weirdness continues. The flip side features the sizzling and chaotic new wave song "Corporate Food," a party anthem for hedonistic robots.*

Both the Mr. Brown and Flat labels would release little more. Though the people behind those labels sensed the need for some organization to release music from the growing number of Olympia bands, they were more interested in publishing *OP Magazine* and playing in their own bands than marketing and distributing records.

Another shift in the Olympia landscape came with the arrival of a new Evergreen student. After a failed attempt at postsecondary education at Blackburn College in Carlinville, Illinois, Bruce Pavitt zeroed in on Evergreen.

"It was one of the few state-sponsored 'alternative' schools in the country," he recalls. "In other words, it was innovative and relatively inexpensive."

---

*"Corporate Food" would be featured the following year on *Let Them Eat Jellybeans!*, the first compilation released by Alternative Tentacles, the Bay Area record label started by Dead Kennedys lead singer Jello Biafra.

When Bruce told family friend Carl Schneider about his plans, Schneider encouraged him to make the move west. As the owner of a small record label, Cowboy Carl Records, Schneider knew about KAOS and even had the first issue of *OP Magazine* on hand. After reading that issue, Bruce wrote a letter to Foster, expressing interest in joining the KAOS crew.

He arrived at Evergreen a few weeks after Calvin left Olympia for Washington, D.C., and in a short time, Bruce had fully immersed himself in the station's culture. By the time Calvin returned, Bruce was singing and playing guitar in Tiny Holes, a band he had started with Fisk and KAOS music director Steve Peters, and had his own radio show called *Subterranean Pop*, which aired from 10 p.m. to midnight on Fridays—Calvin's old spot. Inspired by John Foster's *OP Magazine*, Bruce also published his own fanzine, also called *Subterranean Pop*, in which he wrote about underground bands from the Northwest and the Midwest and gave voice to ideas about the music industry that happened to be consistent with Calvin's.

"When people buy a record, they are not only plugging into the music, but into the values and lifestyles that are implied by that artist," Bruce wrote in the first issue of his zine. "By supporting huge New Hollywood music corporations, you (yes, you) are not only allowing middle-aged capitalists to dictate what goes over the airwaves, but you are giving them the go-ahead to promote macho pig-fuck bands whose entire lifestyle revolves around cocaine, sexism, money, and more money. The '80s need new sounds, but just as importantly, they need new cultural heroes."

It was a Monday morning—the day after Calvin arrived back in Olympia—when the college freshman returned to the KAOS offices for the first time in a year. There, in the music library of KAOS, he came face-to-face with Bruce, whom he had only known through letters from Foster. Bruce had just collected his mail and showed Calvin a 45 by an obscure Texas punk band named the Big Boys. Calvin had never heard of the band before. He knew right away that Bruce was tapped into a whole new sphere of underground music.

"Bruce was sending his zine out to enough labels and bands at that point that he was making something happen," Calvin recalls. "That's what his life was like, getting these amazing cool records in the mail."

Calvin and Bruce spent the morning in the library, talking about music. Bruce showed Calvin the records he had been receiving at the station and Calvin told Bruce about the bands he had discovered in D.C., including the Teen Idles. Peters and Fisk were there, too, but Calvin and Bruce were laser-focused on each other. They left the station and walked around the campus, talking until they arrived at Calvin's dorm room. There, Bruce picked up a guitar Calvin had packed away for school and played a series of notes that made no musical sense but were delivered with authority.

"He really doesn't know how to play guitar, but it doesn't matter," Calvin says. "I was just like, 'Wow, how did you do that? I want to do that.'"

Calvin started his freshman year without a show on KAOS. The station had switched to strip formatting, which maintained the diversity of its free-form past yet allowed for more predictability: folk and bluegrass in the morning, jazz in the evening, and rock from 10 p.m. to midnight. The rock slot was the most coveted, becoming so popular that deejays were forced to alternate, playing just one show every other week. By the time Calvin showed up, all ten spots were full. With his interest even more focused on rock and punk than before, Calvin saw no need to force himself into the rotation elsewhere. Instead, he hung out at the station between classes and got to know his fellow Evergreen students while living in the dorms. A freshman named Heather

Lewis lived directly above Calvin in those dorms. Early in the school year, while visiting his roommate, she met Calvin.

"I totally fell in love with him," she says. "He was extremely compelling and unlike anyone I had ever met."

Heather's reaction was a common one for those who encountered the odd and engaging teen. Calvin used his charm to create a circle of music-minded friends.

"I met this fellow, Tony Traverso; he lived in a different building," Calvin recalls. "He was from the Boston area—Ipswich, actually—and played guitar, and he was interested in music, and I met some other weirdos that were all first- or second-year students who were kind of into weird crap."

At the same time, Calvin managed to stay close to his KAOS roots. Eventually, he would earn back a deejay spot when Foster decided that Calvin should take over Foster's 10 p.m. to midnight spot every other Tuesday. He was also becoming closer friends with Bruce, listening to music with the upperclassman, and even contributing to his zine. In mid-autumn Bruce asked Calvin if he would play a show that Tiny Holes was in at the New Deli in downtown Olympia. If Calvin wanted to get on the bill with Tiny Holes, Foster and his band, the Pop Philosophers, and a band called Mr. Right and the Breadwinners, Bruce said, Calvin should talk to the guy putting on the show, Gary Allen May.

After receiving directions to May's apartment, Calvin jumped on a bus headed toward 207 West Fourth Avenue, in the Barnes Floral building. Calvin walked up to apartment No. 2 and turned the hand-crank doorbell. A voice called him inside. There, Calvin saw "the ultimate rock 'n' roll bachelor pad; it was this old apartment, freezing cold, mattress on the floor, ashtray, a couple coffee cups, guy laying in the bed with some woman. I don't know who she was. *He* knew who she was, though. And he told me to come in and I came in and said, 'Hey, I'm Calvin. I hear you're puttin' on a show and I want to talk to you about it.' And he says, 'Okay, I'll tell you what. Why don't we meet down at the Spar in about twenty minutes? I'd love to talk to you."

Half an hour later, Calvin was talking with May at the counter of the Spar Café downtown. May, an Evergreen alum, had spent a couple years working at a local cinema before moving on to his job as a dishwasher at the New Deli, one of the few live music clubs that embraced something besides rock 'n' roll, which they actively avoided.

"They had this long-standing folk and jazz thing going on," May recalls. "It was doin' okay but not doin' that well."

The venue was the site of an acoustic-appreciation music club called Victory Music, which brought folk and jazz artists into the sixty-capacity venue. May himself—a member of Mr. Right and the Breadwinners—was more inclined toward the Victory sound, until punk rock changed his mind.

"He was like a jazz-bo guy, like all the other jazz-bo guys," Calvin says. "But somewhere along the way, he had heard the Cramps and decided that rock 'n' roll was where it's at, and he started his band and decided they should have rock 'n' roll at the New Deli. Somehow he talked them into this idea, which they didn't seem that enthusiastic about."

Calvin told May that he was interested in playing the show. May invited him onto the bill. Calvin was ecstatic, but there was a problem: he had no band.

Traverso and Calvin had played music together, but never really solidified into a group. After meeting with May, Calvin announced to Traverso that they would start a band called the Cool Rays and would play at the New Deli in a few weeks. The duo got to work, until the Washington State Liquor Board ruined everything.

After hearing that the New Deli was putting on a rock 'n' roll show, the authorities informed the venue that, while folk and jazz shows could be all-ages with alcohol service, this rock show was off-limits to anyone under twenty-one. The New Deli's owners informed May, who passed on the word to the bands.

"That was so painful to go tell Calvin, 'You know what? You can still play the show, but you won't be able to watch the show, because you're underage,'" May recalls.

Remembering the hassle that D.C. bars had given him, Calvin dropped off the bill.

"I only wanted to play all-ages shows," Calvin says. "Gary felt that, 'Well, you committed to play the show, so you should play the show.' But then I said to him, 'You committed to me that the show was going to be all-ages.' For many years, Gary held it against me, because he thought I should play the show. So, they had the show, and not only did I not play it, I couldn't even go."

Despite not having a show to play, the Cool Rays were united, adding lyricist and saxophonist Ed Gaidrich, bass player Cathy Watson, and drummer Tracy Taylor; the band even recorded a batch of songs with Fisk. One of those songs would show up on *Absolute Elsewhere*, a tape compilation that capped the catalog of Mr. Brown Records & Tapes. Another appeared on *Sub Pop 5*, a cassette compilation mailed out to subscribers of Bruce's zine, which had shortened its name from *Subterranean Pop*. The band played a number of all-ages shows on the Evergreen campus. The Cool Rays' boy-girl makeup, primitive understanding of rock 'n' roll, and Calvin's poetic jumble of tongue twisters and pop culture references, delivered with childlike simplicity, appealed to a few early adherents.

That spring the band was invited to play a punk cooperative in southeast Portland called Clockwork Joe's for the first ever "Olympia Goes to Portland Weekend." But when the Cool Rays performed, the place was almost empty, as it was for every other band that weekend. The Olympia bands weren't bad—it was just that no one in Portland knew anything about them.

"It was an important lesson to always have local bands play," Calvin says. "It was just Olympia bands. Who is gonna go? No one's ever heard of us. Why would they go to our show?"

Despite the low turnout, Calvin watched every band. The first night, he slept on the floor of the studio space where the concert was held until Leesa Anderson of popular local punk band Sado-Nation offered the band a place to stay.

Anderson wasn't the only Portland luminary Calvin ran across that weekend. He also met Fred Cole, who fronted the Rats, and Greg Sage, the enigmatic lead singer of the Wipers. But the connections made and lessons learned would ultimately be of no benefit to the band: in June of 1981, the Cool Rays disbanded after all its members, except Calvin, left Olympia for the summer.

For the next year, Calvin concentrated on his studies and his radio show. He rented a tiny studio in the Capitol Theater building. His neighbors were Bruce and his burgeoning Sub Pop empire and a fellow Evergreen student named Stella Marrs, who moved into the building at the same time as Calvin after living with him in a house on Legion Way the previous summer.

In her four-room studio Stella and a handful of fellow female artists created a nascent arts collective; members of the community could create and sell their own artworks and crafts. They called it Girl City. In the tavern culture of downtown Olympia, there was very little feminism on display, but thanks to the sagging economy, there was plenty of space for new ideas to take root. And Stella had a wealth of ideas.

"I got the tools and identity of being an artist at Evergreen," Stella recalls. "And I had the politics of feminism. I just wanted to make work and to make work in the community of other women. When I first started that process, I was shocked at how inhibited and self-conscious my peers were in terms of expressing their voices, so I was very driven to make this mini-universe of girl production."

That universe was mostly populated by women, but not exclusively. Stella believed in creating an inclusive environment and was welcoming of men. One of those men was Calvin. From the time that Stella first saw Calvin, wearing sunglasses and a string of pearls in the campus library where she worked, she knew that, like herself, he was interested in challenging perceptions of what was permitted in normative culture. As she came to know Calvin through various shared friends, she grew to understand that the two had something in common.

"This is what our link is," Stella says. "The ground was pulled out from under us when we were younger. I lost my primary gender parent model, as did Calvin, at really the same age. I think something like that really ends up shifting what you assume is the ground beneath your feet and the borders around you. You really start to realize how arbitrary those things are and you don't really pay attention to them the same way. We weren't afraid to reinterpret anything."

Stella was interested in reinterpreting feminism. By 1981 the women who had come to power during the second wave of feminism in the '60s were mothers, and their ideas were forming a strict code of formalized behavior for feminists—from the manner of their activism (direct) to their form of dress (asexual), to their preferred title (woman). Stella and her fellow artists were interested in a different type of feminism, one that embraced the traditional roles of women in Western culture and turned what were once strictures into modes of expression.

"There was this kind of feminism in Olympia at the time, particularly through the work of Stella," recalls Rich Jensen, a new student at Evergreen that fall and another one of the men who ventured into Girl City. "They were really embracing a kind of housewife culture. There were women who thought that there in fact was a unique kind of power in girlhood and that there was amazing cultural knowledge and power in the way that, say, '50s housewives had run their home, that was their power to be recovered. So, they made aprons, and learned to cook, and did domestic arts, and reclaimed this cultural territory that had been the province of womanhood."

Stella kept an odd schedule in the autumn of 1981, what she called "winter artist hours": working until three or four in the morning. While she worked, Calvin would hang out in the studio, surrounded by the Christmas lights she had hung for the season. That December, Stella opened her studio every Saturday and invited the public inside to buy artwork in what was a kind of Christmas bazaar. Calvin's contribution to the inventory was found in the first-ever Girl City calendar.

"He had drawn a picture for one of the months," Stella remembers. "He cut it out and he needed something to stick the picture to another piece of paper. We didn't have any glue, so he just used some jam. That's how he resolved the problem."

That autumn, Calvin met another woman who would become a fast friend, a freshman from Phoenix, Arizona, named Lois Maffeo. Lois was catholic in her taste of music, which endeared her to Calvin almost immediately.

"I remember that she had Nick Drake albums in her collection," he recalls. "Now, this is thirty years ago, before anyone knew who Nick Drake was. I knew him because of working at KAOS, but for this seventeen-year-old girl to have all three of his LPs—that was something else. But then, she also had all of these Gene Vincent records and she loved pop culture. And I loved pop culture, so we got along really great from the start."

While spending time with Lois, Calvin also got to know her dormmate, Krista Forcast. Krista was a native of Anacortes, a small fishing town on Fidalgo Island, an hour north of Seattle. That December, Krista's boyfriend, Bret Lunsford, stopped at Evergreen to visit on his way to Tucson, where he would winter, spending his days fishing with his uncle Roy. During that visit, he met Calvin.

Bret was still living in Anacortes but was beset with wanderlust and had spent the year after high school graduation traveling from Mexico to New York and on to Los Angeles rather than going to college. Calvin and Bret didn't speak much, but Bret did see something they had in common.

"I was intrigued by his record collection," Bret recalls. "It was expensive and hard to find those punk seven-inches, and it was cool to be exposed to other people's records; their history was often shown in what they had in their collection."

In that collection, Bret saw the earliest records from his favorite band: the Jam. That spring, the Jam announced a show at Kerrisdale Arena in Vancouver, B.C. In early June, Bret drove his mom's station wagon from Anacortes down to Olympia; the next day, he, Krista, Lois, and Calvin headed north on I-5 to see the Jam play for the first and last time. The Kerrisdale Arena show was the Jam's last show on North American soil. Within a year, the group would disband.

A BRIEF HISTORY OF THE EVERGREEN STATE COLLEGE

The Evergreen State College was founded by the Washington legislature in 1967, following a request from the presidents of the state's colleges for a new institution to serve the growing student body. But Evergreen was different from the rest of those schools. A product of the culture of experimental education that arose in the '60s, the school was founded on the idea that, as the state senator who crafted the legislation stated, it "would not be bound by any rigid structure of tradition."

In the fall of 1971, the first freshman class arrived at the thousand-acre campus located ten miles outside of Olympia and was greeted by an educational platform built around interdisciplinary education and student-determined coursework. There were no majors to be declared at Evergreen; instead of a series of required courses, the students signed up for a single interdisciplinary "program," which would make up the full sixteen-credit course load for a quarter, with some programs lasting as long as three quarters. Multiple instructors taught each program, delivered evaluations rather than grades, and awarded credits based on student participation. The school also offered Individual Learning Contracts, which were used by students, like Dean Katz who started KAOS, to complete a project of their own determination in lieu of a program of study.

The school's approach to postsecondary education was not without its detractors and has been a flash point for controversy among students and faculty throughout its history. Despite criticism, Evergreen has received high marks as an institution and as a successful model of experimentation, even at times when interest in alternative forms of postsecondary education has waned.

5

IN THE SUMMER OF 1982, a postcard from Reno, Nevada, arrived at the Capitol Theater building. It was addressed to Calvin.

The postcard, sent by a woman named Bessie, was the continuation of a correspondence Calvin had been carrying on with her and another woman named Jone, both of whom published a fanzine called *Paranoid* that claimed "Blind and Illiterate Punks" as its audience. The first issue jokingly advertised itself as "Only $29.95"; later issues were only fifty cents. In its newsprint pages were stories about bands in the Reno punk scene and the latest on U.K. punk, the D.C. scene, and the West Coast's more well-known bands, from Southern California's hardcore groups to D.O.A. and the Subhumans, bands that were creating a scene of their own in Vancouver, B.C.

It was in Vancouver a year earlier that Calvin had discovered *Paranoid* sitting in a pile of publications at a party he attended during a brief visit. After writing the publishers of the zine, Calvin discovered that they were in an all-girl punk group called the Wrecks. The postcard was an invitation to Calvin to finally see the Wrecks when the band opened for Black Flag at a hockey rink in Vancouver.

Despite Black Flag's popularity, Calvin was suspicious of the band. The year before, Dez Cadena, Black Flag's third vocalist in its five-year history, had given up his lead singer role to focus on guitar playing. In his place, the band brought on Henry Rollins. Rollins was a product of the D.C. punk scene that Calvin had witnessed two years before. As the lead singer of S.O.A., Rollins performed at the Unheard Music Festival where Calvin first heard Minor Threat. Calvin remembered the singer well.

"I had never actually seen Black Flag before. But I had seen Henry play with S.O.A.," Calvin recalls. "When I heard that he was going to be the new lead singer of Black Flag, I was just like, 'No, that can't be.' He just seemed so random to me. He just seemed to me like he was some football player whose best friend was into punk, so he ripped the sleeves off his T-shirt and decided to be in a band. It just seemed so wrong; it just seemed so off, and ungood, so ungood. So I was really unhappy that he was in the band."

In late 1981 Black Flag released its first studio album, *Damaged*, which featured Rollins punching a mirror on its cover. The album was not a commercial success, but it did succeed in impressing Calvin. Still, the young punk was more interested in seeing his pen pals in the Wrecks play than seeing Rollins lead Black Flag.

Lacking a car or money for the bus ride, Calvin hitchhiked the entire two hundred miles. Sam Hendricks, his friend and traveling companion on the trip, suggested that they visit Bret in Anacortes on the way up. The Friday before the show, Calvin and Sam packed their bags, went out to the nearest I-5 on-ramp, and stuck out their thumbs. Only four cars blew by before one slowed to a stop. At the wheel was Jon Turnbow, an Olympia musician that Calvin recognized. Three years before, Turnbow had released *Alien City*, a glam rock concept album that Calvin had seen on the shelf at Olympia's Rainy Day Records shop. While Turnbow wasn't the greatest singer, his vision was grand in scope, as revealed in the liner notes to his album:

> *Alien City* was composed over a period of five years. It is a song cycle of epic proportions centering around the incarnation of Celestial Visitors to this planet. They take youthful

bodies with the soul mission of increasing the intelligence of the human race. Alas, in their compassionate endeavors they become trapped in the pernicious web of the world and their aim becomes warped and sarcastic. In taking mortal bodies they lose their reference point, their center of gravity, and they eventually become as depraved and stupefied as the very people they initially intended to illuminate. There is no story line; no characters are introduced. The work is arranged in four movements.

It was rumored that, after releasing *Alien City*, Turnbow was committed to a mental institution. If that was true, he had managed to gain release and a wife by the time he met Calvin and Hendricks on that I-5 on-ramp. Turnbow asked Calvin where he and Hendricks were heading.

"Oh, going to Anacortes, so we just need a ride as far north as you can go. Mount Vernon would be perfect, or Burlington."

"We're stopping in Mount Vernon to meet this friend of ours. He's going to Anacortes—maybe he can give you a ride."

"Great!"

Two hours later, they arrived at the small town of Mount Vernon. Turnbow pulled into a restaurant parking lot full of cars and next to a man leaning against his car, waiting. The four Olympians exited the car and, after a brief conversation between Turnbow, his wife, and their friend, Calvin and Hendricks were ushered into the stranger's car.

"It was almost as if they were only meeting their friend to pass us off to him," Calvin recalls. "They didn't sit and talk with him, or anything. They just said, 'These guys need a ride to Anacortes, bye!' And they left."

An hour later, Calvin and Hendricks pulled up to Krista Forcast's Anacortes home. After saying farewell to the stranger who drove them there, the two college students entered the house to find Forcast and her friends plotting plans for the evening. The big event was a show at the Summit Park Grange Hall, right outside the city limits. While Grange Halls were built in most rural communities to house events for farmers who belonged to the fraternal organization, they also served as community centers where events could be staged.

In this case, the event was a concert by a band called the Spoiled.

As far as punk rockers go, the Spoiled was straight out of central casting. Brash and uncompromising, the band had made its start as the Outcasts, covering early punk songs by the Sex Pistols and the Clash. When they started writing and performing their own material, which was as loud and obnoxious as any of the songs they were covering, the band changed its name. The newly christened Spoiled booked its debut gig through a family connection. The band was to serve as the entertainment for a gathering of the Rainbow Girls at the local Masonic Temple.

"The people who booked the band didn't know what they were getting," recalls Bret Lunsford. "Maybe the band knew what they were getting into, but I think the show lasted for three songs."

The members of the Spoiled had graduated from Anacortes High School the year before, in the same class as Bret and Krista. Instead of heading off to college or traveling, though, the members of the Spoiled stayed in town and played music. They all rented an old house together, where they hung an American flag in the living room, their band name written in black spray paint across the stars and stripes. And they played shows wherever they could and for whoever would show up.

Being a small town, Anacortes offered little in the way of entertainment for residents under the age of twenty-one. So when Forcast and her friends were planning their Friday night, there was little doubt that they would go see the Spoiled play a show. The plan was to meet Bret at the Summit Park Grange Hall. First, though, Forcast and her friends would take Calvin and Hendricks to "cruise the gut," the ritual teenage experience of driving up and down Commercial Avenue, the main strip that led from the main highway to the docks. After acquiring some beer, the girls and their guests made off in one of their parent's muscle cars. "Don't tip when you see square headlights," Forcast advised her passengers, informing them that the county cops all drove cars with headlights in that shape, and that they would pull them over if they saw anyone drinking beer. Calvin needed no warning.

When the car pulled up to the Grange Hall, Calvin saw a teenage paradise. There were kids in the parking lot, and past the doorman, who was also a teenager, were a couple hundred teenagers on the dance floor. And on stage was the Spoiled, teenagers as well, dressed in U.S. Army fatigues and leather jackets and wearing their hair short. The band played a combination of covers and original songs. Calvin found Bret standing against the wall and talked to him for a while before taking to the dance floor. For him, this party in the middle of the country with other teenagers was reminiscent of the early Beatles shows he had read about.

"It's like normal kids appreciating local music, local culture," he says. "That seemed exciting to me because it was not something that was going on anywhere. Local bands did not play and have people show up, you know? Even though it was mostly covers, still, it was just the idea that they were having a local scene. That was really exciting. And also the idea of having it at the Grange Hall. Crazy. I was like, 'This is such a great idea!' Because that's what the Grange Hall is. It's a place where people congregate. Yeah, it's a trade organization, but it's also a social organization. And it just made sense that here in this small town you would go to the Grange Hall to see the local band. So I was just like, 'Why don't we have this in Olympia? This doesn't happen in Olympia.'"

The surreal experience ended abruptly when the town sheriff and a handful of deputies showed up. "Okay, party's over," the sheriff announced, but the party continued. As the deputies ushered the young revelers out, the Spoiled kept on playing. The deputies finally pulled the singer off the stage.

"He wouldn't stop playing," Calvin recalls. "He just kept rockin'. It was so awesome. And so they arrested him, put him in the back of the police car."

Outside, Calvin, Bret, and their friends watched as the police ushered the rest of the teenagers out, placing a few of them in the backs of squad cars. Calvin was energized by what he had just experienced. Before that night, he had only been in a Grange Hall to attend Cub Scout meetings. Now, he saw community halls and the possibilities of punk rock in a whole new light.

"Anacortes has had a connection to the history of K, maybe dating back to that moment," Bret says. "I didn't know it at the time, but I do recognize it now that something clicked for Calvin about Anacortes and about what was going on."

The morning after the Spoiled show, Calvin and Hendricks woke up early at Bret's house. Bret had invited them to go strawberry picking with him and his younger brother Jonn to make some extra money. The four teenagers trudged out into the early morning rain and down to the strawberry patch. After picking fifteen dollars worth of berries, Calvin headed back to Bret's house with Hendricks, changed clothes, and hopped in Bret's mom's car. An hour later, Calvin and Hendricks were back at an interstate on-ramp, their thumbs stretched out in the midsummer rain, hoping to catch a ride sixty miles to the border.

After two hours in the rain and two short rides, a large American car pulled over. Inside, two young stoners greeted Calvin and Hendricks.

"Where you going?" asked the stoners.

"We're going up to Vancouver."

"Oh, so are we!"

"Awesome!"

"What're you going to do in Vancouver?"

"Well, we're going to see this show . . ."

"Oh. Cool. Yeah, yeah . . ."

Calvin and Hendricks settled in for the short ride to the border. It was then that Calvin realized his back pockets were empty. He had left his wallet in Anacortes, which at this point was eighty miles behind them. Rather than alert the driver, Calvin kept the news to himself, hoping for a smooth passage through the border. He had no such luck.

"Whatcha all doin'?" asked the Canadian border agent.

"Goin' to Vancouver," answered the driver.

"Are you all American citizens?"

"Oh yeah, we are. Well, *we* are. I don't know about those guys."

"They're not with you?"

"No, I just picked them up hitchhiking."

"Okay, pull over there, go inside, talk to . . ."

In 1982 the United States–Canada border was fairly lax. No passport was needed for U.S. residents to pass through, but they did require state-issued identification. Calvin's identification was back in bucolic Anacortes, along with the fifteen dollars he had earned that morning. When the border guard asked for his ID, Calvin told him the truth.

"Well, do you have anything with your name or anything that identifies you?" the guard asked.

Calvin reached into his bag, still wet from the morning rain, and pulled out the postcard sent to him from Bessie of the Wrecks. The card was limp and wet, the penciled invitation blurred. Still, the guard could make out the recipient's address.

"And you're Calvin Johnson?" he asked.

"Yes, sir," Calvin replied.

"All right. Have a good time."

Calvin and Hendricks walked back to the waiting car in disbelief. They sat in silence for the short thirty-mile ride from the border to Vancouver. Perhaps aware of his slip at the border, the driver graciously dropped the two young punks at the entrance of the hockey rink where Black Flag was scheduled to play.

The show was a memorable one. The Wrecks played hard, seeming to know that this one-off show with the kings of hardcore would be the band's biggest ever. Later that year, the Wrecks would break up, though its members would go on to form the influential San Francisco independent pop band Imperial Teen. Next, Vancouver's Subhumans, at the height of their popularity, played to an enthused hometown crowd. By the end of the year, that group would disband as well.

Black Flag was a revelation for Calvin. After touring on its debut full-length for a year and celebrating the July release of "TV Party," a single that would become one of its most well-known songs, the band was in muscular form. Black Flag mastermind guitarist and composer Greg Ginn wove the band's tight-knit and brutally fast songs while Rollins, wearing his trademark shorts and nothing else, demanded the room's attention and got it. The show far exceeded Calvin's expectations.

That night, Calvin and Hendricks slept in the alley behind the hockey rink. The next morning, July 4, they walked to the highway and began hitchhiking back to Olympia. Twelve stops and a smooth entrance into the country later, they would settle for a night in Seattle. There, Calvin went again to see Black Flag play at the Nordic Hall before hitchhiking to Olympia the next morning. Later that month, he wrote a review of the experience for *Sub Pop*.

"Henry was incredible," Calvin wrote. "Pacing back and forth, lunging, lurching, growling; it was all real, the most intense emotional experience I have ever seen."

A BRIEF HISTORY OF THE CASSETTE

The audiocassette was first introduced by Philips, the multinational electronics corporation, in 1964 as an audio storage device intended not for music but for dictation. Few record companies bothered with the technology because of its poor fidelity. Even when the quality of the tape improved, the overwhelming majority of cassette players were still configured for dictation and held little promise for a pleasant listening experience. With the exception of flirtations with the eight-track, consumers were content buying their music on wax.

When Sony introduced the Walkman in 1978, that all changed. The portable cassette player was marketed as a must-have for the hip and the young, which hit right into the playbook for major record labels. Soon, all of the majors were issuing their releases on both cassette and vinyl. Car companies began installing tape decks in their factory models, and the cassette became a necessity for any home stereo.

The portable stereo (aka the boom box) was soon introduced, followed by a version with two tape decks, which allowed for duplication onto blank cassettes. That was a problem for the music industry. The British Phonographic Industry launched a campaign to dissuade consumers from duplication, disseminating a skull and crossbones–inspired logo beneath the slogan "Home Taping Is Killing Music." Whether or not the slogan did major labels any good, it gave punk bands a cause and the opportunity to align themselves with the home-taping contingent. The Clash delayed the release of *Sandinista!* in the United States after demanding that its Stateside record label, Epic, remove the logo from the record. The Dead Kennedys went one step further by including a spoof message on *In God We Trust, Inc.*: "Home taping is killing record industry profits! We left this side blank so you can help." For the emerging punk movement, the cassette provided a quick and easy way to disseminate underground music to young fans. As the punk culture quickly grew, though, it abandoned the format for the seven-inch single and eventually the LP.

For a brief period in the late '80s, after it had helped vanquish the LP as a mainstream format, the cassette was the format of choice for consumers. Then the CD came along, quickly replacing the cassette as the most popular format while providing the music industry with a sense of relief that the era of rampant cassette tape duplication was over.

BY THE SUMMER OF 1982, the Olympia music community had made a complete migration from Evergreen to downtown. While there still wasn't an all-ages venue where bands could play, the growing number of groups made due by playing wherever they could. Concerts were put on in alleyways, or groups played small dance parties in each other's apartments. It was at one of those parties later that summer that Calvin first heard the Supreme Cool Beings.

Like many Olympia acts, the band was a ramshackle affair, featuring musicians with limited ability playing whatever instruments were available to them. Gary Allen May, the rock 'n' roll bachelor who had been booking shows at the New Deli restaurant, played guitar and bass and shared vocal duties with a very loud, self-taught saxophonist named Doug Monaghan and the drummer, Calvin's former dormitory neighbor Heather Lewis. The Supreme Cool Beings was Heather's first band.

"I never had any aspirations to play music," Heather says. "I was taking visual art classes at Evergreen. I was over at Gary Allen May's apartment with Doug Monaghan and Laura Carter. I think it was the first time I met Gary. He had a drum kit. I sat down and just started playing. I think he and Doug had been wanting to start a band and they asked me to play the drums with them. It just happened. The next day I went to band practice."

May saw something in Heather that she didn't and as the band developed, the untrained drummer turned into a fierce creative force.

"Heather distinguished herself as a hard-hitting drummer," May says. "She actually could have done anything in that band and done it just as well as she played the drums. She was equally involved in anything creative that was going on. She wasn't just some girl who played the drums. An equal partner; the songs were all by us and the lyrics were all by us."

Undergirded by Heather's drum lines, the music moved many in the Olympia scene, including Calvin, who invited the band to play an in-studio set during his Tuesday night show, now titled *Boy Meets Girl*. The band agreed and arrived at the KAOS studio the next week, where it played a set of eight short songs.

The band started with "Who's That?" Opening with a sinister bass line, the song quickly crackled with a snare hit by Heather, who began hitting the ones and threes as she sang a series of questions in a serious alto voice: "Who's that walkin' on the sofa?" "Who's that hummin' in the kitchen?" "Who's that tappin' on the air?" and "Who's that breathin'?" At that point, Monaghan's saxophone blurted out four brassy notes. The song continued, with May eventually answering all of Heather's questions: "a cat," "the refrigerator," "I don't know," "me!" Wobbling in and out of time, the song never lost steam, moving forward until a flurry of saxophone honks finally gave way to four sharp snare hits. The song was far from perfect, but it was filled with the energy of a band on the verge of discovery. Unlike much punk music, which vacillated between self-seriousness and satire, this music just sounded fun—playful even. If there was any doubt of this, the next song put it to rest.

"Childhood has gone down the drain," May intoned as the band played "Your Name Here." "Mr. Potato Head isn't even the same."

The rest of the set continued in similar fashion, with May taking most of the vocal duties. Halfway through, he switched from bass to guitar while introducing the next song, "Um."

"Are you going to tell us a story, Heather?" May asked, before starting a song that required him to do little more than play two chords over and over. As Monaghan bleated and skronked out a non sequitur saxophone line for two minutes, Heather spoke her verse: "Um, well, um, well, oh I don't know, um, see, uh, well, oh, hmm, well, um, ehh, um, I don't know, um, well, see there was, um, well, oh, um, uh, well, oh, I don't, I don't know, I don't know, oh, I don't know."

The song ended with a syrupy approximation of a surf rock breakdown. It was weird but also charming, a moment of playing dumb for a band that clearly had no problem being smart.

After a brief instrumental called "Liberal Art," the band played the closest thing it had to a mainstream pop song, "Big Bombs."

"Sun goes up, sun goes down," May sang, his voice containing shades of the Talking Heads' David Byrne. "Water goes up, water comes down."

The final song, "Our Advice to You," swung back in the direction of the band's playful songs but was punctuated with subversion.

"This is our advice to you," May said by way of introducing the song. Heather laid down a drum line that managed to be both slippery and tight, while May ground his way through a jangly chord progression and Monaghan wrestled notes out of his sax. After two minutes in this groove, all three stopped and shouted: "Take your clothes off!"

Unbeknownst to the performers, Calvin had taped the entire show. After listening to it again, he had an idea.

Earlier in the year, Bruce Pavitt had released *Sub Pop 5*: a cassette compilation that featured, among others, Jad Fair of Half

Japanese, Steve Fisk, and the Cool Rays. The compilation was meant to expose the *Sub Pop* readers to an array of different artists, and cassettes made the creation, duplication, and distribution of these collections easy. But, despite a growing number of mainstream artists who were moving from vinyl to cassette, very few underground artists had made the leap to releasing full-length albums through the new technology.

Without the financial means to release full-length vinyl albums, most bands in the underground had committed themselves to recording and releasing 45 singles. The prospect of recording a full-length just didn't make sense, and since the cassette was the province of major labels, it carried the additional strike of having a bad reputation.

"On the mainstream, the cassette had completely replaced the album," Calvin recalls. "But on the underground level, cassettes were never really accepted. They were tolerated. But if you made a cassette-only release, it was definitely looked upon as similar to a band today handing you a CD-R with their album burned onto it. It just wasn't viewed as legitimate. If you made your own [vinyl] album, that was more like, 'Oh, that's legit,' but if it was a cassette-only release, that was like, 'Oh, that's not a real record.'"

At the time, though, Calvin had little choice. With the full recording of the Supreme Cool Beings' session in hand, and Bruce's knowledge of cassette reproduction, Calvin saw the opportunity to issue, at little cost, an album that he believed people should hear. He approached May with the idea. After the band agreed to the plan, Calvin got to work. Through Bruce, he connected with Pat Baum, drummer for the all-girl new wave band Neo Boys and a feminist fixture in Portland's underground music culture.

Baum had acquired the most rudimentary equipment to duplicate cassettes, which dubbed each one in real time, and started her own cassette label. She could make duplications for Calvin; he just had to supply the cassettes. With Rich Jensen's help, Calvin found a company on the outskirts of Olympia that carried blank cassettes in bulk. The company used the cassettes to record choral music for religious services but was happy to sell them to Calvin at a slight markup. Baum agreed to duplicate the Supreme Cool Beings tape at a cost of $1.20 each. Calvin sent her 150 tapes.

While waiting for his cassettes to come back, Calvin asked Heather, whose artwork he had seen at Girl City, to create the cover art. She painted three stick figures. Above them, in pencil, she wrote the band's name; below, she gave the album its title, *Survival of the Coolest*. Before photocopying the sleeve of the album, Calvin would add two final touches: On the narrow side of the album, below the band name, he drew a capital "K" with a roughly drawn shield around it. On the back, he drew it again, with a much bolder shield, next to an address: "Box 7154 Olympia Washington 98507."

"It's unclear why the name is K," Calvin says, "but I did have the foresight to realize that a one-letter name can easily get lost. So I thought that if I put this shield around it, it might show up a little better in the text. But it was a concept; it wasn't a design. There wasn't a set 'K.'"

When the shipment arrived, Calvin inserted the J-sleeve into every one of the 150 cassette cases and began distributing the album. He placed a few copies at Rainy Day Records, where he had once seen Turnbow's *Alien City* on display. He sent copies out to the few connections he had in the record business, including one to a former KAOS deejay named Phil Hertz who had moved to San Francisco to work at the U.S. wholesale and distribution arm for Rough Trade Records. He also took a handful to Girl City, which had recently moved out of Stella Marrs's studio and—for a six month stint—was operating out of a storefront in the Angeles Building, downstairs from Heather's apartment and across the street from May's building.

Calvin also sent copies for review to fanzines and publications focused on music, including *The Rocket* in Seattle. Despite the underground credibility of KAOS and *OP Magazine*, *The Rocket* viewed Olympia—and Evergreen State College in particular—with the smiling patronization of an older brother.

Though the cassette was sent in early autumn, a review didn't show up in *The Rocket* until the February 1983 issue of the monthly publication. At the very end of a tape roundup that included a release from another Olympia band described as having the "grating pretensions so often the downfall of so many arty-Oly-Evergreeny type groups," reviewer Ann Powers tackled the first release from Calvin's K Records. She wrote two sentences and never mentioned the unknown label.

> The Supreme Cool Beings sing about Mr. Potatohead [sic] and taking your clothes off. Their sound is kind of sloppy, Heather's vocals come off sort of flat, and it's all kind of silly, but that's really the fun of it.

By the time that review appeared, May had left town and the band had, for all intents and purposes, broken up. That did not help with record sales.

"No one paid attention," Calvin recalls. "We didn't really sell a lot of them. It took a few years to sell them all. I mean, there was a lot we were giving away, but there were a lot of tapes for a long time. Never re-pressed it, I mean, that was it."

The recording wasn't a complete loss. After May left town, Calvin recruited hard-hitting Heather to start a band with him and another Evergreen student named Laura Carter. For the band, Calvin embraced the minimalist aesthetic and instrumental flexibility he had discovered with the Supreme Cool Beings. The three-piece, called Laura, Heather and Calvin, stripped the sound even further, dropping the saxophone and bass in favor of a simple drums-guitar-vocals combination reminiscent of the Cramps.

Musically, the band relied on Heather's crisp, dance-friendly groove and Calvin's deceptively simple lyricism, which had been on hold since his days in the Cool Rays more than two years earlier. The band rarely practiced, but the trio was good at improvising. Laura, Heather and Calvin played a few shows before spring break, and even recorded a few songs, one of which would later appear on the third *Sub Pop* compilation, *Sub Pop 9*.

Around that time, Bret invited Calvin to visit Tucson, where the young wanderer was spending his second consecutive winter. It so happened that Lois Maffeo and Sam Hendricks were going to Lois's hometown of Phoenix during the break as well. Calvin took the train down to Arizona and, after spending a few days in Phoenix, traveled to Tucson on his own to see Bret.

They were still just acquaintances, but Bret was eager to show Calvin around Tucson. That winter, Bret's girlfriend had sent him copies of *Sub Pop* in which Bruce had written about the decentralization of culture that was taking place because of the emerging independent music movement and Calvin had written about his revelation at the Grange Hall in Anacortes. Bret had discovered something similar at work in Tucson and was eager to show Calvin.

"Being from a small town, you kind of develop a real hunger for anonymity," Bret says. "I just wanted to get away from Anacortes and see what's out there and meet people without any prior connection, so that's what attracted me about travel and living in other towns. Tucson resonated with me because it was cool to live in a college town without going to college, 'cause everything is geared towards youth culture and I actually had the time to pursue it. I didn't really have a job when I was down there. I washed dishes at a restaurant on the weekend, that kind of thing."

Thanks to the trailblazing touring schedules of early punk rock bands like Black Flag and Hüsker Dü, by 1982 a number of college towns across the country had developed their own underground culture, with a few businesses that were tailored to young people looking outside the confines of the mainstream. Tucson was no different. In his first year in the city, Bret had discovered an underground rock club called the Backstage and a record shop called Roads to Moscow, which was owned by a man named Lee Joseph. Joseph had started his own record label and was releasing music on cassettes. So, when Calvin arrived bearing the Supreme Cool Beings tape, Bret saw it as part of a larger trend and accepted it with no prejudice. In short, Bret got it.

"When Calvin started K, the medium was part of what he was promoting as much as the music," Bret says. "Part of that had to do with access. 'Hey, now everyone has the equipment to stage this revolution against the corporate ogre, so buy some blank tapes, record yourself in your living room, release it!' It's inspiring to have that kind of decentralized, expressive democracy."

Calvin and Bret spent the next few days wandering around Tucson until late in the night, talking about music and college and girls. The two shared an off-kilter sense of humor: sardonic, wry, and informed by a deep knowledge of pop culture. They also shared a worldliness uncommon to men their age, the product of an unquenchable curiosity and willingness to see their ideas—no matter how harebrained—through to completion. While telling stories of places they had been, the two explored the spots Bret had uncovered in the past two years. One in particular was the dumpy bar at the Hotel Congress, which was located in a bad part of town but had a jukebox that Bret loved. There, the two solidified their friendship while plugging quarters into the juke, listening to Conway Twitty sing his torch song "It's Only Make Believe" over and over again.

As the music played, Calvin told Bret about his trouble booking an Olympia show for Minor Threat, the new band fronted by

Calvin's old D.C. friend Ian MacKaye. The band was willing, he said, but he couldn't find an all-ages venue to host it. There was no such problem in Tucson, where the band was scheduled to play at the Backstage in a few days. Bret implored Calvin to stay, but Calvin declined, deciding to head back to Olympia in time for class. He told Bret to say hello to MacKaye for him.

After Calvin left, Bret listened to the Supreme Cool Beings cassette. He liked it, and for the rest of his time in Tucson, listened to it continuously. A month later, on his way back to Anacortes, Bret stopped in Olympia. He saw Laura, Heather and Calvin play a show with Foster's Pop Philosophers and Rich Jensen, who had started performing spoken word, at the Smithfield Café, a small coffee shop next door to Girl City.

"That's where Olympia clicked for me," Bret recalls. "I had had two years off from high school and I was willing to consider college then and this seemed like a really cool community to be a part of."

Bret went back to Anacortes and applied for admission to the Evergreen State College. He was accepted. Before moving to Olympia, though, Bret wanted to set up a show in his hometown with Calvin's new band.

While Bret was away exploring the world, his high school friends in the Spoiled had continued to pursue their music. Naturally, Bret went to them with the idea of putting on a show with Laura, Heather and Calvin and another popular Olympia group, the Young Pioneers. The Spoiled had limited options when it came to venues for local shows. The lead singer, Bryan Elliott, had found a prime location—an old train depot that had been turned into a meeting hall—but, given its reputation, the band had no hope of securing the space. In need of a citizen in high standing, they called up Jonn Lunsford, Bret's younger brother who was senior class president at Anacortes High School.

In exchange for Jonn's good name and fifty dollars, the owner handed over the space for the night.

The stage was set, but there was a problem. At the end of the school year, Laura had moved, leaving a hole in the band. Undeterred, Calvin told Bret that the band would play the show and that he planned to continue the band under a new name. Inspired by a film called *Beatnik Happening* that Bret's girlfriend Krista Forcast and Lois Maffeo had made, Calvin planned to call the new group Beat Happening. Bret took the cue and made posters promoting the show. Soon, the photocopied sheets showed up on telephone poles and bulletin boards around Anacortes, advertising the three-band bill with a tantalizing promise: "It's a beat happening!"

Calvin was able to salvage the show and cobble together a brief tour with a rotating cast of players that stood in for the missing Laura. The band first played an evening show in Bellingham, preceded by a live performance on the Western Washington University's college station, KUGS. The next night, the newly christened Beat Happening played in Anacortes. The show was a mess, but no one seemed to notice.

Afterward, Calvin took Bret aside. Despite the fact that Bret had not played the show or ever played guitar in front of an audience, Calvin saw something in him.

"You should join the band," Calvin said. "If you do, we'll go to Japan."

A BRIEF HISTORY OF PUNK POLITICS

While the Sex Pistols aimed their disdain for England's societal ills at the Queen, the American punks of the '80s found their true enemy in the guise of President Ronald Reagan. For many hardcore punk bands of the era, Reagan was one of the primary catalysts for their art. Joey "Shithead" Keithley, the lead singer for the Vancouver hardcore band D.O.A., summed it up best:

"Who was the person who did more for punk rock in the '80s than anyone? And I ain't talking about Jello Biafra or John Lydon," the singer was reported to have said at one of the band's shows, before answering himself: "It was Ronald Reagan! Everyone got into punk bands because of him."

For many progressive-minded teenagers becoming politically aware at the time, a union-busting commander in chief who promoted deregulation and tax breaks while instilling fear of a nuclear winter in the populace made for an obvious target.

"When Reagan came into office, it was such a stark divide between what was before and what was after," Stella Marrs says. "I think that almost the rawness and the little bit of militancy that came out of that regional definition of the music scene was definitely a response to how disenfranchised people felt. Reagan was more than a symbol. It really trickled down in a bleak economic way."

In the fall of 1983, musicians from New York organized a tour called Rock Against Reagan to rally the youth of the nation in revolt against its leader. The group drove a large flatbed truck equipped with a sound system to cities across the country and invited local bands to play. On October 9, the truck pulled up to the State Capitol Building in Olympia and the Young Pioneers played to a small crowd of punks. The show would not impact the next election, in which

Reagan carried Washington State on his way to one of the greatest landslide wins in the history of presidential politics.

Where the rally in Olympia did succeed was in introducing the city's political-minded punks, who hadn't had a place to congregate, to one another.

BRET LUNSFORD HAD NEVER played music in public. The seventh of eight children in a second-generation family of Croatian immigrants, Bret spent his childhood like that of most of his neighbors: exploring the island on which he lived, biking to Washington Park on the western edge of Fidalgo Island, and swimming in the chilly salt water of the Puget Sound. As Bret grew older, he and his younger brother, Jonn, organized ball games and pool tournaments with their neighbors. Though Bret and Jonn's grandfather was a music teacher at Anacortes High School, and their six elder siblings all received formal music instruction, music played a minor part in the early part of Bret's life.

By 1980, punk had made enough waves in the mainstream press that Bret and Jonn were aware of it. During Bret's sophomore year of high school, the brothers and a few friends discovered punk rock through the record collection of a senior named Don Yates. Yates would return from trips to nearby Bellingham and Seattle with records by the Clash, the Damned, and the Sex Pistols. One night, Bret and two friends traveled to Bellingham, planning to take in a midnight movie. First, though, they stopped at one of the record stores Yates had told them about. The clerks hard-sold Bret on the latest Jam album, *Sound Affects*, and told the three teenagers about a local punk rock show happening at the V Lounge. Bret and his friends skipped the movie and instead attended their first punk rock show. The seventeen-year-olds watched in amazement as the band X-15 ignited a frenzied crowd. The singer, Kelly

Mitchell, climbed a stack of amps, tearing down a sign for the radio station that was hosting the event before jumping and landing in a pile on the floor. The show ended with the singer gripping his leg, writhing in pain, surrounded by his fans, which now included Bret and his friends.*

The Lunsfords and their friends became punk rock devotees, regularly traveling to nearby cities to watch shows and shop for records. In his final year of high school, Bret bought an acoustic guitar and taught himself six chords, but his playing was never heard outside of his bedroom. He wouldn't dare start a band.

"There was a barrier about musicianship in my mind, and maybe more broadly in the culture, that I didn't have chops," Bret says. "My friends and I should have been in a band. I mean, we were huge music fans going to concerts all the time, hanging out together, listening to music religiously. We were a natural band, but it didn't occur that we could just grab instruments, start to play, and do shows, because that model hadn't quite reached through punk to us yet. Or, if it did, it hadn't quite sunk in yet."

Eventually, the punk ethos would inspire Bret's friends to start the band that would become the Spoiled, and even Bret's brother would form a band in high school. Bret, though, remained simply a devoted fan until the day that Calvin asked him to join Beat Happening, with the lure of a trip to Japan. Calvin's odd promise helped Bret shed his inhibitions.

"It distracted me from my own shyness about pursuing music," Bret recalls. "It was all just this game anyway about this band in Japan, so, yeah, I'll pursue it."

---

*X-15 soon after moved to Seattle and, in 1981, its song "Vaporized" kicked off *Seattle Syndrome Volume One*, a definitive compilation of songs documenting the city's punk and new wave scenes that was highly influential to the bands that went on to form the nucleus of the grunge movement.

That fall of 1983, Bret moved to Olympia. He registered for his first program at Evergreen, the freshman class Great Books of the Western World, and he began a crash course in guitar with Calvin.

Those earliest Beat Happening practices took place without Heather. At the end of the summer, she had moved to Seattle, though she stayed committed to playing shows with the band and would move between the two cities for some years. Calvin had moved as well, out of the Capitol Theater building and into the nearby Ray Apartments, where he and Bret practiced the songs that Laura, Heather and Calvin had written. Those early rehearsals were rough. The first song Calvin tried to teach Bret, "I Spy," was a surf rock number with a lyrical narrative that starred Calvin as the pulpiest of private eyes and ended with the memorable line, "I wear Spanish boots, Brooks Brothers suits, and I don't know how to cry." Though it required little fret work by Bret, the picking pattern caused him problems. Calvin pressed on, and soon Bret had the basics down for a handful of songs, including two of Laura, Heather and Calvin's fan favorites, "I Love You" and "Our Secret."

"It was a challenge to learn," Bret recalls. "Just going from nothing to doing a song was challenging. I guess I got a little bit better over time, but I never could get too inspired to devote a lot of time to increasing my technical ability beyond the rudimentary."

After a few informal practice sessions, Calvin decided the band needed to practice on real equipment. He received permission from Olympia's most popular band, the Young Pioneers, to use their rehearsal space in an old firehouse near the Evergreen State College campus. Calvin and Bret practiced twice a week throughout the fall, with Heather making a handful of trips from Seattle. They managed to work their way through the old Laura, Heather and Calvin songs and even wrote a few new ones.

"When we started working with Bret, we started really formalizing the songs more and we practiced more," Calvin says.

In December, Calvin decided the band was ready to perform in public. Still with no local clubs to play, Beat Happening debuted at a friend's house on the west side of Olympia. Later in the month, they played a party in Seattle at Heather's Belltown loft.

Between songs, the band members would sometimes switch roles. Since none of them were expert at their instruments, the quality of the music didn't suffer. But when Bret or Calvin would sit at the drum kit and Heather would grab the mic, or Calvin would strap on a guitar, the mood that the band created changed dramatically. In its experimentation, Beat Happening had succeeded in overcoming one of the most difficult hurdles facing a young band: the monotony of the unskilled repeating the same formula ad infinitum.

Sloppy and unsteady, the band survived both performances intact.

Confident in their abilities, Calvin brought his bandmates into the KAOS studios for his *Boy Meets Girl* show. He recorded the performance but never intended it to be released as a cassette, as he had done with the Supreme Cool Beings. Instead, Calvin contacted Greg Sage, whom he had interviewed on KAOS earlier that year prior to a show where Laura, Heather and Calvin opened for the Wipers during a rare punk show in a downtown Olympia storefront. He sent Sage the tape and asked if he would record Beat Happening. Sage soon showed up at the old firehouse space with a four-track and an Echoplex, a machine that uses a tape delay to create an echo effect; this technology would make Bret's guitar sound bigger while helping to cover up any notes the novice missed.

In one day, the band recorded four songs: two old ("I Love You" and "Our Secret") and two new ("Down at the Sea" and

"What's Important"). When Greg played the songs back to the band, Bret was shocked.

"We had rehearsed enough that we were smoother than the early sessions, but still not so far in my mind from when we'd begun," Bret says. "But then when I heard what Greg had recorded, it was like, 'We're a band. This sounds good.' That was a real change for me in the way I thought about things. I think every artist, every musician, can transform themselves to a point where they are for real. People don't have to like it; people are going to hate certain things and like certain things, but that was a powerful realization."

Greg Sage had inspired more Olympians than just Bret.

Following the success of the Wipers' storefront show, the organizers of the event planned to lease the space and start an all-ages rock club. That plan fell through when the storefront was leased to a salon, so the organizers set their sights on a space down the street. Within a few months, they had secured the lease, put up gypsum board, painted the walls, spackled, built a stage, installed a sound system, and painted the new club's name on the window. The Tropicana was open for business.

"The TROPICANA can best be described as a multi-media-mecca," read a flyer distributed by the club. "It is open because there are painfully few places where the highly talented but unknown individuals can display or perform their creative endeavors. The TROPICANA is all ages. We encourage, invite, implore, and urge everyone—that means YOU—to participate."

The grand opening was booked for March 3 with the garage pop Young Pioneers scheduled to headline. Second on the bill was Beat Happening. The show was a resounding success, and Calvin—who had never played in any of the city's bars—was vindicated.

"I felt that it was important that shows be accessible," Calvin says. "And people were like, that's weird. One of the arguments was, 'Well, no one under that age would go anyway—what difference does it make?' But I knew what it's like to be that one person who wants to go to a show and you can't go. So even if there's one person who wants to go, I want that person to be able to go. I admitted there probably wasn't anyone who would want to go. But what if there was? And then when the Tropicana opened, all of a sudden out of the woodwork there are these eighty kids we'd never seen before. They were just waiting for this."

While the members of Beat Happening busied themselves writing and recording music and playing shows in those early months of 1984, they were also working behind the scenes to make good on Calvin's promise to Bret. They were going to Japan.

"I don't remember hearing them announce it at a show, but everyone knew," recalls Candice Pederson, at the time an Evergreen freshman and an early fan of Beat Happening. "It just seemed really amazing that people would go to Japan to play shows. It was astounding to me. I remember being so excited that Bret was going to be in my class and then he was never there."

Despite the fact that Washington State and the island nation shared a common ocean, they might as well have been on different planets. While Japan had been exporting electronics to the United States for some time, there had been little export of Japanese culture to the U.S. The little that Calvin knew about Japan came from a friendship he had made the year before with Ai Miyake, a high school exchange student studying at Evergreen.

"The Japanese students became really fascinated with some of the Olympia bands, particularly the Young Pioneers," Calvin recalls. "They would go to all the shows for the Young Pioneers. So, I met some of them, and Ai seemed very interested in it. She came down with some other students to a Laura, Heather and

Calvin show at the Smithfield. And she talked about how it would be neat if we went to Japan."

At the time, very few bands toured the continental United States; even fewer went to Europe, and no one went to Japan. It seemed a natural first international adventure for the band. Beat Happening would start its touring life as trailblazers, if clueless ones at that.

Calvin and Bret were the first to arrive in Tokyo, carrying with them a tiny Fender amplifier, Calvin's acoustic guitar, an old Silvertone electric guitar, and contact information for the Miyake family. When the two American musicians arrived at the family's apartment in the Nakameguro area of Tokyo, they were greeted warmly and given a portion of the tiny apartment in which to get settled. First on the band's to-do list was a visit to the city's electronics district. Calvin and Bret purchased two large matching portable stereos, both with microphone inputs and double cassette decks—technology that was not yet available in Olympia.

Calvin was also beginning to do research for an Individual Learning Contract he had arranged with an Evergreen advisor before he left. The result of his research would be published in an article for *OP Magazine*.

"I was trying to establish what was available in terms of underground music in Japan," Calvin says, regarding his project. "We had no idea if there were any bands because there was no communication between underground Japan and underground America. So I was doing a lot of outreach, I guess you could say. Going to record stores, looking for independent releases, trying to find shows, and things like that. And asking people, 'Are there any bands? Do you know any bands?'"

By the time Heather arrived a week later with her snare drum in tow, the Miyake family had secured an apartment for the group in a vacant building slated for demolition later in the year. As the only tenants in the four-story building, the bandmates could make as much noise as they wanted. They took advantage of the space, practicing a handful of new songs and then recording them onto cassette using their two new boom boxes, utilizing the input on one to turn it into an amplifier for vocals. The other was used for recording and playback. In the first month, the band managed to record five songs, including one titled "Youth." The recording consisted of a simple circular acoustic guitar line, a barely there rapping drumstick, and Calvin singing in an almost bratty baritone, "When I was young, I thought I was old. I sailed across the sea to Tokyo. I thought there must be more to this world than we're being told. When you're young, you can afford to be bold."

The band had arranged no shows before arriving in Tokyo, but Calvin had plans for the band to perform. The year before in Olympia, Ai had told Calvin about Yoyogi Park, an immense stretch of open land in the middle of Tokyo that once served as the athletes' village for the 1964 Summer Olympics. Since then, the park had become a popular destination for street musicians and performance artists eager for an audience. For the band's first performance in Japan, Calvin planned to spend a day at the park, playing for passersby while using one of the new stereos as an amplifier.

"It wasn't really that much louder than just playing and singing without a cassette player," Calvin recalls of the band's afternoon in the park. "With lots of other stuff going on, we weren't really making a dent in anyone's psyche. People had very elaborate sound systems they brought and set up. We didn't realize how established this was. Some of them were quite impressive. We were dwarfed by them."

The second opportunity came straight from Ai: she told Calvin that Beat Happening could play at her high school. Calvin made the arrangements with the contact Ai provided and, when the date came, Bret, Calvin, and Heather boarded the subway with their instruments. When the band members arrived at the given address, they were greeted not by an administrator but by a sixteen-year-old girl in a student uniform. She informed the Americans that she had not received permission for them to play, but since school had just let out, they could play in one of the empty classrooms. As they walked three blocks through the campus, more and more students followed. Soon, Calvin, Bret, and Heather were part of a chain, clearly the strangers in a line of Japanese high school students.

Their host eventually led them into a classroom where students sat waiting as the band set up their equipment. Calvin went to the chalkboards and wrote "BEAT HAPPENING" in large letters. The band played and the students danced. After twenty minutes, a teacher showed up and told the band it had to leave but could play three more songs. Calvin, Bret, and Heather did, packed up their equipment, and walked to the subway station, a line of students following them the entire way to the doors of the train car.

After those two strange shows, the band was determined to play at a club. During his research, Calvin had learned of a number of venues that the Japanese called "live houses." Calvin picked the biggest, and the band headed down to check out a show. By the time they arrived, the show had ended, but Calvin spoke with one of the venue's booking agents. He told the agent that he was in a band and handed him a tape of the recording they had recently made. The agent gave Calvin a show on the spot, scheduled for just a few days before the band would return to the States. He handed Calvin fifteen tickets and told him that the band had to sell the tickets or buy them in order to play. Later, Calvin would recognize this as the abusive pay-for-play scheme used by many all-ages music clubs in America. At the time, though, he took the tickets gratefully. For the next week, whenever they met someone new, the band members would ask them if they would like to buy tickets to the show. Curious about the American band, the Japanese were receptive and the band sold every ticket.

American bands were largely unknown to the Japanese population, but British music was in high demand, thanks largely to the fact that music magazines like *Melody Maker* and *NME* were imported from the U.K. As a result, one of the dominant youth cultures in Japan had been built around the mod subculture of the '60s that a segment of popular U.K. bands were replicating in the '80s in an updated mod revival. Bret, Calvin, and Heather had attended a show featuring Japanese mod bands earlier in their visit. They heard Japanese musicians approximating that '60s sound and met fans who drove scooters and sported other styles found in the British magazines.

Calvin also discovered that the Style Council, the band Paul Weller had formed after the breakup of the Jam, was scheduled to play a show in Tokyo during the final weeks of Beat Happening's stay.

Bret and Calvin went to the venue and tried to buy tickets. The show was sold out, but the Olympians met a young musician distributing flyers outside the venue. After hearing that they were members of a band who loved the Jam, she invited Beat Happening to play a show with her band.

Like that, Beat Happening had achieved its goal. On two nights at two different clubs, the band played to Japanese crowds. The reaction was not nearly as animated as the students' had been weeks before, but the performances did make an impact. Twenty years later, when Calvin would return to the country with a new musical project, fans who had attended these shows would thank him.

Calvin was also nearing completion of his research project. He had contacted a number of labels he discovered while exploring the albums in Tokyo's record stores.

He also connected with Japan's biggest distributor of punk records. The head of the distribution company agreed to see Calvin before the college student left the country. In that meeting, the executive pressed one group on Calvin: an all-female punk trio with a fondness for songs about food called Shonen Knife. Calvin failed to connect with the band before leaving Japan, but he did begin a correspondence with them. Calvin also zeroed in on one label in particular that he would continue correspondence with: Rebel Beat Factory.*

Calvin, Heather, and Bret returned to Olympia a changed band. After two months of practicing, writing, and playing together they still lacked technical ability, but the band members were playing with confidence.

"People told me after they saw us play when we returned that it was clear that we had been concentrating on being a band for two months," Bret says. "At no other time have we spent that amount of time concentrating on music."

---

*Rebel Beat Factory would go on to issue a number of K Records albums in Japan and bring a number of K artists over to Japan to tour, including the Crabs, Lois, Karp, Fitz of Depression, and Dub Narcotic Sound System among them.

A BRIEF HISTORY OF ROUGH TRADE

In the middle of the '70s, a teenage music fan named Geoff Travis traveled from his native England to the United States for an adventure. While in America, he discovered records that were unavailable in the U.K. He bought hundreds of them.

When time came to go back home, Travis faced a dilemma. He had floated the idea of selling the collection he had amassed, but one of his friends had a better idea: why not ship the records back to London and start a record shop?

That is exactly what Travis did. In 1976, he opened Rough Trade Records at 202 Kensington Park Road in the Notting Hill district of London. It was a poor section of the city and therefore home to both immigrants and artists—in particular, punk musicians.

Soon after opening, Travis was approached by musicians who were recording and pressing their own seven-inches but had nowhere to sell them. Travis began taking commissions and, after deciding to fund the recording of some of the artists, started one of the first independent record labels of the era.

Rather than model his business after the major record labels—which had signed punk pioneers like the Sex Pistols and the Clash to multi-album contracts that paid the artists a small percentage of their record sales—Travis chose to take a more egalitarian approach. The agreement went as follows:

> *Clause 1*
> *Rough Trade and [artist] agree to make records and sell them until either or both of the parties reasonably disagree with the arrangement.*

> *Clause 2*
> *We agree that once agreed recording, manufacturing, and promotional costs have been deducted, we will share the ensuing profit equally.*

This arrangement, which later became known as the "punk rock split," would be applied to almost all of the records released by the label, including those by the Raincoats, Swell Maps, Pere Ubu, the Fall, and Scritti Politti, as well as the early releases by the Smiths.

As the Rough Trade label roster grew, so did its influence. Before the end of the '70s, Rough Trade expanded once again, adding a distribution arm that would help the U.K.'s growing number of independent record labels get their albums and seven-inches in stores around the country.

In the early '80s, Rough Trade opened a record shop in San Francisco where it could sell imports. Soon after, the company started a U.S. label and distribution center that allowed it to expand its reach to record buyers across the country.

LIKE MANY FIRST BANDS, the Spoiled didn't last for long. A year after Calvin first saw the Anacortes punks get shut down at the Summit Park Grange Hall, the band had split up. Two of the members, Nilo Madeja and lead singer Bryan Elliott, moved to Guam. A year later, Elliott moved to Arizona, where he attended art school and taught himself how to play guitar.

When Elliott returned to Anacortes in the summer of 1984, he was a very different musician. No longer identifying as a hardcore punk, and now endowed with some technical abilities, Elliott's edge started to soften. He formed a more poppy, acoustic-based group called the Few, and he and his bandmates rented out an old cabin on nearby Guemes Island where they could live and practice in relative peace. One day, Bret showed up with the boom box he had just brought back from Japan. Elliott told Bret about his adventures in Guam and his time in Arizona. Bret told Elliott about his trip to Japan and the band he was now playing in. Bret handed Elliott a cassette. The sleeve was made of red construction paper and featured the photocopied images of three sets of clothing on the cover: two for boys, one for a girl. The tape, issued by K Records, was *Three Tea Breakfast*, Beat Happening's first EP, which featured the five songs the band had recorded in Tokyo.

"What kind of band are you?" asked Elliott.

"We're a punk band."

"Great."

Bret told Elliott the story of the tape's creation. Gesturing toward the boom box, he invited Elliott's band to do the same. "I want to record you guys," Bret said. Soon after, the band had set up its instruments and played twelve songs. Bret recorded every one.

After Bret left with the recording, Elliott put the Beat Happening tape in his own cassette player, expecting to hear punk rock. He found something very different.

"In the Spoiled, we played hard punk rock," Elliott says. "Punk rock was new back then, and I really thought it was more of an attitude. But I remember listening to that tape and thinking, 'What the fuck is this?'"

The sound grew on the recovering punk rocker. By the time Calvin offered to put out the Few's twelve-song recording on K Records, Elliott was a full convert.

"As I grew and started getting the K newsletters and started listening to more of the stuff they were putting out, it started to make sense," he says. "I understood that we were part of this generation, that we were part of this really cool sound. So then I wanted to turn people on to these different bands."

Some time later, Calvin would show up at a Few performance in Anacortes with the Few's debut in hand. Again, the label owner had gone against convention.

"He said that it was kind of new packaging they were trying out," Elliott recalls. "He hands me it and it's in kind of a Ziploc baggie with the cassette and then this picture of us and these splotchy paint things. I thought, I want to see a formal kind of cassette tape, make it seem a little more real, but that's how he put it out."

Now back in Olympia, Calvin was building on the momentum from the Japan trip, and putting more effort into his fledgling record label. Since releasing the Supreme Cool Beings recording in 1982, Calvin had issued only one other tape tagged with his

K logo, a compilation called *Danger Is Their Business*, which featured crudely recorded a cappella performances by Calvin, John Foster, Lois Maffeo, and Rich Jensen, who helped Calvin record the project.

After releasing *Three Tea Breakfast*, though, Calvin put out a handful of albums, including a full-length retrospective of songs recorded by Foster's Pop Philosophers and two compilations. The first, *Let's Together*—named for a broken-English phrase Beat Happening had seen on a poster in Tokyo—was a collection of songs curated by Bret that included the Young Pioneers, the Wrecks, his brother Jonn's group Public Service, and a new band out of Aberdeen, Washington, called the Melvins. The second, *Let's Kiss*, was put together by Calvin and included one song from Bret's recording session with the Few, a new band out of Tacoma called Girl Trouble, and another track from the Melvins.

Calvin also released a self-titled cassette from Beat Happening, which contained the songs the band had recorded earlier in the year with Greg Sage. Calvin was so proud of those recordings that he decided to use two of the songs—"Our Secret" and "What's Important"—to launch K into the world of reputable underground record labels, placing both on K's first 45 single. By the end of the year, all of the new releases were available from the record label for two dollars each. And anyone who wanted to know about future K releases could sign up to receive the K Records newsletter, a semi-regular publication that featured the label's catalog with colorful descriptions written by Calvin.

The beginning of the newsletter coincided with the loss of *OP Magazine*. Earlier in the year, Foster announced that the magazine would end publication with its twenty-sixth issue, "Z." That July, he held the first and only Lost Music Network Conference, inviting *OP*'s readership to Olympia for three days of music and discussion about where the community would go from there. Out of that gathering, two new publications would emerge: *Option* and *Sound Choice*. Unfortunately, neither would be published out of Olympia and both would disappear, with little fanfare, before the end of the century.

The departure of *OP* wasn't the only loss Olympia had experienced. While a student at Evergreen, Bruce Pavitt had experienced great success with his *Sub Pop* fanzine and sold two thousand copies of the *Sub Pop 5* compilation. Another successful compilation, *Sub Pop 7*, followed, but it would be the last issued from an Olympia address. In March 1983, Bruce moved to Seattle.

"The economy in Olympia was very challenging," he recalls. "I had been out of school for two years, and felt there were more opportunities in Seattle, but I did miss the intimacy and the creativity of Olympia."

From his new Seattle home, Bruce put out *Sub Pop 9*, a compilation that included a few Olympia bands—including Laura, Heather and Calvin, Rich Jensen, and John Foster's Pop Philosophers—mixed in with a slew of obscure underground bands from around the country. After the release of *Sub Pop 9*, he stopped publishing the fanzine.

In Seattle, Bruce continued his work as a radio deejay at the University of Washington's college station and, in April 1983, he began writing a new monthly column for *The Rocket* titled "Sub/Pop." Bruce used the column to continue exposing his readers—now Seattle residents—to the best in obscure underground music culture. His first two columns focused on the Portland and Washington, D.C., scenes, breaking down those cities' best under-the-radar bands, labels, clubs, and publications. In December of 1983, Bruce introduced readers of *The Rocket* to K Records, making the paper's first explicit mention of the label in a brief review of *Danger Is Their Business*, which the columnist called a "novelty item." Bruce would mention Olympia every so often, even devoting his entire May 1984 column to the Tropicana, but the discerning tastemaker did not give the city a pass. In the August 1983 issue, the Sub Pop column featured brief descriptions of the West Coast's best underground scenes: Seattle, Portland, Vancouver, B.C., Los Angeles, and Sacramento were all mentioned. Olympia didn't make the cut.

When Beat Happening started its post-Japan assault in 1984, though, *The Rocket* did take notice. In the June issue of the magazine, the band was spotlighted as one of "Eight Hot Ones" to watch. The unidentified reviewer wrote, "Beat Happening is a now, happening, beat-hip trio that plays a drum and a guitar and rhymes *banana* with *pajama* and *Baltic Sea* with *KGB*. They switch their instruments and occasionally play out of key, but their fresh, naïve love songs are a great antidote to sterile synth pop and nihilistic leather."

After returning to Olympia, Calvin and Bret reconnected with Heather, and Beat Happening continued playing to growing audiences. The band's biggest show yet came on September 24, when it was scheduled to open for Black Flag at the Tropicana. The show, Black Flag's first appearance in Olympia, placed Calvin and Beat Happening in direct connection with the hardcore movement that helped spawn the band. But when Beat Happening began playing that night, Black Flag's lead singer did not see a reflection of his own culture. Watching from the side of the stage, Rollins became angry at Calvin's performance because he thought the lead singer's decidedly non-macho stage show was a mockery of Black Flag's aggressive approach. He took a spot in the audience, front and center, and began jeering. Undeterred, Calvin continued with his performance, dancing about the stage and rubbing his tummy. Frustrated, Rollins reached up and put his hand over the singer's crotch. Calvin broke. "Didn't your mother teach you any manners?" he asked before proceeding with the show.

Rollins relented and after its performance, Black Flag moved on, but Beat Happening continued to court an audience with the Olympia crowds at the Tropicana, playing two more shows before the end of 1984.

The Tropicana was running into some resistance of its own. The punks who congregated in and around the venue stood out with their ripped jeans, leather jackets, dyed and shaved hair, and creatively altered thrift store finds. The teenagers added some color to Fourth Avenue, but they were not welcomed by all of their neighbors. From the Tropicana's opening in March to early July, the Olympia Police Department received twenty complaints about activity at the venue, ranging from vandalism to noise to liquor violations. Downtown business owners filed a petition with the city in an attempt to shut the Tropicana down, and the city gave the club ninety days to clean up its act. The punks responded by designating a few regulars to patrol the nearby streets and alleys, keeping an eye out for trouble of any kind.

The self-policing worked, and the club continued to operate after its three-month probation was over. Though the city backed down, its citizens didn't. One night a car continually circled the block where teenagers were gathered, its occupants throwing a different object at them with each pass: a beer can, a broomstick, a tire iron. Some patrons, including the friend of a purple-haired fifteen-year-old interviewed by the local daily newspaper, were harassed. "You're going nowhere," a man said as he shook the teenager. "Why don't you conform with society?" Others were beaten.

Despite the club's success at controlling the crowds of teenagers, the publicity was too much for the building's owners. When the venue was forced to close at the beginning of 1985, Beat Happening played the farewell show, earning a spot second on the bill behind only the Young Pioneers.

The band had lost a venue in its hometown, but it continued to tour and record. In the summer of 1985, Calvin decided it was time for Beat Happening to release its first full-length record. But what to release? The band had just finished another session with Sage, recording a handful of songs at Yoyo Studios, a recording studio that Calvin's friend Pat Maley had just built at a farm west of Olympia. Without enough new material for a full-length album, Calvin decided to combine the new recordings with the stronger songs from the previous cassette releases and a second, live version of the song "Bad Seeds" that Jensen recorded with a handheld Panasonic tape recorder. The final album was a patchwork featuring ten songs recorded in five locations by four producers. It was a precarious collection of the band's best work, and Calvin wanted to make sure that it sounded right. The process of recording a full album the right way was expensive, and none of the band members had much disposable income, but Bret did have one line of credit. He donated a portion of his student loans to fund the printing of the album at a plant in California.

The quality of the 45 Calvin released the year before had left him frustrated, so he traveled, accompanied by Rich Jensen, to Los Angeles to oversee the mastering of the album himself. There, he saw the inner workings of a process that went so much deeper than pressing "record" on a boom box. The first stop was K-Disc (no relation to K Records), where a man named John Golden showed him how to turn recordings into records.

"It was all done on reel-to-reel tape," Calvin recalls. "And it was a beautiful process. Then we went to Bill Smith Custom Records, the place where the records were getting pressed, and we sat in with him. I had never seen how records were made. That was different than with the 45 or the cassettes, because we actually went and tried to connect with the physical process of making the record."

On his way back to Olympia, Calvin made a stop at Rough Trade's U.S. headquarters in San Francisco. After receiving the first Beat Happening EP from Calvin, Phil Hertz asked Calvin to send more with the promise that Rough Trade would sell the albums on consignment through its wholesale division. Calvin did so, but had never received any royalty checks from Rough Trade. Calvin went to the Rough Trade shop to get his money, with a handful of new K releases in tow. When he arrived at the shop, which was physically connected to the distribution warehouse, he asked for Hertz. Hertz wasn't in, so the store clerk suggested he meet with Steve Connell.

Just as it had started in the U.K., the U.S. branch of Rough Trade was a nonhierarchical business, meaning that Connell received the same pay as the other employees and was not technically in charge. "In theory it was a collective and everybody got the same and decisions were made by the group," Connell says. Still, he was the problem solver. Connell had worked for the distribution arm of Rough Trade in the U.K. for a number of years before being sent to San Francisco. His job was to fire a small faction of employees who were pushing for greater autonomy for the U.S. division of the label, and to keep the wholesale and distribution arm up and running. Connell made sure that imports from Rough Trade's U.K. operation, as well as the American titles—both those that had been released on Rough Trade U.S., as well as those from other select independent labels—made it into record stores across the country.

"I'd met quite a few people by then running labels and they were all interesting. None of them were really like Calvin," Connell says. "He was an unusual-looking guy with an unusual voice—that deep voice—and obviously somebody with a kind of different idea."

Connell settled up Calvin's account and then asked him if he had anything more. Calvin pulled out the handful of tapes and the 45 he had brought along. Connell was interested and told Calvin that Rough Trade would distribute those as well.

The visit made an impression on Calvin.

"The point was that, okay, we can't put out records like a real label does," Calvin recalls. "But we can work with other labels and try to find a way to just be creative in how to keep the label going."

The relationship was a symbiotic one. Soon after, Connell started asking Calvin advise on running *Puncture*, a well-regarded music magazine that he published with his girlfriend, Katherine Spielmann. Calvin was not trained in business, but he did have an idea about how to treat his customers, which was embodied in his practice of sending personal notes with each of the orders he sent out. Each one was signed "Love, Calvin."

"Calvin was always quite shrewd about business stuff," Connell says. "I remember him giving me very good advice about how it was very important to hang on to and respond to everyone who wrote to you. His reasoning was that if these people were interested in writing to you and interested enough to buy something then that was someone who you could probably sell more stuff to in the future. It was important not to blow people off, but always to follow up. Obviously it was a lesson that he had learned from K."

While Calvin was delving deeper into the intricacies of the record business, Bret was getting more involved at Evergreen. He and Denise Crowe, a fellow Evergreen student he had started dating earlier in the year, were both involved in student groups: he with the Evergreen Political Information Center and she with the Expressive Arts Network. With the Tropicana closed, the couple saw the opportunity to create a new kind of club that would bridge the gulf between Evergreen and the downtown scene.

"We recognized that enough students lived off campus that they deserved to have a campus-sponsored community center in town where there could be this cross-pollination between campus and town," Bret says. "So, we started G.E.S.C.C.O., the Greater

Evergreen Student Community Cooperation Organization. We just thought it would be—not a rock club exclusively—our ideals were to have it be something of everything, from art gallery to theatrical space to political speaking arena."

Through an Individual Learning Contract, Bret and Denise opened the space in a storefront near the old Tropicana. They were determined not to make the same mistakes as the old hangout, so before opening the club's doors, they invited the people with the power to shut it down in for a peek.

"We were still under the idea that we were the weirdos and that people were going to throw bricks at us," Calvin says. "But Bret and Denise had a different approach; they went to the city and they invited the mayor and the city council down to G.E.S.C.C.O. and said, 'Hey, check out what we're doing.' And they never had any problems."

One day in November, while Bret and Denise were busy setting up for a show, Calvin popped in with a surprise: Beat Happening's first full-length album had just arrived. Calvin handed a copy to Bret. The cover was brilliant yellow with a crude drawing made by Calvin of a cat riding a rocket ship.

"It was a dream come true," Bret recalls. "I think it takes a certain amount of bravery and pretentiousness to actually create something like a record. I had been, maybe, conditioned against pretentiousness, but I learned to ultimately rethink that. Yeah, there are a lot of annoying parts of pretentiousness, but without arrogance and ignorance, what gets tried? What attempts get made? I started to understand it as part of the search, part of the way that people motivate themselves to go beyond what they thought was possible."

With the opening of G.E.S.C.C.O., Olympia once again had a guaranteed space where the punk fans could invite touring bands to play. So when two friends of Calvin's returned from Vancouver,

B.C., with a full-length record by a powerful new band called Mecca Normal, Calvin encouraged them to book a show at the venue. The music was unlike anything Calvin had heard before. It consisted of only two elements: aggressive guitar riffs churned out by a man named David Lester and the intense and overtly political speak-sing lyricism of a woman named Jean Smith.

The timing was perfect. Mecca Normal had just teamed up with another performance art duo from Montreal called Rhythm Activism to create the Black Wedge Tour. The name was inspired by the Red Wedge, a group of U.K. artists who supported Britain's Labour Party during the waning days of conservative prime minister Margaret Thatcher. The Black Wedge, though, championed no political party; rather, the two duos, along with three poets, were touring the West Coast to spread a message of antiauthoritarianism. "One step easier than punk!" their literature read:

> The Black Wedge is out to spread the word of how to combine poetry, music and politics and have a fun time doing it. Hardcore poems and shredding guitars, radical voices crushing sexism, militarism, poverty and conformity. The Black Wedge wants to set wild hearts and imaginations free, to release a riot of emotion—opening up a new arena for activist resistance culture.

The tour was booked by David's brother Ken Lester, one of the poets and the manager for D.O.A., the band that is credited with creating the term *hardcore* after the release of its album *Hardcore '81*. Hardcore meant something different in each city where it took hold, and Vancouver was home to the most political strain of the music. In 1981, five ecologists and feminists acting under the banner of Direct Action were arrested and convicted for firebombing a plant that manufactured missile guidance systems. One of those arrested was "Useless" Gerry Hannah, bass player for the Subhumans, the Vancouver hardcore band that Calvin saw play with the Wrecks and Black Flag years before. The Vancouver Five, as the activists became known, were supported by the punk community, including D.O.A., which told *The Rocket* that "what's really interesting is the issues they've brought out. It's not really important whether or not they're guilty."

Mecca Normal did not form until 1984, but the band members were already a part of the scene. Thanks to his brother, David was able to land the band a number of shows opening for D.O.A.

But Mecca Normal was doing something very different with its music. Not only was the composition of the band and the style of the show—David's manic guitar playing paired with Jean's vacillating poetic vocal delivery and imposing stance—unlike the accepted punk formula, but the lyricism of the songs was unapologetically feminist. Critics and fans were deeply split. In one instance, the band held the top position on the chart at the college radio station at the University of Alberta in Edmonton. When the band came to town, though, the student newspaper ran a review of its album, stating that it was an abysmal failure and that the band should consider actually killing the singer. Threats were a rarity, but some fans at shows where Mecca Normal opened for D.O.A. were not impressed, often walking out in the middle of the set.

By early 1986, though, Mecca Normal had cultivated enough of an audience that it managed to sell out the Black Wedge Tour's first two nights at the Venue in Vancouver. After those shows, the group of artists packed up a bus it had borrowed from D.O.A. and drove down to Olympia for the June 1 show at G.E.S.C.C.O. The ensemble cast of nonconformists played an afternoon show. Rhythm Activism called on the modest crowd to raid the Safeway grocery store next door. They didn't, but the gesture was appreciated. Mecca Normal closed the show, performing "Strong White Male," "Women Were King," and "Smile Baby," a song where

Jean chastises another woman for dressing for the eyes of men before conceding that "it hardly matters, I suppose. My cold heart beats and looking tough and they still tell me, they still tell me, 'Smile baby.'"

Calvin enjoyed the entire show, especially Mecca Normal. Afterward, he approached Jean, told her he was in a band, and asked if she would like to trade the self-titled *Mecca Normal* album that she and David had just released on her own Smarten UP! label for his own Beat Happening release. Jean thanked him and accepted.

"I looked at his record cover and just thought, 'What the fuck is this?'" Jean recalls. 'This doesn't have anything to do with me or my hardcore, punk, heavy-duty, anarcho-feminist thing. This has got a cat on a rocket ship to the moon.' I didn't really want to give him one of my records, but I did."

Jean put the record underneath a seat in the tour bus and left Olympia, heading south into the California heat.

With records to sell and some momentum, Beat Happening planned a tour for the fall. There were two problems, though: first, Heather had moved to Los Angeles to do some soul-searching while living with the sister of Supreme Cool Beings saxophonist Doug Monaghan and working at an internship.

While she was still committed to being a member of the band, there was no way she could take the weeks off that the tour would require. In her place, Bret suggested his girlfriend Denise. She had never touched a drumstick, but that didn't matter to Calvin. She was in.

Denise had two weeks to learn the drums, and Bret was responsible for teaching her. The couple traveled to his hometown and spent their days at Bryan Elliott's cabin on Guemes Island. They practiced on the Few's drum kit for hours, sometimes with Denise playing along to Beat Happening's recordings, other times with Bret playing guitar.

The second problem was that none of the band members owned a car and they were all still too young to rent one. Calvin contacted a local drive-away company, a service used by people to move their automobiles long distances. By signing up to handle a drive-away, a driver agreed to deliver a car to a specified location on a specified date. Calvin located a car that needed to be driven to Boston and signed up. The band now had a week to get to the opposite coast—plenty of time to play a few shows on the way. Bret, Calvin, and Denise packed up a snare drum, a tom drum, a guitar, and two small amps and made their way east.

The first show was scheduled for Ellensburg, Washington, the small college town where Calvin once lived. Ellensburg was also Steve Fisk's hometown, and the former KAOS deejay had since opened his own studio, Creative Fire, there. Fisk offered to set up the show at his studio, placing Beat Happening on a bill with local bands.

The night of the show, a slew of the city's teenagers showed up. The band set the stage with its modest equipment, and Denise sat behind the drums on stage for the first time. The band started playing and the crowd was rapt. By this point, Calvin had found his rhythm as a front man. He danced feverishly and continuously, in a style similar to the U.K. punks in the *Weekend* news report he had seen years before. He would pogo, hula, and shimmy, his arms swimming through the air in a seemingly manic fashion as he recited his deceivingly childlike lines. While his baritone was steady, Calvin was clearly moved by the music his band was playing. Denise watched this all unfold from behind, working desperately to keep the beat. Midway through the show, after the band performed a newer song called "Jamboree," Calvin turned to her.

"He had tears running down his cheeks," Denise recalls. "He looked me right in the eyes and said, 'I love you.' I was kind of in shock and just looked at him. 'I love you,' he said again. That time

I think I said, 'Calvin, what are you talking about?' And then he said, "I Love You." The song. Let's play "I Love You" next.' I was a little more on my toes after that."

When the show was over, Calvin had one complaint about Denise's drumming. "You're smiling too much when you drum," he said. "You can't smile when you're playing rock 'n' roll." The new drummer took the note into consideration and the band packed up its equipment. The next day, the three bandmates were back on the road. The next show was in Columbus, Ohio, twenty-three hundred miles away.

After a nonstop cross-country drive, the band arrived at the home of Nancy Bonnell-Kangas, the publisher of *Nancy's Magazine*, a zine that, in its creator's own words, "combined the meatiness of *Scientific American* with the sassiness of *National Lampoon*." She set up a show for the band at a coffee shop with checkerboard floors. Next, Beat Happening headed to Philadelphia, where it played on the street in front of a record store. After that, the band stopped in New York's Lower East Side at a club called Rio, where the band witnessed a heroin addict shooting up in the doorway to the club.

"It was a very good education for me," Denise recalls. "It was the first time that I had ever been east of North Dakota and I had a lot of perceptions of the East Coast, but to be able to view it from a West Coast perspective was pretty instructive. Just the poverty in Philadelphia was unbelievable. But I never felt threatened in New York. It still felt like a safe place."

After New York, the band played in Boston, where it dropped off the drive-away car. For the rest of the trip down the coast, the bandmates traveled by train and bus, carrying their equipment along with them. Before the trio headed back to the West Coast, again in a drive-away car, it played in Washington, D.C. After the show, Calvin's mom, who had watched the entire performance, gave the three weary travelers a ride back to her home in Silver Springs, Maryland. "You are a wonderful drummer," she told Denise, as they drove down the highway. "But you should smile more." Calvin just looked out the window.

A BRIEF HISTORY OF
PUNK ROCK TOURING

For rock stars, touring has always been a rarefied affair, consisting of either airplane or bus travel paid for by promoters bringing the artists in to concert halls filled with paying fans. The punk rocker of the '80s experienced "the road" in a much more pedestrian manner. Outside of the largest cities—New York, Los Angeles, and Chicago—there were virtually no established venues to play and absolutely no money to be made. But there were fans. Those fans only increased throughout the coming years as college radio stations, fanzines, and independent record stores showed up in cities both large and small. And wherever there were willing listeners—no matter how few—bands would follow.

Black Flag, a pioneer in so many other facets of the punk rock world, was also among the first bands to map out tours into uncharted U.S. territory. The still-new interstate system helped connect the dots, but bands needed a way to get to their shows with all their gear. Traveling blindly to faraway cities and playing pickup shows with borrowed equipment, as the Teen Idles did when they took the Greyhound to California in 1979, was not sustainable. And neither was traveling by way of drive-away car, as Beat Happening did for its first tour. Fortunately, the earliest models of cargo and passenger vans—first made by American car companies in the early '60s and used mostly for plumbing, électrical, and HVAC contractors or church congregates—were within the limited price range of poor punk bands like Black Flag. Years before Calvin Johnson saw his first show at a Grange Hall, Black Flag was driving its van to community centers, fan's basements, and local Grange, VFW, and union halls, creating a rudimentary tour circuit that bands would build on for years to come.

During the '80s that circuit became formalized as the audience for underground artists grew and clubs like Olympia's Tropicana started to pop up in smaller cities. By the early '90s, the underground had grown large enough that a network of freelance tour bookers in cities across the country was able to make a modest living helping bands set up tours. Publicists—either independent or on the staff of record labels—helped get the word out to an increasing number of interested publications in the cities along the punk rock circuit. At the start of the twenty-first century, business at clubs became lucrative enough that the corporate concert promoters began booking shows at them, employing some of the early independent bookers and disgusting others.

The advent of the Internet and the cell phone made touring much more convenient, and as the underground blossomed, the potential audiences in even the smallest cities held promise. Still, touring was never easy. In order to make a profit—or as was more often the case, to lose less money—tours were booked tight with shows every night in sometimes-distant locales. Accidents due to long overnight hauls on little sleep remained on occupational hazard to independent musicians.

CANDICE PEDERSON GREW UP on a farm ten miles outside of Olympia under the watchful eye of strict parents. She graduated from Olympia High School in 1983. The only time she ever went into the city was on Saturdays to go shopping or to the library.

"I didn't have any way of going to shows," Candice says. "I didn't even know that stuff like that existed. In fact, I wasn't really aware of music until I could get KAOS, and then suddenly it was like, 'Oh, now I can hear music I like.' I don't think I liked any of the contemporary things that my peers were listening to."

Candice could only pick up KAOS on some clear nights, when the signal from the low-wattage station traveled farther through the air into the surrounding country. She started listening to the station her sophomore year and, like Calvin, started working there while she was in high school. During her junior year, she helped host one of the weekday rock shows with a friend. In the music library at KAOS, she began her musical education. At the same time, Candice also discovered Girl City.

"It was really intriguing," she recalls. "I remember the first time I went—and I'd go at least once a week—I never bought anything, I couldn't. I just would look at everything. It was female run, a lot of art stuff, just something really different from anything I had ever heard of. And I didn't really know anything about San Francisco scenes, or L.A. scenes, or New York City scenes. I just knew what was in the record collection at Girl City."

During one of her regular visits to the store in the summer of 1982, the soon-to-be high school senior saw a flyer for a show at the Evergreen State College. The headlining band was the Young Pioneers. It was her first show, and her second would be a long time coming. Candice stopped working at KAOS after graduating high school when her cohost, who was her only ride to the Evergreen campus, quit. Staying at KAOS would have been tough anyway, because she was expected to work on her parents' farm that entire summer.

In the fall of 1983, she enrolled at Evergreen. Soon after, she saw her second concert when the Wipers played at the college. It changed her.

"That was the first time I was like, 'I like music, this is amazing,'" she says.

That first year of school, Candice lived in downtown Olympia because it was cheaper than living on campus. From that unique vantage point, the young college student had the opportunity to witness the Olympia scene flower as punk infiltrated its landscape. That was also the year that Beat Happening began playing. Candice was a fan of the entire band, though she found Heather and Bret, the more unimposing and elusive performers, more intriguing than the showman Calvin. Heather, in particular, was fascinating. Like Candice, she was very shy, a trait that made some people think of her as a snob. Heather was also a talented visual artist, which Candice respected deeply, though she would never tell Heather.

"I was seventeen," she recalls, "and really immature. So anyone two or three years older seemed very mature and I was just very starry-eyed. And I remember I'd see Calvin on the bus with Lois. Of course, I didn't know them at the time, but one day he introduced himself to me."

In her sophomore year at Evergreen, Candice continued to integrate herself into the community while working her way through school. In addition to a job she held at the college, Candice transcribed tapes for an elderly woman and worked at the Smithfield Café, which was located next door to Girl City and often hosted concerts by Olympia's growing cast of musicians and performers. There, her relationship with Calvin continued to grow. One day near the end of 1985 Calvin approached her with a proposition.

With the recent release of Beat Happening's debut full-length album, a growing distribution business run through his K Records newsletter, and plans for future albums, Calvin needed help with the business side of the label. Clearly a hard worker, Candice seemed a good fit. But without much money, Calvin couldn't ask her to give up her other jobs. Instead, he encouraged her to turn K into a learning experience by applying for an Independent Learning Contract through Evergreen that would give her course credit for assisting in the operation of the fledgling independent record label.

"I was sure I'd had my fair share of college at that point," Candice says. "And I just went from there."

Candice agreed and, in January of 1986, began working for Calvin in exchange for a weekly paycheck of twenty dollars. At that point, the K office consisted of a kitchen table in Calvin's new home at the Martin Apartments. K's two sole employees would open the incoming mail, catalog orders, and send out tapes and the Beat Happening seven-inch single. Each order was accompanied by a handwritten thank-you note.

"When we were first doing it, it was just little bits and pieces," Candice recalls. "Calvin had just produced the first single. So, we were hand-coloring the single's cover and stuffing those and putting up cassettes and doing a lot of cassette distribution."

Distribution for non-K releases actually took up a majority of their work. While working for KAOS, Calvin continued to discover singles from labels and bands that didn't know the first thing about distributing their music. If Calvin liked what he heard, he would write a letter asking if those bands wanted to be included in the newsletter in exchange for a small percentage of their sales.

Even as distribution was becoming a focal point of the K newsletter, Calvin continued to slowly build up his label's catalog. Through his correspondence with the distributor in Tokyo, Calvin was able to secure the rights to release Shonen Knife's U.S. debut, *Burning Farm*, as a cassette on K Records. Capitalizing on Calvin's East Coast connections, K released a live split cassette by D.C.'s Velvet Monkeys and Half Japanese, the Maryland band that Calvin had missed seeing because of the first day of his senior year of high school. K also released full-length cassettes by an upbeat electro-pop band from Australia called the Cannanes and Fisk's new band Pell Mell, and recorded and released a cassette EP with a musician named Tim Brock, who played with Lois Maffeo in the short-lived group Lumihoops.

Calvin was also continuing to cultivate relationships with bands through K's cassette compilations. In the months after meeting Jean Smith on the Black Wedge Tour, Calvin started a correspondence with the Mecca Normal singer. Jean sent him a tape of demos that Mecca Normal had recorded; when Calvin traveled to Vancouver later that summer to buy tickets to a Tracey Thorn show, he asked to meet with her.

"He wanted to get together for something called 'tea,'" Jean recalls. "But I was a pretty heavy drinker back then, so that seemed kind of boring."

When Jean cleaned out D.O.A.'s bus after Mecca Normal's Black Wedge Tour, she carried away numerous political tracts, volumes from anarchist bookshops, and gifts from fellow poets and activists that the group had encountered in coffee shops, soup kitchens, and clubs all along the West Coast. In with all of the radical anarchist literature was Beat Happening's full-length album, warped from the summer sun but still playable. Despite her initial response to the childish cover, Jean listened to the record. When Jean met Calvin at the Railway Club in Vancouver, she ribbed him about his music. Calvin must not have minded the mild mockery, because he asked Jean if Mecca Normal would appear on a cassette compilation from K. Jean agreed. Mecca Normal was included on the third of K's Let's compilation series, *Let's Sea*. In addition to Mecca Normal, that comp added a few more names to the K stable, including Screaming Trees from Ellensburg, Fastbacks from Seattle, and Snakepit from Eugene.

The year before, Calvin had been introduced to a fifteen-year-old girl named Tobi Vail at the Tropicana. Tobi was a precocious youth who wanted little more than to be a musician—and she could play the drums. Calvin first thought she could join Beat Happening as a possible fill-in for Heather. Tobi declined the invitation, but only because the band's demanding touring schedule—which would soon be taking the band overseas—could end up interfering with her schoolwork. Calvin soon enlisted her as a collaborator on a different project that, by its nature, would demand much less travel.

Like many in the London punk scene a decade before, Calvin was deeply influenced by reggae, having listened to the music since his days at KAOS. In particular, he was fascinated with the subgenre of dub, a style of music that consists mostly of instrumental remixes of already existing songs. So when Calvin started the Go Team—his project with Tobi—he decided to translate dub to the Olympia underground. Traditionally, the catalyst for dub reggae was a producer who would take music created by other bands into a studio and remix it. Since the recording technology available to Calvin was limited, and there were still relatively few local bands with recorded material to work with, the Go Team's version of dub would be a little different. Calvin and Tobi planned to record songs and then hand the cassette of the recording over to various musicians in town, telling each to add whatever they wanted to the recordings. It was a difficult sell.

"No one knew what I was trying to do," Calvin recalls. "They just didn't understand that they could just do whatever they wanted with the recording. They didn't realize that there weren't any rules or constraints."

After a number of failed attempts to get artists to take up the dub template, Calvin simplified his original concept; instead of other artists remixing the Go Team's music, Calvin asked a rotating cast of artists to collaborate with the duo. In 1987 the band released its first EP, a K cassette recorded with former Tiny Holes member Steve Peters called *Your Pretty Guitar*. Around that time, Calvin decided to take the Go Team on the road. He arranged a tour down the West Coast to San Francisco with Mecca Normal, Rich Jensen, and another Olympia band called Spook and the Zombies.

The first stop was at the University of Oregon. The show was set up by Robert Christie, a Eugene musician who played in Snakepit with lead singer Al Larsen, and who had helped spread the music and ideas coming from Olympia to the burgeoning Eugene music scene. Calvin knew of Snakepit from meeting Al a few times; the first was at the "Olympia to Portland" concert that the Cool Rays and Tiny Holes had played years earlier at Clockwork Joe's in Portland. It wasn't until a fortuitous tour late in 1986 that Calvin saw Al perform, though.

After seeing the music that was coming out of Olympia, Al subscribed to John Foster's *OP Magazine*. In those pages, he read about a diverse array of music, from American folk songs to the exotic sounds of world music. When *OP* announced its demise,

Al traveled to Olympia for the Lost Music Network Conference, which marked the publication's end. There he saw a more confident Calvin play a show with Beat Happening.

"I thought that was fantastic," Al says. "I had never heard an American band with that kind of shambling and friendly feel to it."

Soon after, he subscribed to the K newsletter, started ordering the releases, and traveled to Olympia whenever he could. Shortly after starting school of the University of Oregon, Al brought his bandmate Robert with him to the Washington State capital. They had hoped to connect with Calvin, but after looking his name up in the phone book were connected to another Calvin Johnson. On another trip, inspired by Beat Happening's first seven-inch single, "Our Secret"—where Calvin sings that he "went to the Smithfield Café, there she was again, so I said, 'Hey, we should go swimming in Capital Lake'"—Al planned to go for a swim in the lake. There his plans were again thwarted by a sign that read, "Polluted. Do Not Swim."

Eventually, after running into Calvin at a comic book convention in Portland, Al and Robert started to correspond with him, sending the music that they were making in Snakepit with another musician named Mike Johnson. When planning the first Go Team tour, Calvin contacted Robert and asked if Snakepit would like to play. Unfortunately, Robert and Al were already booked for that night, playing at an art gallery in a new band called Some Velvet Sidewalk. But Robert did set up another show for the Olympians at the University of Oregon.

Since Some Velvet Sidewalk wasn't playing until later in the night, Al, along with six other people in the audience, was able to take in the entire bill of K artists. Afterward, Al invited Calvin to the Some Velvet Sidewalk show, the band's first ever.

Some Velvet Sidewalk was a duo consisting of Robert on drums and Al playing guitar and singing. A two-piece band was an oddity then, and it wasn't the only thing that was different about the group.

"In Snakepit, Mike was this amazing guy, but very much a classicist," Al says. "He cared about guitar tone and tempo and things like that. I wasn't so focused on that. I was more concerned with questions like, 'What is the gesture?' 'What does it mean?' 'How do we go out on stage?' and 'How do we look at the audience?'"

At the gallery, which was packed, Calvin and his tourmates saw a completely different style of punk rock than they had before. In the middle of a noisy and discordant set—during a song called "Dinosaur"—Al put down his guitar, picked up a crayon, and drew a dinosaur on a large pad of paper while Robert continued to play.

"The question was, 'How do you do something different while keeping the form, but challenge the form at the same time?'" Al says.

His answer was to replace the traditional rock 'n' roll guitar solo with a drawing solo.

"His energy was just great," Calvin says of Al's performance. "He was just out there. He had a crayon and a piece of paper on the wall, and he would draw pictures while the band was playing these great songs. It was just sort of youthful."

After the show, Aaron Stauffer, 15-year-old lead singer of Spook and the Zombies, exclaimed his love for the band.

"I later learned that Aaron was known around Olympia as the guy whose favorite band was whichever one he saw last," Al says. "He was really excited about us, talking nonstop. And then they all got in the car, and as they headed down to San Francisco, I was told that he kept talking about us. He might have just convinced them all."

Though it was a Go Team tour, Calvin was still focused on Beat Happening, his primary musical outlet. The final stop on the West

Coast tour was San Francisco. They played a show at the Rough Trade Record Store to a near-empty room, but Steve Connell was there. Calvin, Tobi, and the members of Mecca Normal spent that evening at Connell's place, hanging out with him and his girlfriend and *Puncture* copublisher and -editor, Katherine Spielmann. The next day, the three tourmates returned to the Rough Trade shop. As the rest bought records, Calvin met with Connell to negotiate the future relationship of Beat Happening and Rough Trade U.S. It was a future that Tobi wished she were a part of.

"Bret and Heather probably don't even care," Tobi wrote in her tour diary the day that Calvin met with Connell. "I should have joined that band when Calvin asked me, but I would have had to quit high school and my dad told me I had to earn a bunch of money before he would let me do that. So, I didn't get to go to England on tour. Being on tour and playing in bands is all I ever wanna do. I don't understand why Bret and Heather don't feel like that. They don't want to be famous I guess."

Whether or not they wanted to be famous, the members of Beat Happening were definitely gaining recognition. In an instance completely separate from Calvin's dealing with Rough Trade U.S., the Beat Happening full-length debut had made its way to the Rough Trade offices in the U.K. Of the seven hundred copies of the album that Calvin had pressed, the band had only sold about three hundred. So when his friend David Nichols told Calvin he was going to be traveling to England, Calvin had no problem giving him a few copies of the album to give to anyone who might be interested along the way. Nichols found that person in Jerry Thackery, a U.K. music critic who was then publishing a fanzine called *The Legend!* Thackery loved the album and took it to the Rough Trade offices where label head Geoff Travis heard it. Travis called Calvin personally and offered to release the band's debut in the U.K. The record was well received by the

British music press, charting at No. 27 on a year-end critics list that was topped by the Beastie Boys' *Licensed to Ill* and filled with names like Elvis Costello, Run-D.M.C., the Smiths, and Billy Idol. During the meeting Steve Connell offered to release the band's next album through Rough Trade's Stateside label. More than a distribution deal, the move would put Beat Happening in the company of labelmates Pere Ubu, Stiff Little Fingers, the Raincoats, and Young Marble Giants. The band would also now be associated with Rough Trade royalty like the Smiths, who after reaching No. 55 on the Billboard chart with their third album were at the pinnacle of their popularity in the United States. The band had signed on with a major label for its U.S. releases, but in the eyes of its fans, was more closely associated with Rough Trade, which continued to release its records in the U.K.

"When Beat Happening got picked up by Rough Trade, that was cool," Jonn Lunsford remembers. "We always thought that Beat Happening was interesting and pretty cool. You know, their melodies were simple, but long lasting. At least that's what we thought. So when Rough Trade picked them up, that was kind of a watershed moment."

The downside was that Rough Trade wasn't interested in releasing the album with its U.K. division. Fortunately the band had already forged another connection in the U.K. that was excited to put out the record there.

When the Beat Happening debut full-length was released on Rough Trade in the U.K., it garnered a glowing review in *Melody Maker*. Calvin and Candice managed to get their hands on a copy. "Calvin, Bret, and Heather unlock the kind of magic open only to the incompetent," the review read. "An unexpected masterpiece." After absorbing those words, they both read the rest of the issue. One item stood out: a review of two singles by an Oxford band called Talulah Gosh. Lois was in England at that time, so Calvin wrote her and asked her to look for the two singles. Weeks later, a letter arrived from Lois. She had not only bought the singles, but also managed to catch Talulah Gosh in concert. Just as Calvin and Candice had suspected, the band was great.

Eager to hear the group, Calvin went to a record store in Portland that sold imports. He found one of the singles, took it back to Olympia, put it on, and studied the sleeve. The record was released by 53rd & 3rd, a label Calvin had never heard of, but he immediately recognized the name as a reference to the Ramones' second single, "53rd & 3rd," a dark and gruesome pop tune about male prostitution.

The two singles from Lois soon arrived at K's headquarters, and neither Calvin nor Candice was disappointed. The music burst with a light energy. Over an insistent swinging rhythm, guitarist Peter Momtchiloff played loose, jangly lines while Amelia Fletcher sang high-and-light singsong melodies. Their musicianship was clearly more advanced than Beat Happening's, but the two bands were closer in sound to each other than they were to their punk forbearers. Plus, Calvin and Candice loved them; the spare delivery and cultural references (Talulah Gosh's first single was "Beatnik Boy") appealed to Calvin's musical sensibility, while Fletcher's vocals bowled Candice over. The band made it onto Calvin and Candice's wish list of groups to work with, a list that had been growing longer by the month.

With the relatively simple machinery of K Records in place, Calvin and Candice could get music out through the cassette compilations advertised in the pages of the K Records newsletter. Those compilations, though, were not ideal. While they helped create an audience for the bands—and bring a modest income into K's kitchen office—using tapes was still a compromise in Calvin's eyes. Now that K was bringing in some money, he was able to think about moving away from the lowly format and further into the production of 45s. It was a move in contrast to the rest of the underground, which—with the increasing ease of putting out full-length records and the emergence of the CD—was abandoning the seven-inch single as a format.

"I always loved the single," he says. "I always felt like it was the ultimate format. And that's one of the things I loved about punk rock, was that it brought the single back in the '70s and saved us from album-oriented radio. When you look at the history of rock music as written by *Rolling Stone* magazine, it's totally from this perspective of album-oriented radio, like an album is a real work of art, a single is something you did because you had to as a commercial . . . a marketing tool. It's so condescending because the dominant idea was that singles are what little girls listen to. But that's the reason they're cool. I always felt like rock 'n' roll is about two-and-a-half-minute songs. So that's what was great about punk rock. It came along and said, 'Singles!'"

In late 1986 Calvin began contacting his favorite bands from around the Pacific Northwest and the world, asking if they would like to release a single as part of a new series he was curating. Starting in January of 1987, K began issuing those singles under a new moniker, International Pop Underground.*

"I still wanted K to be a regional label," Calvin says. "But I wanted to have this outlet to connect with other people as well who were outside of the region."

The first year brought a number of releases from a collection of bands that were not only diverse in their zip codes but also in their sounds. The second single by Beat Happening ("Look Around")

---

*While it wasn't the only factor, the singles series helped give the label a significant bump of income. While K brought in $1,947.15 in the first quarter of 1986, it collected $2,414.49 in the same period of 1987, its best quarter to date. "With the release of up to ten seven-inch 45 releases in 1987, we will be in much more direct and regular contact with distributors," Calvin wrote in the quarter's financial report, "which should lead to an increase in their interest in K products generally."

kicked off International Pop Underground and was soon followed by contributions from Bryan Elliott's punk-folk band the Few ("Rollin' Like the Tide"), Tacoma's decidedly heavy rockers Girl Trouble ("She No Rattle My Cage/Riverbed" and "Old Time Religion/Tarantula"), the Australian pop group Cannanes (the EP *No One*), a more hard-bopping pop group from Britain called the Flatmates ("I Could Be in Heaven"), and the acerbic, political Canadian Mecca Normal ("Oh Yes You Can").

"It seemed as though, with underground music in the '80s, there was a lot of identification with genre," Calvin says. "You were hardcore or you were paisley underground or whatever. There were these genres. But when I was working with *OP Magazine* or *Sub Pop*, there was just a lot of great music that just doesn't fit. Like we used to say, 'They don't really fit the suit.' So I knew we needed a catchall thing. All of these people who are making interesting music that is powerful, but it's not easily categorized."

In order to promote the new venture, Calvin put together a tour of small Northwestern towns. For the first show, in Bellingham, Calvin invited Mecca Normal to play, but the rest of the tour featured a three-band bill of Beat Happening, Screaming Trees, and Girl Trouble, a tour that Bret dubbed the "Screaming Trouble Happening Tour." The bands played small halls—like the one where Calvin first saw the Spoiled years before—in Bellingham, Anacortes, Eugene, Olympia, and Ellensburg. The absence of Seattle from the tour itinerary was intentional, because the options for playing the city were too few for Calvin's inclusive ethic.

"At that time, it was really difficult to get shows in Seattle because we only played all-ages shows," Calvin says, "and there were no shows like that in Seattle. And we were like, 'Well, all of our favorite bands are in Aberdeen, and Tacoma, and Ellensburg, and Anacortes, so why don't we just play those places?' That's where all the cool bands are anyway."

The tour also served to connect Calvin with artists in the small Northwest communities that were managing to create inventive, genre-defying versions of punk rock. During the tour's stop in Eugene, Calvin invited Snakepit to open the show. Afterward, Al Larsen told Calvin that the show would be the band's last. From then on, he would be concentrating on Some Velvet Sidewalk. Calvin was thrilled and asked Al if his new band would like to be included in the International Pop Underground. Soon after, the band was recording the next two volumes of the IPU series with Calvin at Pat Maley's Yoyo Studios in Olympia.

Calvin spent a lot of time at Maley's studio that year. Though Mecca Normal had pressed its debut album on its own Smarten UP! label, Jean and David decided to release its second record with K. The band had recorded that first album in a practice studio with a four-track recorder and was willing to do it again, but Calvin had a different idea.

"Why don't you come and record here?" he asked Jean. "I'll record it."

Despite the fact that he had released a number of full-length records and even recorded a few of the IPU singles at Yoyo, Calvin had never recorded a full-length record in a studio before.

"He made things happen by simply making it sound like it was all possible," Jean says. "We were similarly predisposed to just doing things. Nobody knew probably quite exactly what to do or the right way of doing it, but Calvin created opportunities and invited us into those opportunities."

The band arrived at the Yoyo studio for its session only to find that it was recording in an old chicken coop. Inside, David and Jean set up their equipment and Calvin, with the help of Maley, tried to set up the mics. Mecca Normal had recorded much of its debut album live, with David playing guitar as Jean sang, and they insisted on taking this same approach with their Yoyo session, even though the vocal and the guitar would be recorded onto two separate tracks. This wouldn't have been a problem, but David and Jean also insisted on being close together in the studio space so that they could take visual cues from one another. This made it nearly impossible to isolate the band's two component sounds and keep David's guitar shredding from bleeding into Jean's vocal track. Eventually, the production team managed to engineer an acceptable solution. All set, the band recorded its first song. When they finished, Jean looked expectantly to Calvin.

"So, how is that?" she asked.

"Oh, it was okay."

"Well, what do you mean by that?"

"Well, maybe . . . how do you like it? I thought it was pretty okay."

"But, you know, do you see anything you might want to say about it?"

"Well, did you want to do it again?"

"No, if it was kind of okay, then what would we be doing again? Like what would we be doing differently?"

"Well, you might just want to do it again."

Later in the day, Calvin picked up a book—Jean contends it was a spy novel, Calvin recalls an issue of *Betty and Veronica*—in the middle of a song and started reading as the band played.

"I've got the words that I need to sing," Jean remembers thinking. "They're in my head, and directly in front of me is the guy who's recording us and he's reading a book. The upshot of that can be perhaps he got better performances out of me by a process of gently aggravating me."

The group finished recording the album in a single day.

"For the most part Dave and Calvin and I joked around a lot," Jean recalls. "There was a lot of levity and cleverness, a silly kind of humor, just to keep it light. So as a group of individuals, I would say that's where we probably all find the most comfortable rapport."

The next day Maley and Calvin mixed and mastered the record. Despite the fact that K had no other full-length releases scheduled, the album wouldn't be pressed for more than a year. It wasn't the only album to sit on K's shelf. Pounding Serfs, a twangy acoustic surf rock band led by the Few's Elliott and Bret's brother Jonn, also recorded a full-length album at Yoyo that year. The album wouldn't see the light of day until two years later. Some Velvet Sidewalk's debut would also languish on the shelf for some time before being released. While Calvin had willing bands that he was excited about and the tools to record them, he lacked the financial means to do anything with those recordings.

"I'd recorded these records, but I couldn't afford to put them out," Calvin recalls. "And they sat around for what seemed like forever. Now a year and a half doesn't seem like forever anymore, but when you're twenty-five, it seems like forever. And I felt really bad, I felt guilty, and the bands were like, 'When is our album gonna come out?' And I'm like, 'I don't know.'"

In the summer of 1987, Calvin received a letter from a man named Thomas Zimmerman, who ran a touring agency for bands in Germany. Zimmerman had recently booked a tour for a British band called the Pastels. When the Pastels came through Germany, a guitarist named Norman Blake, who was briefly touring with the band, played the first Beat Happening record for Zimmerman. He was impressed. He wrote to tell Calvin that he was coming to America and would like to stay in Olympia for a week. Calvin wrote back with a formal invitation.

While visiting, Zimmerman told Calvin about the Pastels, a band that had gained some notoriety after releasing a series of well-received singles on a number of labels, including Rough Trade. The band's sound was an oddity at the time; decidedly amateurish, the Pastels' songs featured themes of childhood, a melodic sensibility that harkened back to '60s pop groups, and a lead vocalist who could not sing, at least in the traditional sense. If Beat Happening had a British cousin, the Pastels were it. Zimmerman then told Calvin that the lead singer of the band, Stephen "Pastel" McRobbie, had started his own record label, 53rd & 3rd. At that moment, Calvin decided that he needed to hear the Pastels.

Before he could track down one of their releases, though, Calvin received a letter from McRobbie, asking if Beat Happening would be interested in releasing an album on 53rd & 3rd. Since Rough Trade had passed on distributing the band's second full-length in the U.K., there was an opening. Calvin said yes.

Despite the increased exposure that Beat Happening was experiencing, the band maintained its casual approach to the craft of writing, practicing, and recording songs. With Bret in Anacortes and Heather in Seattle, the trio could only physically collaborate every so often. When they couldn't get together, they just used cassettes to write and rehearse their songs.

"Some bands need to get together five nights a week to do their thing," Bret says. "We were more, okay, here's these songs that we are thinking of doing for an album; send out some cassettes of some rough home recordings with some lyrics sheets and then we'll use that as a base to get together to do some rehearsals. Then maybe we'll write some more songs; then maybe we'll start to do some shows so that the songs get to blossom a bit before we record them."

For its second album, Beat Happening traveled to Albright Productions, the recording studio that Fisk was running in Ellensburg. Fisk had been a musician in the K Records world since he met Calvin at KAOS, and their relationship culminated in the release of his band Pell Mell's first full-length cassette on the label. Since moving back to Ellensburg, though, he was building a reputation for his production chops. By the time Beat Happening came to his studio, Fisk had already recorded the first two full-length albums for Screaming Trees, the second of which was released on SST Records.

Despite Fisk's reputation, Calvin arrived with his own game plan. Fisk took a step back, allowing Calvin to call the shots when it came to staging the recordings and dialing in the instruments, and did his best to see that Calvin's ideas were fully realized in the end product. At one point, Calvin wanted to record a couple of the songs on a porch outside the studio, an unconventional way to use that space. But the band ended up outside with all of its equipment, and Fisk stayed in the booth with his assistant, Screaming Trees leader Mark Lanegan, trying desperately to capture the sound. None of the band members can remember what songs they played outside. Thanks to Fisk's production, it is impossible to tell those porch recordings from the in-studio songs on the resulting album, *Jamboree*.

No manner of studio experimentation could have resulted in *Jamboree* sounding as uneven in its fidelity as the patchwork of songs that constituted the band's debut, but Fisk's production did more than even out the band's sound. It gave Beat Happening some punch. The band's wobbly amateur musicianship might have maintained the music's lo-fi reputation, but the actually fidelity of the new recordings was far from low. The music sounded full, deep, and crisp.

Jamboree was different for more reasons than its sonic clarity, a fact that was announced with the long, warped peel of feedback that introduced the first track, "Bewitched."

Musically, the band was a tighter unit than on its early releases, though Bret was guilty of a number of noticeable missed notes. Calvin's voice was still sometimes aggressively off-key, but his lyrics had matured, sharpening Beat Happening's dual touchstones of innocence and danger.

Despite its pink cover, *Jamboree* was a much darker album, although its darkness, found in songs like "In Between" and "Hangman," was often cartoonesque or couched in catchy sing-song meter.

"I remember when my parents met," Heather sang on the second song, "In Between." "It was years before my birth. And I can see them years from now, their ghosts fly above the earth. And let's not talk about what makes us die, let the jokes make the years go by, 'cause it's a burden and it's hard to bear. It's too easy to not even care."

Calvin was mastering the come-on song with the tracks "Bewitched" and "Midnight a Go-Go," but he also showed a tender side to his romantic persona, most remarkably on the blissful ballad "Indian Summer" and the self-ingratiating kiss-off track, "Cat Walk." The album ends with its one inconsistency, a live track recorded by Rich Jensen called "The This Many Boyfriends Club." The song starts with a crowd of girls yelling for the band to play a song from the *Three Tea Breakfast* cassette called "Honey Pot," interrupted by a squelching line of feedback that continues through to the end. Calvin speak-sings his lines: "This many boyfriends walk her home. This many boyfriends ring her home. Laurie, Laurie what's the story." At this point, a bloodcurdling scream comes from the crowd. Undeterred, Calvin continues, "All those boys think you are boring. They just see those bobby socks, not what's beneath those curly locks." The song continues for two minutes, with Calvin blurting out lines of quiet devotion as the screaming continues in the background. After reciting the final lines, "But there's one thing I forgot. I love Laurie a lot," he drops the mic and the crowd of girls scream as if they were attendees at a 1964 Beatles concert.

The song was a testament to the idea that Beat Happening was best experienced live, where the band's inconsistencies were overshadowed by an enigmatic lead singer whose fits of dancing and deep voice were—for those not eager to judge—overpowering.

Still, for all of the album's depth, it was difficult for some critics to hear past the juvenilia and amateur musicianship. One of them was influential *Village Voice* critic Robert Christgau. In his weekly "Consumer Guide" column, he gave the album a B-, which translated to "a competent or mildly interesting record that will usually feature at least three worthwhile cuts." His review reads harsher than the grade:

"Some find their calculated simplicity and semi-unrehearsed spontaneity recombinant, their unadorned lyricism and rude guitar doubly tonic," he wrote of the release. "I find their adolescence-recalled-cum-childhood-revisited doubly coy and their neoprimitivist shtick a tired bohemian fantasy. Catchy, though."

A BRIEF HISTORY OF ZINES

Independent publishing and revolution have been intertwined since Johannes Gutenberg invented the movable-type printing press in 1440. The mass reproduction of the printed word allowed ideas to flourish and literacy rates to soar, providing the intellectual fuel that gave rise to the Renaissance.

Technological advancements that led to cheaper means of printing put the power of the press into the hands of the otherwise powerless. As a result, the written word continued to fuel political and religious revolutions through the centuries, including the Protestant Reformation of the sixteenth century, the American Revolution of the eighteenth century, and the French Revolution of the nineteenth century. This lineage would continue into the twentieth century with the birth of the zine.

There is no clear definition of what constitutes a zine, except that its circulation is generally minimal (most often fewer than 5,000 copies) and its creators are more interested in spreading a message than making a profit. The earliest zines—called fanzines—appeared in the world of science fiction in the middle of the twentieth century. Fans unhappy with the output of established sci-fi magazines created their own publications, first using mimeograph technology developed late in the nineteenth century before the emergence of the cheaper and more ubiquitous photocopier in the '60s.

The rise of punk rock music ran parallel with the rise of punk zines. While the music press that was born the decade before recognized this new strain of rock and the mainstream press quickly focused its disapproving gaze on the subculture, the punk zine was the only required medium in the underground. The zines established the culture of punk rock—often through spirited manifestos—while also spreading the word about new bands, styles, and clubs.

The first of the punk fanzines was *Punk*, a semiregular New York–based publication started in 1975 by John Holstrom, Legs McNeil, and Ged Dunn. It would publish fifteen editions before ending its run in 1979. English punks kept up with the underground through the zine *Sniffin' Glue*, a monthly publication that lasted for only a year, but grew in that time from a circulation of fifty to fifteen thousand.

Despite the demise of those initial efforts, thousands of punk zines from first-time publishers would continue to connect and shape the underground. Of those, a few became standard bearers with lengthy runs and religious readers, including *OP Magazine, Puncture, Maximum RockNRoll,* and *Flipside*.

Zines also became the creative launching points for larger projects. Before starting Mecca Normal, Jean Smith shared her ideas through her *Smarten UP!* zine (which later turned into a record label). Bruce Pavitt's *Subterranean Pop* zine created the initial audience for his Sub Pop record label. *Bikini Kill*, a zine created by Evergreen student Kathleen Hanna, shared its name and its politics with her band. The riot grrrl movement to which Hanna's zine helped give rise serves as the last, and perhaps the greatest, testament to the power of the zine before the Internet turned the photocopied pamphlet from a revolutionary tool into a novelty.

"All across the country, girls wait to hear from the fanzine network," *Chicago Reader* writer Emily White wrote of riot grrrl in September 1992, "a phantom community they belong to but never see—it's an underground with no center, built of paper."

10

G.E.S.C.C.O.'S DAYS were numbered from the start. As a student project headed by Bret and Denise, it would only last as long as the couple was enrolled in school. It was possible that it could have lived beyond that, but Bret and Denise had different designs.

With his tour schedule feeding the same wanderlust that had previously made him a nomadic young adult, Bret started to focus his studies and experimentation more toward community development. G.E.S.C.C.O. was an example of that, but Bret didn't feel that downtown Olympia was the best place for him to discover the keys to building community.

"Olympia was cool," Bret says. "But when I am in Anacortes, I feel that I am home. So, I decided to respond to that feeling and go back. And also I thought that if I'm interested in how community works, it makes sense to go to where I am from and have all the insights I already have and have all the connections that I already have to help me figure out whatever it is that I am trying to figure out."

In 1987 Bret and Denise began taking the steps to move to Bret's hometown. Bret was still committed to playing in Beat Happening, but his departure meant that Calvin was the last member left in Olympia. However, the recent success of the band assured that, unlike Calvin's earlier bands, Beat Happening would not let distance destroy it. Fortunately, since part of the band's established pop formula was a primitive playing style, having regular practice was not a necessity.

Touring, however, was. With *Jamboree* scheduled for U.K. release in the summer of 1988, Calvin arranged a European tour through Zimmerman. Because Norman Blake had turned the German booking agent on to Beat Happening, it was only natural that the band should tour with Blake's new band, a much-buzzed-about group called Boy Hairdressers. Filling out the three-band bill was the Vaselines, a little-known Glasgow band that had just released its first single on 53rd & 3rd. When Beat Happening arrived in Europe, Zimmerman had some bad news: Boy Hairdressers had broken up.

"Because they were the most well-known band, a lot of the shows just got canceled because they didn't want to have just the Vaselines and Beat Happening," Calvin says. "They were like, 'Who the fuck are these guys?'"

The tour wasn't a complete bust. Beat Happening toured the continent, playing shows in Germany, Sweden, and Holland before traveling to the U.K., where they played three shows with the Vaselines.* The shows were spotty, but the band did find a modest fan base in the U.K., where Rough Trade had already sold fifteen hundred copies of its first album.

"There were some people who knew about us, but not really a lot," Calvin recalls. "In Scotland, there were a lot more people who seemed to know who Beat Happening was. I think there was a word of mouth there, and more people seemed to be aware of Beat Happening. So the Edinburgh show was by far the biggest and the most exciting show of the whole tour, really well attended.

---

*In 1991 K Records issued a recording of Beat Happening's and the Vaselines' June 16, 1988, show in London as a split cassette. Side A featured the Vaselines performing "Dying For It," "The Day I Was a Horse," "Sex Sux," "Let's Get Ugly," "Molly's Lips," and "Teenage Superstars." The B-side featured Beat Happening performing "I Love You," "Knick Knack," "Sea Babies," "Cast a Shadow," and "Bad Seeds."

Pretty exciting. But the other shows, like in England, nobody had any idea who we were."

For a few stretches, though, the band had no shows to play. One occurred the week that *Jamboree* was scheduled for its U.K. release. With nothing else to do, Beat Happening traveled to Glasgow to finally meet the Pastels and the owners of 53rd & 3rd. To actually witness the operation behind the *Jamboree* release, however, Calvin was told to go to Edinburgh and visit the offices of another record label called Fast Forward. While McRobbie and David Keegan ran 53rd & 3rd and were responsible for scheduling releases, they had outsourced the administrative tasks of getting the records pressed and into the hands of radio, the press, and record buyers. When Calvin visited Fast Forward's offices, he wasn't interested in chitchat. He was there to work.

"I went down to the office at Fast Forward to try to get people to know about our record," Calvin says. "I think at first they were like, 'What are you gonna do? Why are you here? Who are you?' But I was like, 'I want to do whatever we need to do.' I was just calling the stores and making sure they had our record, or knew about our record, and calling the distributor and making sure they knew, because so many records come out, and we're just like another band no one's heard of . . . Once they saw that I really wanted to do this, they were like, 'Oh, well you should call this person too.' And they had some journalists come in and interview me."

The combination of the band's touring and Calvin's extra work helped raise Beat Happening's overseas profile enough that Rough Trade offered to release its third album in the U.K. Before that could happen, Calvin had a number of other projects to undertake in the Pacific Northwest.

After returning to the United States, Beat Happening entered Fisk's studio again to make an odd seven-inch with Screaming Trees. Instead of each band recording its music on a different side of the album, as is the case with most split releases, Beat Happening and Screaming Trees collaborated on all four songs, with Calvin taking vocal duties on two songs and Lanegan and Heather splitting the other two (and singing backup vocals for each other). The seven-inch came out later that year, released by New York–based Homestead Records in the United States and 53rd & 3rd in the U.K.*

K Records had continued to grow, even without the advantage of having the latest Beat Happening release in its catalog, but with Calvin's focus on that record and the tour, the K newsletter had little to report. Before the end of 1988, the label had added a few more releases, including Some Velvet Sidewalk's International Pop Underground singles, another Go Team tape titled *Donna Parker Pop*, and the Mecca Normal full-length record *Calico Kills the Cat*.

By the time of *Calico*'s release, Mecca Normal had become a fixture in the Olympia scene. Jean had come to visit Olympia more often since her band played G.E.S.C.C.O., even moving to the city during a romance with a spoken word artist named Slim Moon. Though the outspoken nature of her art and her passionate embrace of the political was not in line with most of the Olympia scene, Jean did feel accepted in the community. Still, she didn't quite understand what they saw in the band.

"I was very surprised at the people who liked us, based on their orientation," she says. "I didn't really see the connection. It seemed like everybody had children's toys in their apartment, you know, either masking taped to the wall, or sitting on their bed, or in the middle of their dining room table. And to me, that was an

---

*Homestead Records was owned and operated by the Dutch East India Trading music distribution company. Starting in 1984 it was managed by Gerard Cosloy, who also published the fanzine *Conflict* and hosted a radio show on WFMU. In 1990, Cosloy became the co-owner of Matador Records, which would become one of the most successful independent record labels of the '90s.

unknown, unheard-of sort of aesthetic choice. I was married and divorced by the time I ever set foot in Olympia. And I didn't have kids' toys around my house as decoration or as a way to connect to my childhood. My childhood was absolutely over, and that seemed how best to proceed through life."

The conflicted feeling was mutual for the young Olympia fans. In the spring of 1989, Mecca Normal went on a cross-country tour with Some Velvet Sidewalk and the Go Team. After playing a show in Minneapolis to a near-empty coffee shop, Tobi reflected on the band's performance.

"No one does what Jean Smith does," she later wrote. "I just wish it was more accessible . . . I looked up to them because I had seen them on the Black Wedge Tour . . . when I was sixteen and was blown away, but they seemed like authority figures to me, because they were older and serious."

Despite the hurdles that Mecca Normal faced as artists, the band now had the ability to reach a larger audience, thanks to the K newsletter and the distribution Rough Trade provided to K in the U.S.

"Steve Connell was interested in what K was doing, and fairly supportive, although he wasn't really a fan necessarily of the music that we were putting out," Calvin says. "Some of the bands were either too normal—like, Girl Trouble to him was just like a rock band—or they just didn't make sense to him, like Mecca Normal didn't. But he was supportive of K. And I could understand, you know, having worked at KAOS and *OP*. *OP* wasn't about loving a lot of weird kinds of music; it was about supporting the idea that you could put out lots of weird kinds of music. KAOS was a community radio station; it wasn't saying, 'Here's a lot of really good music'; it was saying, 'Here's a lot of different kinds of music, independent music.' And so I understood the difference between supporting something and liking it. And I certainly understood

Steve feeling like he could make the distinction in his life that he liked the idea of K even if he didn't necessarily like all the music on it. So I appreciated that."

Although it was hard for Connell—or even Jean—to see the appeal of Mecca Normal, the band was now officially a cornerstone of K, the only artist besides Beat Happening to have a full-length record out on the label.

In the summer of 1989, Calvin decided to relaunch the "small towns tour" that he had organized two years prior. Together with his brother, Streator, and Bret, Calvin started a new organization intended to spread music to the small communities of the Pacific Northwest: Sound Out Northwest. Its mission was to institutionalize the practice of having regional rock bands tour small towns around the Northwest, playing all-ages shows at fraternal organizations and community centers. The maiden tour would be a brief one, along the western edge of Washington State.

Naturally, Calvin asked Mecca Normal to join Beat Happening on that first S.O.N. tour in August of 1989. Also on the bill was Mudhoney, a Seattle band that hadn't worked with K but had released a seven-inch single with Bruce Pavitt's Sub Pop operation, which had metamorphosed from its modest fanzine beginnings into Seattle's top record label.

In 1986, the label's first official release, another compilation called *Sub Pop 100*, landed Pavitt an on-air interview with a DJ at the University of Washington radio station named Jonathan Poneman. Soon after, Poneman partnered with Pavitt, making a financial investment that helped Sub Pop rent an office space in downtown Seattle and begin producing singles and full-length albums.

The single "Touch Me I'm Sick" was a hit on college radio and made Mudhoney the label's flagship band. Immediately after the S.O.N. tour, the band would enter Jack Endino's Reciprocal Studio and record its full-length, self-titled debut for Sub Pop, a record that became the pioneering album in a new genre of music that would soon after be known as "grunge."

The fourth spot on Calvin's tour bill was meant for a band from Aberdeen called Nirvana. In June of 1989, the band had released *Bleach*, its debut album, through Sub Pop. Following a July 18 show at the Pyramid Club in New York City, the band canceled the remainder of its summer dates, including the S.O.N. shows. Calvin's tour went on without the band as Nirvana prepared for a long string of tour dates through the Midwest and eventually to the U.K., where thousands of new fans were waiting to hear the band perform its hit record.

Calvin arranged one more tour before the end of the year, this time taking the Go Team out to the East Coast to play a few dates with the Boston power pop band the Blake Babies. Three weeks into the six-week tour, the band's '64 Ford Falcon broke down and that was it, not only for the tour, but for the Go Team as well.

"We were on the East Coast and it was really hard to find someone to work on old cars," Calvin remembers. "The van was only twenty-five years old. So, the car was not gonna live and we weren't getting along, so it seemed like the tour needed to end. We didn't have a mode of transportation and there really wasn't a spirit of 'the show must go on' at that point."

The Go Team was gone, but the rest of the K roster was busy making more music. While the musicians at K were far from grizzled vets, they had gained some perspective throughout their triumphs and travails of the '80s. As the decade came to a close, Al Larsen decided to put that perspective to use and attempted to define exactly what it was he and his fellow artists were doing, and how they might proceed into the next decade. He submitted his thoughts in an article titled "Love Rock and Why I Am" to *Snipehunt*, a monthly tabloid in Portland published by an old friend from Eugene.

"We had used and reused the term 'punk' enough," Al remembers thinking. "I felt that we kept trying to redefine punk. Like, Punk isn't hitting people in the face; punk is giving people free food. Or, Punk isn't sloppy musicianship; punk is speed metal bands. Punk had been redefined so many times that we would be better off using a different word. I was trying to write a manifesto that would draw a circle around things that were important to me with the idea that this was 'love rock.' This was a vision for the future."

That vision was rooted in the power of music.

"When Sonic Youth do 'Kool Thing' they are love rock," Al wrote in his manifesto. "Or when Beat Happening trade roles, singer to guitarist to drummer. When Nation of Ulysses makes an absolute sincere mess or when the Melvins play, three people as one. These people create music about the most important thing going: the transformation of society. And each one suggests possibility."

But love rock was more than just music. In his tract, Al pointed to the '80s as a decade of despair, evidenced by the fact that "Levi's began making black jeans! The brutal world of Dark Knight Batman was the movie mega-sensation that closed the decade."

Love rock was the hope that Al saw in the coming decade. "It's a scary world, but we don't need to be scared anymore," he wrote. "We need active, visionary protest, we need to grab hold and make the transformation, from complaining that there is NO FUTURE to insisting there be a future."

He declared the key word of the decade as "Let's," the same word that had started the three earliest K Records compilations: *Let's Kiss*, *Let's Sea*, *Let's Together*. Borrowing from Stella Marrs's reappropriation of forgotten cultural rituals, Calvin's ethos of inclusion, and his own proclivity toward political engagement, Al created a vision of a future that moved past the dominant culture of the '80s and embraced the industriousness of the past while looking toward a radical shift in the way people lived their lives. Through love rock, he concluded, the future would be one filled with "Cooking. Canning. Composting. All-ages shows in Grange Halls across the land. Engaging. Enacting. Ennobling. A dance party on the docks. Root cellar. Dry pack. Do it yourself. A free press. Custom bicycles, streamers flying, cards clacking in the spokes. Let's. We. Free. Go, love rocker."

PART II

REVOLUTION
COME AND GONE

*A double shot of International Hip Swing is the goal.
Barbecues, parades, disco dancing, picnics and wild screaming teenage rock 'n' roll are the means. Revolution is the end.
Revolution is the beginning. No lackeys to the corporate
ogre allowed.*

—Advertisement for the International Pop
Underground Convention, written by Calvin Johnson

IN MARCH OF 1983, Calvin received a phone call from a man named Buzz. The lead singer of Nerve, a band from the seaside town of Aberdeen, Buzz contacted Calvin after seeing Laura, Heather, and Calvin open for the Wipers at an empty storefront in downtown Olympia. Buzz wanted to book a show with them for his band and was hoping that Calvin could help.

"I was just thrilled that somebody from Aberdeen was calling me," Calvin says. "I just thought that was so cool that there was a band in Aberdeen. So I was psyched."

Calvin passed Buzz's number on to the organizers of the Wipers' show and soon after sent them a song from the band under its new name, the Melvins. It would be a year before the people behind the Wipers' show would open the Tropicana, but when they did, the Melvins were on the bill for the venue's second show. The band played there five times before the venue closed.

At those shows, Candice became both a fan of the band and friends with the members and their Aberdeen neighbors. By the time she was working at K, Candice was traveling to Aberdeen on a weekly basis with two of her coworkers at the Smithfield Café, Tracy Marander and Tamra Ohrmund. They would hang out at the house of the Melvins' bass player, Matt Lukin, to engage in sober evenings of teenage silliness with the band and their friends. Matt's roommate was a young musician named Kurt Cobain, who was playing in a band with a bass player named Krist Novoselic.

The band had yet to settle on a name in the spring of 1987, when it was invited to play its first club gig in Olympia. The performance was to be the final show ever at Bret and Denise's G.E.S.C.C.O. venue and would also feature two Olympia bands, Danger Mouse and Nisqually Delta Podunk Nightmare. Kurt and Krist would play with drummer Aaron Burckhard under the name Skid Row.

After the show, the band was invited to play a midnight radio show at KAOS hosted by Donna Dresch and John Goodmanson, two local musicians who had also performed at the final G.E.S.C.C.O. show. Kurt and Krist would use the tape from the in-studio session as a demo to secure future shows.

By the time Kurt had given Tracy a copy of the tape, the band had decided on a name: Nirvana. Each week when Tracy, Candice, and Tam drove the Olympic Highway from Olympia to Aberdeen and back again in Tam's two-door Datsun, they listened to the tape over and over. Candice was enthralled with the recording and thought the band would be a good fit for K. She took it to the office to let Calvin have a listen.

"I don't think Tracy ever told Kurt, like, 'Oh, I took your tape over to K,'" Candice says. "She just gave it to me and I said, 'Hey, I got this tape from Tracy. It's her boyfriend's band.' But Calvin had a lot of tapes. So, it could seem like, 'Really, another tape?' I remember putting it on the windowsill in the office, and saying, 'You should listen to this.'"

What happened to that tape is a point of contention. Calvin says that the tape was lost in the growing pile of demos at the K offices. Candice says that Calvin listened to the tape, but wasn't interested. "Calvin's quote was, 'I'm not gonna put out some girl's boyfriend's band,'" Candice recalls. "And that was it."

The next fall, Kurt moved out of Aberdeen and into Tracy's house in Olympia, while Krist settled in Tacoma with his girlfriend. Now in Olympia, Kurt hoped Nirvana would start playing more shows. But following the closure of G.E.S.C.C.O., Olympia was again without an all-ages venue. Kurt had to travel thirty miles north, where Nirvana would play on Krist's turf at the Community World Theater, something the band did often throughout the next couple of years. The band also played at a number of Olympia house shows, dorm parties, and even a day-time festival on the Evergreen campus, but did not return to a downtown Olympia club until April 1, 1989, when it played a new feminist art gallery called Reko/Muse started by an Evergreen student named Kathleen Hanna.

The shows at the Community World Theater had paid off for the band, which began playing at Seattle's hippest clubs and even found an outlet for its music through Sub Pop. For Kurt, though, the label was a second choice.

While the band's first single, a cover of a song by the Dutch band Shocking Blue called "Love Buzz," was being prepped for release on Sub Pop, Kurt wrote a fan letter to Mark Lanegan. In it, he told the Screaming Trees singer that he had heard all of the band's records, including the collaboration it had done with Beat Happening the year before. He also sent Lanegan a cassette tape filled with new Nirvana songs.

"This stuff on the tape I sent is some 4trk mello, pretty sleep music we've been doing for the past couple months," Kurt wrote. "It's obvious that it has been inspired from Beat Happening/ Young Marble Giants music. If you like some of it or if you have something of your own in which you thought I would be appropriate for collaborating then I'm willing.

"Nirvana is planning on asking Calvin if he wants to put a K cassette of these songs & a couple of obscure heavy songs too," Kurt wrote before complaining that Sub Pop was having financial difficulties and that he doubted the label's ability to release a full-length record with the band anytime soon. It's not hard to read between the lines and see Kurt's true wishes for his music.

"It was always really clear he had a lot of respect and a lot of interest in the label," Candice says.

Calvin had warmed to Nirvana, giving the band its first ever review, for "Love Buzz," in his fanzine *sand*. A few weeks after the Reko/Muse show, Calvin invited Kurt to record a single with his side project, the Go Team. The record was the seventh of a seven-inch series that the Go Team was releasing through K on a monthly basis. Kurt, credited as "Kurdt Cobain" in the liner notes, is only featured on one of the release's two songs, playing guitar with Calvin as Tobi drums on the instrumental track "Bikini Twilight."

The record would be the only K release that Kurt would ever play on.

Nirvana was not the only subject on which Calvin and Candice disagreed. Candice served as an assistant when she was in Olympia, but with Calvin on the road for much of 1987 and 1988, she kept K running, fulfilling the orders that arrived from readers of the newsletter and corresponding with the various bands and labels that had come to count on the newsletter for distribution. The label had come to count on the distribution business as well. The cost of providing the service was negligible, consisting mostly of the time that Calvin spent curating the titles and the cost of printing the newsletter, but the return was keeping the label afloat.

"More of what we were doing, for the most part, was distribution than releasing our own stuff," Candice says. "We just wanted to—there was so much out there."

Candice had the business acumen to run a tight ship on a small budget, but she didn't have the time or the amount of control to do so effectively. While Olympia was cheap to live in, the twenty dollars a week she was paid for her work was not enough; Candice still had to work three other jobs to make ends meet. She also wanted more of a say in the overall operations. As the years went by, Candice began digging deeper into some musical circles that Calvin was only able to skim as his touring schedule became more demanding. While Calvin was on the road, Candice was going to shows. She was making connections and discoveries of her own that she wanted to add to the K family, but she had no official right to push Calvin to pay attention. Something had to change.

In the summer of 1989, Candice left Olympia and K behind and moved to San Francisco. Since 1986, the farm girl—who had gone out of the state only once before—had been visiting the Bay Area two or three times each year, building up a network of friends and connections who were prepared to give her the support she would need to start a new life. She took a job with Steve Connell at the Rough Trade label, working alongside two fellow former Olympians, Donna Dresch and Billy Karren, and she lived in Chico, California, with Barbara Manning, a well-known musician who had played in a jangly psychedelic rock band called 28th Day and was then part of a darker pop outfit called the World of Pooh.

While Candice was settling into her new life, Calvin returned from the first Sound Out Northwest tour and faced the realities of his record label. While the distribution arm of K was faring well, the label itself was in a difficult period of transition. No longer the scrappy upstart promising a "cassette revolution," K was now beholden to bands that had come to expect more from an independent music industry that was gaining influence. But as the growing number of independent record labels in the United States were discovering, entering the world of legitimate record sales was not easy.

"The whole thing with multiformats—it was confusing," Calvin recalls. "For a while, the single was a way to just keep the label going, but not having to deal with albums and three formats. Let's just forget about albums, let's just concentrate on these 45s."

Calvin knew that he could no longer concentrate on the single alone, which may have been his aesthetic preference, but offered very little chance of a financial return—bad for both the label and its bands. K Records was beginning to issue full-lengths, including the Mecca Normal debut and a recently released album by the Pounding Serfs, but Calvin didn't know what to do with them.

"I finally put out both those records, but they were limited by my ability to press very many copies." Calvin says. "They were also limited by their appeal to the general public. Nobody cared about Mecca Normal or the Pounding Serfs. So, just like the first Beat Happening record, we sold a couple hundred, then we had many boxes sitting there that no one wanted. The bands were like, 'How's my album doing?' And it was hard."

Calvin had forever been the face of K, a mesmerizing he-man in a small music world. Through his performances, his radio show, and the K newsletter, Calvin served as both the inspiration for an increasing number of young bands and as a gatekeeper whose approval was something akin to a knighting. But there were limits to Calvin's powers. As the independent music scene became more sophisticated, it was necessary for the label to have someone at the helm at all times, managing relationships with customers, bands, media, and potential distributors. Calvin's growing commitment to numerous musical projects of his own, as well as his increasing role as a producer, meant he could not provide that care. Candice could, and Calvin knew that. He called her and told her that he needed her back. Candice, no longer the shy music fan who first met Calvin, was resolute in her demands.

"I said, 'Either this is a full-time thing and we're partners, or I'm gonna stay down here,'" Candice recalls. "It wasn't mean or anything. I just wasn't going to be an assistant."

In the end, Calvin agreed to a partnership with Candice. In keeping with the way they did business with the bands on K, the pair did not sign a contract. It was a handshake deal.

Candice had planned to return at the end of October, but after experiencing her first major temblor in the middle of the month, she hastened her return. Three days after she arrived in Olympia, a slip occurred along the San Andreas fault, resulting in a magnitude 6.9 earthquake that left buildings and bridges in shambles.

Back in Olympia, Candice stepped into her new role without hesitation. The first order of business was to get more office space. In early 1988, Calvin had moved the K offices out of his two-room apartment in the Martin and into a rented room above the China Town restaurant, two blocks away at 213 Fourth Avenue East. The rooms were cheap, which meant that the record label had a number of artists as its neighbors, including Stella Marrs, Calvin's old neighbor from the Capitol Theater building, and another artist named Mikey Dees, who had just started playing in a hardcore punk band called Fitz of Depression. It wasn't long before the label had outgrown that room and acquired another to store its stock of cassettes, singles, and records. By the time Candice returned from San Francisco, the new business partners decided it was time to expand yet again.

"We just kept expanding, getting more and more rooms," Calvin recalls. "We needed warehouse space, and we needed more office space. So we just said to the people at the China Town, 'Why don't we just rent the whole floor? And we'll just sublet to the artists that are still here.'"

By the end of 1989, the label had added a number of new titles to its catalog. In addition to the seven-inch series from the Go Team and the debut full-length from the Pounding Serfs, K had issued a cassette full-length by the Go Team called *Archer Come Sparrow*, the first seven-inch from Fitz of Depression, two more entries in the International Pop Underground series from Some Velvet Sidewalk and Girl Trouble, and yet another full-length album by Beat Happening, *Black Candy*.

For its third album, Beat Happening shifted back to the arrangement it had with its debut: K released the album in the United States while Rough Trade released it in the U.K. Beat Happening again went to Steve Fisk to record. This time, Calvin suggested that the band forgo the studio and instead record to a four-track in Fisk's apartment. Again, Fisk obliged and invited the band to his home for a recording session. Calvin, Heather, and Bret arrived with a carload of equipment borrowed from Maley's Yoyo Studios. Calvin and Fisk set up to record the album.

What followed was a comedy of errors, with equipment shorting out and tension rising. Eventually, the band and the producer called off the plan and moved back into the studio.

As the title implies, *Black Candy* found the band still straddling the line between dark and sweet, though there clearly had been a move into more morose territory. The album started out with an upbeat, jangly chord progression, the sound that had become a Beat Happening trademark. In that first song, "Other Side," Calvin proposed a shift. "Let's fly away to the other side," he sang. "Wipe the slate clean for the umpteenth time, starting again on a life of crime on the other side."

The album's title track followed with a similar plea, spiked with a sinister sexuality and delivered over a decidedly dark and stormy bed of guitar noise. "Suck my blood, join the club, breakfast dub, cross my heart, hope to care, pull my hair, take me there, black candy." The rest of the album followed in that darker vein, filled with ghosts, tombstones, and grave diggers. The childlike, singsongy parts were still there (in particular, the catchy-yet-infantile "Playhouse"), but almost every song was haunted by a specter. The album's most tender love song, "Cast a Shadow," was shot through with darkness, the object of affection gone missing from the real world, seen only in dreams and able only to cast a shadow on the song's bereft narrator.

Around the time that Beat Happening released *Black Candy*, the debut album, *13 Songs*, from Ian MacKaye's new band, Fugazi, was released. Since the brief encounter between Calvin and MacKaye in the nation's capital a decade earlier, the tie between Olympia and Washington, D.C., had continued to strengthen. The two communities had become so close that recent Evergreen graduates were relocating to D.C., including Lois Maffeo, who in 1989 moved into the house where MacKaye and his bandmates stayed while not on tour. They were often away: in the two years since the band had started touring outside of D.C., Fugazi had played more than 150 shows across the United States and Europe.

In December of 1989, Calvin and his brother, Streator, made their annual road trip to Washington, D.C., to spend Christmas with their mother. Calvin dropped by MacKaye's house to visit with Lois and reconnect with the Fugazi lead singer, who had just returned from the band's first European tour. MacKaye invited Calvin out to a show featuring three new bands on his Dischord label. The headliner was Fidelity Jones, a hardcore band that, like Fugazi, was maintaining the intensity of hardcore while experimenting with other musical forms—in this case, funk and jazz. The other two bands on the bill, Hazmat and Ulysses, were even stranger. But they were the bands that MacKaye wanted Calvin to see.

"Hazmat had four girls and a guy singer," Calvin says. "And in D.C. at the time, there were no girls in bands. So having girls in bands was very different. I had seen girls in bands before. But still, I was like, 'This band is good, and not because there were girls in the band, but because they're good.' And I was like, 'Wow, this is refreshing. I've never seen anything like this in D.C., like a good kind of punky, kind of party pop girl band with a guy singer.' And they looked cool."

When Ulysses took the stage, Calvin recognized the lead singer, Ian Svenonius. During the Go Team tour the previous year, Calvin had met him at the Dischord house. On stage, Svenonius looked different. He was dressed in a suit jacket. He looked sharp. When the band began playing its set—a blistering punk rock take on R & B—he appeared possessed.

"It was just like, whoa, that's hardcore, only more so," Calvin remembers. "Plus they had this sense of style that was really cool."

Two days after the show, Calvin returned to the Dischord house. There, he and MacKaye talked about the new bands. Ulysses, in particular, was causing MacKaye some pains. The band definitely met the requirements to be on Dischord, where the only rule was that you had to be from the D.C. area, but MacKaye felt that the band was out of place on the label's roster. Calvin offered to put the band's record out on K. MacKaye liked the idea, but didn't want to walk away from the band. A compromise was reached: Ulysses would release its first record, a seven-inch, on a new record label, DisKord—a joint venture between Dischord and K. The co-release consummated the partnership of the East and West Coast labels.

That relationship would be made public before the release of the Ulysses EP, during Fugazi's spring tour. The band had a series of West Coast dates scheduled, and MacKaye invited Beat Happening to open for the band. It was an odd pairing, and MacKaye knew it.

"That primitive, jangly guitar and no bass didn't work too well with me initially," MacKaye has said, before admitting that the band's live performance grew on him. "Seeing Beat Happening and seeing the way that Calvin performed, seeing how intense their performances were and their songs were so crazy, just guitars, drums, and Calvin singing these weird campfire songs."

Though Calvin and MacKaye shared West Coast punk influences, a sober lifestyle, and a strict business ethic, their bands could not have been more different. Fugazi differed from MacKaye's earlier band, Minor Threat, in its sense of dynamics and instrumental experimentation, but was still fueled by the aggressive and fast hardcore approach that played well to teenage boys searching for release. It was hard to imagine Beat Happening's anti-macho posture and pop sensibility playing well to that crowd. Still, Beat Happening seldom turned down a chance to tour, and with Fugazi only playing all-ages shows, there was no good reason not to go on the road.

During the tour, the conflict between the K sound and hardcore—which had been acted out between Calvin and Henry Rollins at the Tropicana years before—continued. Beat Happening was jeered and abused by Fugazi fans who were not amused by the band's simple pop songs and Calvin's dancing. While playing a venue called the Country Club in Los Angeles, a Fugazi fan threw an ashtray at the singer, opening a gash on his nose. Without skipping a beat, Calvin responded by reciting a line spoken a decade earlier by the Germs' lead singer Darby Crash and captured on a live album. "Somebody broke my nose," he said. "Dump the whole balcony."

While the Fugazi shows were an extreme example, things were never easy for the band.

"The band as a whole was being harassed in general," Heather says. "My being a girl, a drummer, and not a particularly good drummer was just one part of it. People were totally freaked out and pissed off that we were up on stage. They were very threatened by Calvin. It was really hard. Sometimes it made me want to quit and sometimes it was as if that was what drove us forward."

The next year, Fugazi again invited the band out for a series of dates and, perhaps driven by a masochistic urge to challenge the hardcore crowds, the band agreed. The response was no better.

"I first saw Beat Happening up in Seattle in 1990, opening for Fugazi," remembers Doug Martsch, a guitarist at the time in the Boise rock band Treepeople who was unfamiliar with Beat Happening, but went to the Lake City Concert Hall in Seattle's University District to see Fugazi. "I wasn't that impressed with it. It didn't do much for me, but I liked Calvin and what he was doing. It was a really tough crowd. They were throwing shit at him. They were definitely yelling shit at him. It was really hostile. I loved the way he just pressed through it, though."

Things were better at home. Between tours Calvin returned to a label in full swing. Though K had only released three singles in the last two years, the International Pop Underground series added seven titles in 1990, and the label was finally able to release a full-length by Some Velvet Sidewalk. With Candice at the helm and the Go Team done, K was able to continue releasing albums despite a heavy touring schedule that would take Beat Happening back to the U.K. Perhaps most importantly, Candice and Calvin were surviving on the label alone.

"Of course it was Olympia, so it wasn't that expensive," Candice recalls, "but we were both able to live off the label. It was totally miraculous. We were very lucky."

12

IAN SVENONIUS AND CALVIN JOHNSON talked on the phone a lot in the spring of 1990. Since Ian MacKaye had reintroduced the two at the end of 1989, they had been making plans for the first single by Svenonius's band, which the singer had renamed the Nation of Ulysses. Then one day, *Sassy* magazine came up.

"Of course we all read *Sassy* magazine," Calvin remembers. "It was this cool teenage magazine that talked about birth control and just real things. So we saw the Sassiest Boy in America contest and we thought, well this is cool."

Sassy's Sassiest Boy in America contest would become best known through a 1993 *Saturday Night Live* sketch called "*Sassy*'s Sassiest Boys," which featured Phil Hartman as fictitious senior editor Russell Clark interviewing teen heartthrobs including Christian Slater, Mark Wahlberg, and Andrew McCarthy while saying the word "sassy" as often and in as many different manifestations as possible. *Saturday Night Live* was slightly off the mark. While the *Sassy* magazine contest was a search for the "most perfect boyfriend material a girl could ask for," its aims were slightly more substantive than a pretty face.

Sassy was launched in 1988 with a national newsstand circulation of 250,000 and was edited by Jane Pratt, a twenty-four-year-old graduate of Oberlin College who had spent time as an intern at *Rolling Stone* and an assistant editor at *McCall's*. Despite a lack of underground bona fides, Pratt did pass the test of influences that

Sandra Yates, the forty-year-old president of Fairfax Publications, had set out for all of the magazine's employees. "You can't fake tone of voice with kids," Yates told *New York* magazine in 1988. "If they said *Time* or *Smithsonian* or any rock group I'd heard of, I knew they were hopeless."

With the encouragement of Calvin, Svenonius decided to enter the contest. Rather than write a letter explaining his qualifications, Svenonius took a tape recorder around to his friends, bandmates, and family and had each say what made him the perfect candidate for the job. He sent the tape in, along with a photo.

"I did not think he actually would," Calvin recalls. "Everyone's always saying they'll do stuff, and they never do. But he did. And then he got it. And everyone was kind of freaked out."

By the time the editors told Svenonius that his entry beat out the other 150 they had received, copies of the Nation of Ulysses single were sitting in boxes in the K offices. While *Sassy* wasn't a music magazine by any means, it had started to expose its mostly teenage readership to little-known artists earlier in the year when arts and entertainment editor Christina Kelly started her regular "Cute Band Alert" column. Calvin took the opportunity to expose K to a whole new audience. He called up the *Sassy* offices and spoke with Kelly, informing her that his label had just released the first single by the Sassiest Boy in America's band.

In October, *Sassy* magazine officially crowned its Sassiest Boy in America. "As soon as we opened Ian Svenonius's entry to our Sassiest Boy in America Contest, we just knew, the way you know it's time to change your tampon," Kelly wrote by way of introduction.

As the Sassiest Boy in America, Svenonius received a two-page feature in the magazine, a trip to New York chaperoned by Kelly, a plug for his hair product of choice, Murray's Superior

Hair Dressing Pomade, and a kiss from Jane Pratt. As his label, K received a sympathetic ear in the mainstream press.*

"Here's a totally mainstream magazine treating this underground, totally uncommercial band not condescendingly, but as a real, relevant thing," Calvin says. "It would have never, ever happened in the '80s."

Excited about his new musical friendship with Svenonius, Calvin invited the Nation of Ulysses to come to Seattle for the second edition of Sound Out Northwest. Around the same time, Calvin was contacted by the proprietors of a small cassette label from Hertford, England, that had arranged a show for Beat Happening and the Vaselines at a community center in their town two years before. The owners of the label had a band called McTells who wanted to come to the United States to tour. Calvin was happy to return the favor and booked Beat Happening, the Nation of Ulysses, and the McTells for a five-show tour through various small towns around Washington State.

The Nation of Ulysses was as out of place in Washington State's Grange Halls as it had been in Washington, D.C.'s punk clubs. Teenage music fans throughout the Northwest, in particular the fans that would come out to see a band on Dischord, had adopted a personal style that embraced ambivalence, taking great pains to look as though they didn't care. Svenonius and his bandmates, on the other hand, had made it a point of pride to dress like they gave a damn. Fortunately they played like they gave a damn as well and were able to bridge the gap of personal style.

---

*Calvin continued to correspond with Kelly throughout the early '90s, sending *Sassy* records for review and visiting the *Sassy* office while on tour. During one of these visits, Kelly told Calvin that she thought there should be a band named Chia Pet. Calvin encouraged her to start the band herself. Kelly did, inviting other staff members to join. The band, which also featured editor Jane Pratt on violin, played a single show at Bard College and then disbanded.

"I remember seeing those Bremerton-type people at several shows," Calvin recalls, describing the young men with shaggy hair, oversized T-shirts, and big "ugly" shorts. "They would go to like four nights of Nation of Ulysses, because they were like, 'Yeah! This is it!' People liked them. That was a good omen. I felt really renewed by Nation of Ulysses."

After the tour, Svenonius invited Beat Happening to tour with them around D.C. Calvin showed up with his band plus two Evergreen students in pursuit. Allison Wolfe and Molly Neuman had first gained notice in the Olympia community for publishing a zine called *Girl Germs*, but had just played their first show as Bratmobile. Wolfe and Neuman were willing disciples of K and decided to follow Beat Happening to D.C., where they would attend the Nation of Ulysses and Beat Happening concerts while continuing to work on their nascent group. In D.C., Calvin introduced the two women to Erin Smith, herself a fledgling guitar player and the publisher of a pop culture zine called *Teenage Gang Debs*. The three women found a place to practice, and Wolfe and Neuman showed Smith what they were doing. By the time the tour ended, Bratmobile was an intercoastal pop rock trio.

Although women had been a welcome part of the Olympia music formula since Heather Lewis first played with the Supreme Cool Beings, bands featuring exclusively women were still rare and generally lasted only long enough to play a party or two. Even the radically feminist Mecca Normal had a man as its instrumental anchor. With Bratmobile, Olympia gained its first fully female group.

The underground was changing in other ways as well. In 1986 an eighteen-year-old poet named Slim Moon moved to Olympia to attend Evergreen. Slim's interest in Olympia had been aroused in the summer of 1984 after his family moved south from Seattle to a small suburb closer to Tacoma. There he discovered the

University of Puget Sound's college radio station, KUPS, which played enough underground rock that a punk record store in Seattle called the Bomb Shelter advertised on the station After hearing the Butthole Surfers and the Long Ryders one night, Slim decided to seek out the record store. He went to the address advertised on the radio. The shop was closed, but a sign on the door directed shoppers to a new store called Fallout Records.

When Slim arrived at Fallout, he was intimidated by all of the records. Rather than hunting for the singles he had heard on the radio, Slim gravitated toward a display of K Records at the front of the store. At the time, K had only released cassettes and the first seven-inch single by Beat Happening. To Slim the tapes seemed homespun, but the single looked interesting. While he was perusing the section, one of the store's co-owners came over and introduced himself. It was Bruce Pavitt, who had recently opened the shop with a friend named Russ Battaglia. Bruce gave the single his approval. Slim bought the single, took it home, and put it on his turntable.

"I thought it was awesome," Slim recalls. "Especially Calvin's voice. It reminded me of the Cramps because that was my reference point. I didn't know very many bands yet. So the Cramps was the closest thing I knew to that sound. That was the first time I heard K, I guess, but I didn't really know what it was."

For the next few months, Slim continued his punk rock education at Fallout. Bruce turned him on to West Coast punk through the releases on SST Records, as well as the sounds coming out of D.C. on Dischord. He played Slim punk records from all over while continuing to stock K Records' releases.

As Slim was building up his punk rock record collection, his life was falling apart. He was a senior in high school, but all of his friends had graduated the year before and gone off to college. Depressed and self-destructive, Slim dropped out of high school and dove headfirst into the punk rock lifestyle. He drank and partied and attended numerous hardcore shows in Seattle. Eventually he formed a band called Eights and Aces and played shows at Seattle's main punk club, Gorilla Gardens.

After two shows, Eights and Aces broke up and Slim began using poetry as an outlet for his frustration. After writing some poems he was proud of, Slim sought out Jesse Bernstein, the most well-respected poet in the city's underground arts scene. Bernstein was also a punk, largely reviled by many for his caustic style, which was best exemplified by the time he cut his penis with a switchblade in front of a live audience in an attempt to silence a heckler. After reading some of Slim's poetry, Bernstein encouraged Slim to perform it live. Slim did read his poetry a couple times at Seattle clubs, but never received much attention.

Then one night, the young poet heard about a punk rock show happening at the Community World Theater in Tacoma. Slim went south for his punk rock this time and, during the performance by the Tacoma band Girl Trouble, witnessed something very different from what he had seen in Seattle's punk scene.

It was strange enough that there were girls near the front of the stage, rather than in the back holding their boyfriends' jackets. Instead of the violent slam dancing that was customary at any raucous Gorilla Gardens show, the teenagers in the crowd at the Community World Theater were gleefully bouncing off one another, smiling, laughing, and trading barbs with the band between songs. At one point a fan fell to the ground and screamed, "I broke my leg!" before spinning in a circle and tripping everyone around him with both his perfectly healthy limbs.

"They all fall on top of him laughing," Slim recalls. "It was this huge pile of humanity. And Girl Trouble is just ignoring it and is just continuing to play their song. I was just really intrigued. I was like, 'These people seem like they're really enjoying themselves.'"

After the show, Slim talked to the happy strangers and asked them where they were from. Almost none were Seattleites, tending instead to be from Tacoma and Olympia. When he asked the Olympians if this was the only place they came to see shows, they told him that there was also a club in Olympia called the Tropicana.

Slim's focus turned almost completely toward Olympia. In the next few months he drove to Olympia three times to see bands play at the Tropicana and to visit a few of his old high school friends attending Evergreen. On his third visit, this time to see the Melvins, Slim was invited to read his poetry on the air at KAOS. The door was opening, and after passing his high school equivalency exam, Slim applied to Evergreen. In January of 1986, he started class.

Slim didn't last a year. The college freshman was unable to pay his bills following the recent death of his father and was too depressed to go to the school and advocate for himself. Slim stayed in Olympia and started a garage rock band with Donna Dresch called Nisqually Delta Podunk Nightmare. Over the next two years the band played numerous shows, including the final G.E.S.C.C.O. show with Kurt Cobain's band, Skid Row. Still searching for a stable artistic outlet, he formed a band called Earth with a few friends and moved to Seattle in 1989. Within eight months he had quit the band and moved back south.

When he returned to Olympia, Slim formed Witchy Poo, a band in which he was the only permanent member. The goal was to maintain a band, even as creative partners fell off, instead of creating a new band each time someone decided to move away. Slim had also continued writing and performing his poetry, maintaining good standing in an Olympia underground scene that demanded participation.

"Olympia had a reputation of being elitist," Slim says. "But if you got off your ass and did something—started a band, or did a zine, or got a radio show, or put on shows, or made your own handmade postcards, or any damn thing that was meaningful—you got respected. I watched all those people that felt that they were being left out, going to the parties, and hanging out at the shows; but they were mostly getting pressured to do something. The whole community value was to push people to do stuff. People who got pushed and just didn't respond were just consumers."

With so many fledgling artists joining in, the demand for outlets began to mount. K Records and Sub Pop continued to bring bands into the fold, but they couldn't accommodate the growth of the artistic community. Slim saw the opportunity to step up and create a new label, but he wasn't interested in music.

"My idea was to start a record label to just put out spoken word," Slim says. "I just wanted to put out seven-inch singles of spoken word. I felt that a whole album of spoken word was too much for a lot of people, but that the perfect three-minute poem was kind of a really cool idea. So that was the concept."

With no clue how to turn that concept into reality, Slim called Calvin and told him about his idea. Calvin was eager to help. He described the entire process to Slim, from mastering a record and plating it to printing the covers and buying the bag to slip it into. He provided Slim with the addresses and phone numbers for every business he would need to work with. The distribution would come from K.

Slim was doing something new, so he knew he had to be the guinea pig. But he also feared that it would look like a vanity project if he released a record of his own performance. After deciding that he would release a split seven-inch, he approached Kathleen Hanna, the Evergreen student who had made an impact through both the fiercely feminist art she displayed at the Reko/Muse gallery that she owned with two friends, and her zine, *Bikini Kill*. Continuing to stretch her artistic bounds, Hanna had recently taken to spoken word poetry. Slim thought her charged feminist dissertations were perfect for the seven-inch format. Hanna agreed and soon they both walked into a studio to record their poetry. After reciting a poem called "Mean," Slim Moon ceded the microphone to Hanna, who performed a disturbing piece called "Rockstar" that ends with its protagonist on her hands and knees, wiping up her boyfriend's vomit after telling him she was raped by her brother. "You don't answer my question," she said in the final stanza of the seven-minute poem. "You sit down, you pick up your guitar, you remind me I'm ultimately mysterious, and you sit down to write a song about it. Fuckin' rock star."

In February Slim released both poems as *Wordcore: Vol. 1*, the first seven-inch from his new label Kill Rock Stars. That month Slim and Hanna took the single on the road when Witchy Poo went on a brief tour to Portland and Eugene with Hanna's new band Bikini Kill—a quartet named after her zine featuring former Go Team drummer Tobi Vail, bass player Kathi Wilcox, and a former Snakepit guitarist and the only male member of the group, Billy Karren.

With Vail's insistent drum lines setting the pace, the band played an aggressive style of pop music that Olympians could dance to while Hanna sang and screamed her way through songs that were not far in content from her poetry. In her bold, honest lyrics and forceful delivery, it was possible to see shades of Jean Smith, the Mecca Normal front woman Hanna had watched since she moved to Olympia. The influence was definite.

"Jean Smith was really poetic and had feminist ideas at the core of a lot of her songs, and she wasn't ashamed of it," Hanna has said. "She wrote a song about street harassment and the male gaze. When I saw her I was just like, that's it. I'm done. I'm sold."

One week before leaving on tour with Witchy Poo, Bikini Kill joined Bratmobile for a February 14 show at the North Shore Surf

Club headlined by Some Velvet Sidewalk. Calvin printed up posters for the evening. On a sheet speckled with hearts, he wrote the band's names in an oval around a drawing of a teenage couple dancing. Below the dancing couple, Calvin employed the terminology Al Larsen had coined a year before, with an added word. "Love Rock Revolution," it read.

Yet another powerful female voice emerged from Olympia in 1990. Lois Maffeo had been dabbling in music for years, ever since she bought her first acoustic guitar from a store called Captain Whizeagles while living in Portland in 1985. At that time Lois was living with another aspiring artist named Courtney Michelle Harrison. Accounts differ on where it came from—one alleging a friendly discussion of potential rock star names, another a stolen diary—but when Lois moved back to Olympia, she arrived with an idea for the perfect rock star name: Courtney Love.

Back in Olympia, Lois began studying a chord chart that Calvin had drawn for her and collaborating with other musicians. Lois was not new to music. She had been featured on one of K's first compilations, the all–a cappella *Danger Is Their Business*. After she moved back to Olympia, Calvin invited Lois to sing on one of the Go Team recordings. She also formed her first band, Lumihoops. The three-piece recorded six songs and even played an in-studio session at KAOS, but dissolved soon after.

Before moving to Washington, D.C., in 1989, Lois partnered with the owner of Yoyo Studios, Pat Maley. Lois and Maley had collaborated before, filming a series of conceptual music videos for a number of Beat Happening singles.* Transitioning into being a two-piece band, with Maley on drums and Lois on guitar,

---

*Beat Happening had planned to submit the videos, shot on Super 8 film, to a regional music video television show that might play them. When the band discovered it would have to duplicate the film at an exorbitant cost, the plan was abandoned. The videos resurfaced in 1998 as part of a collection on VHS titled *Hand-Held: Super 8 Films on Video by Patrick Maley and Lois Maffeo*.

wasn't hard. Neither was coming up with the perfect band name: Courtney Love. The duo's first single, "Uncrushworthy," released as part of the International Pop Underground series, revealed Lois to be a poetic songwriter with a pure, pop alto voice. The simple song, on which Maley hit his snare on the second and fourth beats as Lois strummed major chords, had the DNA of Beat Happening and was a huge hit with K adherents. Unfortunately for fans in Olympia, by the time the single was released, Lois was living in Washington, D.C.

While Calvin was busy inspiring Maffeo and others to become musicians, Candice was working on recruiting known entities. In 1990 she made her first trip to England, intent on visiting the many friends she had only been able to write and call before. One of her visits was with Jerry Thackery, the music critic who had given the head of Rough Trade his first listen to Beat Happening. In 1989 Sub Pop had flown Thackery, who had since started writing under the name Everett True, to Seattle to write about the growing scene around bands like Mudhoney and Nirvana that were playing grunge. During that stay, the critic spent some time in Olympia, even lending his voice to one of the Go Team's songs, on which he is credited as "The Legend." In England, Candice told Thackery about a new band that she wanted to put out on K: Heavenly, which was made up of members of the since-disbanded Talulah Gosh. He told Candice to call the band. Candice looked up the number for the lead singer, Amelia Fletcher, and called.

"I was very surprised that she answered the phone," Candice recalls. "In my mind, she was famous. Why would she even be home, let alone answering her phone?"

Candice worked out a tentative agreement for a future release with Heavenly and then traveled to Glasgow. There she spent ten days with the Pastels, going to their practices and shows, and seeing other concerts, including one by the Vaselines, who had released two EPs and one full-length album on 53rd & 3rd by that time. She also attended a show by Sonic Youth, a longtime underground favorite that had just released *Goo*, the band's sixth album and its first on DGC Records—a sublabel of Geffen Records, which was run by MCA, one of the now-six major record labels. *Goo* was the first of a five-album deal. In exchange, Sonic Youth received a $300,000 paycheck.

13

BY THE MIDDLE OF 1991, Beat Happening had recorded its fourth album, *Dreamy*. The band held to its formula. Calvin and Heather wrote simple pop tunes with a dark undercurrent and Bret provided the jangly guitar sounds. The band also kept Steve Fisk as its producer, and Candice and Calvin planned to release the album on K, as it had done with *Black Candy*. Beyond that, though, nothing would be the same.

Amid turmoil, Rough Trade, which had distributed K Records in the United States and released Beat Happening's self-titled album and *Black Candy* in the U.K., had cut ties with both the band and the label. At the height of its influence in both the independent and mainstream music worlds, the entire company had gone into a rapid decline. From its beginnings as a small record shop and boutique punk label in revolt against the corporate monopoly of the music industry, Rough Trade had become a behemoth stretched between a board that didn't understand the passion of the company's founder, and a founder who didn't understand anything but. In March of 1991, Rough Trade laid off two-thirds of its workforce. By summer the company had declared bankruptcy and entered into receivership. Everything was sold to the highest bidder, including warehouses full of other labels' records that were being managed by the company's distribution arm and master recordings of albums that had been released on the Rough Trade record labels. Even the name, Rough Trade, was sold at auction.

Since K still relied largely on its own mail-order service for distribution, the inventory of K releases held by Rough Trade in the U.S. was modest and the label survived the downfall largely unscathed. The dissolution of Rough Trade did cause problems for Beat Happening, though. The band lost U.K. distribution for both its debut album and *Black Candy*. Fortunately, while on tour the year before, Calvin had dropped by the Rough Trade U.S. offices—by then located in New York City. Unsatisfied with the attention the album was receiving and sensing that something was amiss, Calvin asked for the masters to *Jamboree*. The company handed the tapes over without incident.

Lacking the funds to reissue the record, K turned to one of its earliest proponents, Bruce Pavitt. Sub Pop Records had continued to grow in relevance and power in the last few years, manufacturing incredible publicity for its bands in Europe while becoming one of the United States' most successful independent labels. Bruce agreed to co-release the album with K. Bruce also offered to help the band with its presence overseas, inviting Beat Happening to put *Dreamy* out on the label's new European outpost, Sub Pop Germany. Since the band's only other option, Stephen McRobbie's 53rd & 3rd Records, was still a label in name only, Calvin accepted the offer.

With its record coming out of Germany, Beat Happening again worked with Thomas Zimmerman, setting up a three-week European tour. Unfortunately Zimmerman's influence did not stretch to England, and Sub Pop Germany's U.K. distribution and promotion was almost nonexistent for a band that didn't have a large fan base or rabid press coverage.

"I don't think that there was much of an interest in us," Calvin says. "Yes, we had three albums come out in Great Britain between the 53rd & 3rd and the Rough Trade records. And then the Sub Pop record came out. But, for most of it, people weren't showing up to the shows."

Beat Happening's momentum in the U.K. had stopped, but Calvin hadn't. Though he was unable to travel to England as a musician, he was still the cohead of a record label that drew from an international pool of talent. When Bret and Heather went home, Calvin headed for the British Isles. After touching down in Scotland, Calvin headed to Bristol, where Heavenly was playing a show. Finally, after four years of fandom, Calvin saw the core members of Talulah Gosh perform. Even though they were a new band, vocalist Amelia Fletcher, her brother Mathew Fletcher, and guitarist Peter Momtchiloff were creating the same hard-bopping melodic pop music that Calvin had first heard on Talulah Gosh's first seven-inch, only better.

The band was expecting Calvin and invited him to Oxford to visit. There, Calvin formed a close friendship with the members of the Heavenly, in particular with the Fletchers. They solidified the plans initiated by Candice to record a few songs for K's International Pop Underground series. Calvin went further, offering to release Heavenly's next full-length album, the band's second, in the United States and to set up an American tour after its release. Then he added that, if they were free, the band should come to Olympia at the end of that summer. K was planning a convention and everyone would be there.

A year before Calvin's trip to England, and just a few months after Candice's trip, the K Records bosses threw an end-of-the-summer barbecue. They invited their growing community of artists and organizers to eat, play music, and dance late into the night. The party was a success, but something was missing. For each connection that Calvin and Candice had made in Olympia, there was one they had made out in the wider world. There were the K bands from Oxford, Sydney, Vancouver, B.C., and Washington, D.C.; there were the myriad music fans from around the world who subscribed to the K newsletter; and there were the artists from across the country who counted on that newsletter to distribute their music. It was possible to see some of those people during their travels, and others if they happened to tour through Olympia, but there had never been a time when the community of artists and enthusiasts that K had cultivated in its near-ten-year history had gotten together and celebrated what they had created together. Candice and Calvin decided to change that and began planning the International Pop Underground Convention.

"We called it a convention, because we were convening," Calvin says. "It wasn't a festival. It was a gathering of folks who had an agenda."

That agenda was made clear when K Records announced the event on the back cover of its newsletter, printed twenty thousand copies, and distributed them to K fans, journalists, musicians, and independent record stores across the country. The advertisement contained no pictures and mentioned no bands by name, likely because Calvin and Candice were still figuring out who would play. Instead, the ad's author, Calvin, couched the invitation in a call to action. The advertisement was a manifesto.

> As the corporate ogre expands its creeping influence on the minds of industrialized youth, the time has come for the International Rockers of the World to convene in celebration of our grand independence. Because this society is sick and in desperate need of a little blood-letting; sand, sidewalk and punk pop implosion. Because the corporate ogre has infected the creative community with its black plague of indentured servitude. Because we are the gravediggers who have buried the grey spectre of rock star myth. Because we are the misfits and we will have our day. We won't go away. Hangman hipsters, new modrockers, sidestreet walkers, scoot mounted dream girls, punks, teds, the instigators of the Love Rock Explosion, the editors of every angry grrrl zine, the plotters of youth rebellion in every form, the Midwestern librarians and Scottish ski instructors who live by night, all are setting aside August 20-25, 1991 as the time. Olympia, Washington

is the place. A double shot of International Hip Swing is the goal. Barbecues, parades, disco dancing, picnics and wild screaming teenage rock 'n' roll are the means. Revolution is the end. Revolution is the beginning. No lackeys to the corporate ogre allowed.

Gatherings of independent musicians were not uncommon at the time. The New Music Seminar had been held in New York City every summer since 1980, and Seattle had its own Northwest Area Music Association Conference. But these gatherings, focused on artist showcases and boring panels, were geared toward the industry and how a band might go about "making it." The IPUC, on the other hand, was a celebration of the underground for the fans and bands that, for the most part, weren't interested in "making it." Most of the bands that were playing weren't even interested in making money.

"The bands that we asked to perform at this event are all bands that we happen to think are incredible," Candice told a reporter for the *Seattle Times* before the convention. "They also have a similar attitude about making music that we do, which is not always for a profit, but because it's fun and they like to do it. In fact, many of the bands we approached didn't even ask about money and most didn't even expect to be paid at all. But they all will be, we made sure of that."

Anyone who wanted to attend the convention was asked to send a thirty-five-dollar check and a passport-size photo for their personalized passes. In exchange, they would gain access to all of the convention's festivities, including a peace vigil at a local park, a cakewalk, and a *Planet of the Apes* movie marathon. The focus, of course, was the music.

Calvin and Candice would not be accused of false advertising. The lineup that greeted the music fans in Olympia was a decidedly international one. Heavenly wasn't able to play, but the Pastels were, representing Scotland. English trio Thee Headcoats, which had just released its debut on Sub Pop, was scheduled to headline Friday night at the Capitol Theater. The Canadian delegation included Mecca Normal, as well as an instrumental rock band from Toronto called Shadowy Men on a Shadowy Planet.

The domestic lineup didn't disappoint in geographic reach either. Doug Martsch's band Treepeople arrived from Boise, while Scrawl hailed from Columbus. L7 came north from Los Angeles, while Kicking Giant headed west from New York City. A large contingent arrived from D.C. as well, including Half Japanese's Jad Fair, the Nation of Ulysses, and Fugazi.

Representing the Northwest were the core K bands—Beat Happening, Some Velvet Sidewalk, and Lois's Courtney Love— as well as a couple dozen of the bands that were friendly with the label's proprietors, including Fastbacks, Unwound, Seaweed, Girl Trouble, the Melvins, Witchy Poo, and Steve Fisk. Overall, the lineup was balanced between quirky pop and noise rock. The one oddity was High Performance, a hip-hop group from Tacoma that Calvin was fond of.

The lineup was filled with almost every artist that Calvin and Candice had hoped would play. Only three bands that received invitations didn't show up. The Cambridge, Massachusetts, band Galaxie 500 never returned Calvin's calls, likely because the band was in the process of breaking up. Nirvana was scheduled to play but had to cancel after being drafted to open Sonic Youth's European tour. Jandek, a mysterious Houston musician who distributed his homemade cassettes through the K newsletter, had expressed interest when Calvin first called him, but never returned any phone calls and never showed up.*

---

*When Calvin later told friends familiar with Jandek's reputation that the secretive artist hadn't shown up, they responded, "How do you know he didn't?"

The bands that did make it performed throughout the four-day festival at venues in downtown Olympia. In order to ensure that anyone who attended would have the opportunity to see every performance, Calvin spaced the shows throughout the day. Some days the shows would start at 10 a.m. at a house venue called the Alexander Berkman Collective, known to Olympia residents as the ABC House. On other days, the Smithfield Café hosted the earliest shows at 2 p.m. Each night of the convention the North Shore Surf Club hosted a 5 p.m. performance, followed by the set of headlining bands who took the stage of the Capitol Theater at 9 p.m. Anyone who had not gotten their fill by then could head back to the North Shore Surf Club, where there was dancing into the early morning.

Calvin and Candice went to great lengths to make sure that the convention was affordable and welcoming. All shows were all-ages and cheap; anyone who didn't have a full-access pass could gain entry to a performance for four or five dollars. For out-of-town bands and fans who didn't have friends to stay with, the organizers arranged a convention rate with a local hotel, the Golden Gavel. Calvin worked with the management of the Capitol Theater to make sure that the concession stand was stocked with cheap vegan candy. He had also decided that there would be no official security at the convention.

"What I thought was, we don't want that," Calvin says. "What we want is to create an atmosphere where people wouldn't consider doing anything other than enjoying themselves. So I thought the best way to go about having that is to not have security guards. I had never seen a security guard at a movie at the Capitol Theater, so why would we have them for a music event?"

Two weeks before opening night, the bands had been booked and the volunteer staff assembled. Stella Marrs was making posters, one for each night, while another Olympia artist named Nikki

McClure was busy creating four large banners, each featuring a different word from the event's name, to hang from the windows of the Martin Apartments building. Things were well under way. But to a segment of the community, something didn't feel right.

"I was reading the newspaper," Stella Marrs remembers, "and there were all these things that were happening that were shutting down the female voice. One in particular was that one of the television networks had written a new policy that they would only show cartoons that starred boys, because if they had cartoons that starred boys, then girls would watch them, but if they had cartoons that starred girls, boys wouldn't watch them. The idea was that you get a larger audience if you have a male leading role. I was just so fed up and outraged by this and IPU was coming up, so I went to Calvin and said, 'This is ridiculous. You need to have a night of girls playing music.' He was like, 'That's weird. Tobi just told me the same thing.'"

It is possible that Tobi and Stella weren't the only ones making the request. Through differing accounts, the idea for a night devoted to women has been attributed to Molly Neuman and Allison Wolfe, both from Bratmobile, Lois Maffeo, a KAOS DJ named Michelle Noel, and the owner of a vintage clothing store named Margaret Doherty. Despite what was potentially a chorus of voices, Calvin wasn't convinced.

"Calvin was a little bit resistant," Candice recalls. "I don't think because of the idea, but how do we make it fit?"

The organizers had already fit a lot into the convention. In addition to numerous shows from underground pop bands, the schedule included a Thursday afternoon spoken word event at the Smithfield organized by Slim Moon and featuring Kathleen Hanna, Juliana Luecking, and Thee Headcoats leader Billy Childish. Wednesday evening at the Capitol Theater was devoted to members of Olympia's experimental music crowd, each of whom was given short sets to perform works of new music. The experimental musicians wanted to be included on the punk bills with longer set times and accused Calvin and Candice of shutting them out. Calvin was worried that the same might happen with an evening devoted to female artists.

"I was against the idea, because I had that experience with the experimental music people," Calvin says. "I didn't want it to be like a ghetto for the women, and then there's the *real* convention."

And the "real" convention did make room for women. In keeping with K's inclusive ethos and its estrogen-friendly roster of artists, the lineup already featured a number of acts with female members, including Kicking Giant, Fastbacks, Mecca Normal, the Pastels, Bikini Kill, Courtney Love, and Beat Happening. There were even three all-girl groups on the bill: Scrawl, L7, and Neuman's Bratmobile outfit.

Calvin offered a compromise, telling the women that he would add more artists to the set lineups if there were additional women who wanted to play. The women were resolute: They wanted their own night. In the end, Calvin and Candice decided to expand the convention by adding one more day. The women would open the International Pop Underground Convention with a Tuesday night show at the Capitol Theater. The event was called "Love Rock Revolution Girl Style Now," a conjunction of two phrases: one, the name constructed by Calvin for the Valentine's Day show earlier that year, and the other, a declaration that had been circulating in the community of young inspired women who were starting to make music in Olympia.* Word went out that any woman who wanted to take the stage that night could and should.

---

*A mouthful, the name was eventually distilled to the colloquial "Girls Rock Night." "Revolution Girl Style Now!" became the battle cry for Bikini Kill as well as the name of the band's debut self-titled cassette, which came out in 1991.

The event hit another potentially disastrous snag when Calvin and Al Larsen went to pick up the sound system they were renting for the theater. When the clerk ran Calvin's card for the deposit, it came up declined. After charging a number of plane tickets for his international bands, as well as other expenses for the convention, it was no surprise that his credit was low. Still, Calvin acted surprised.

"Really?" he said. "Do you mind if I use your phone to call my credit card company and see what's going on?"

The clerk dialed the number and handed the phone to Calvin, who said a few words to the person on the other line, nodded, said, "Okay, I'll do that," and then hung up.

"Everything has been taken care of," he told the clerk.

"After we left with the PA I asked Calvin what the credit card company had said," Al remembers, "and he said, 'Oh, they said my account was frozen and I have to pay my credit card bill.' It was amazing. Classic Calvin. He never blinked."

With the PA in place, the convention was ready to go. On the first night, a crowd converged on the Capitol Theater for Love Rock Revolution Girl Style Now. Members of both sexes were in the crowd, but it was the girls who were up front. From that vantage point, they watched as their peers took the stage. Each of the evening's twenty-five acts was allowed to play three songs, though some chose fewer. Many of the artists were familiar. Bratmobile made its first of two appearances at the conference that night, as did Lois Maffeo, Kathleen Hanna, and Jean Smith. Christina Billotte came from Washington, D.C., where Calvin had first seen her play with the band Hazmat. She was also a member of recently disbanded Autoclave, a band that had released a seven-inch on the DisKord label, the second and final collaborative effort between K and Dischord. Billotte didn't have a band when she arrived in Olympia, so she formed an impromptu group with her friends and played the show. Stella Marrs also formed a one-off group with Margaret and Maureen Doherty. In response to the United States declaring war on Iraq earlier in the year, Stella sang the anti-war song, "Where Have All the Flowers Gone."

Other groups were less familiar, including Seattle's 7 Year Bitch, a high school duo called I Scream Truck, and Kreviss, a band that featured eight women, most of them playing guitar. Also largely unknown were the Spinanes, a duo from Portland fronted by Rebecca Gates.

Then there were the two acts that had never before played music in public. One was Rose Melberg, a shy teen from Sacramento who had intended to play with a friend of hers in their first show as Tiger Trap. Melberg's friend wasn't able to make the trip, so she stepped to the microphone with an electric guitar, said "Hi," and without even telling the audience who she was, began playing a song she had written called "My Day" by herself. "I've got a really good feeling, running through my blood like hot Strawberry Quik," she sang as she strummed out a fast chord progression, her amp crackling with distortion. Then, with a cascading melody, she sang. "Happy day, happy day. Hip-hip-hooray, what a glorious day is today. No price to pay for sunshine, love. Today is my day. Happiness day, no-nastiness day. All I can say is that I'm gonna go out and play today. Everything I want is so near. Everything I am is so clear. Everyone I like is right here, today." The crowd erupted. It was the only song she played.

The other debut performance that night came from Heavens to Betsy, a duo from Evergreen featuring Tracy Sawyer on drums and Corin Tucker on guitar and vocal duties. Tucker had first discovered the underground at the age of fifteen when she bought a Beat Happening single at the local record store in Eugene. Many more K releases followed, as did shows, including a powerful performance by Beat Happening, Fugazi, and Mecca Normal at the

WOW Hall the summer before her senior year of high school. Standing on stage at the Capitol Theater, she and Sawyer played to a crowd filled with her friends and the musicians she would watch play later that week, including Calvin Johnson, Jean Smith, and Ian MacKaye, who would ascend the stage with Fugazi for the final performance of the convention four nights later.

"I couldn't believe that I was playing these songs that I wrote in front of these musicians I loved so much," Tucker says. "It was just about the best thing I could have ever imagined happening."

The band played two songs. Tucker walked off the stage and into the arms of Kathleen Hanna. The lead singer of Bikini Kill cried tears of joy.

The convention had started off on an astonishingly high note.

"I don't think we ever thought about it as a big kickoff," Candice says. "We were lucky that it was first, though. It set the tone in terms of energy and expectations. They set the bar high."

On the logistical end, the bar was pretty low, though not for lack of trying by the sound engineer Nelly Corn. Calvin had discovered Corn working sound during a Beat Happening show at Portland's Reed College earlier that summer and, noticing her meticulous approach, asked her to run sound at the Capitol Theater. Corn had gladly signed on, but after the first night of the convention she was not happy.

"I thought we were organized, because we had stage managers, but my laissez-faire style was not going over well with Nelly," Calvin says. "Nelly was like, 'This band is great. They gave me a diagram that shows how many mics we need and where they're going to be standing and who's singing and what time they will start. *This* band—I don't even know who's *in* this band.'"

Calvin promised to get more organized, much to the appreciation of Corn, but there was another problem.

"The first night was tough because it turned out that there were more who showed up than we thought," Calvin recalls. "And the sound system wasn't quite adequate. So we had to bring in more sound."

Borrowed equipment bulked up the PA in time for Beat Happening to take the stage two nights later, after a set from the Nation of Ulysses but before Scrawl and the Pastels. Dressed in a plain white T-shirt and fitted blue jeans, Calvin started the band's set with a message about concessions. The manager of the venue complained that no one was buying the twenty-five-cent boxes of Ferrara Pan candy that had been brought in for the event, so Calvin made a sales pitch.

"I was talkin' to Candice, also known as Candi—she's, like, sort of putting on this whole big shindig here," Calvin said to enthusiastic applause. "And we were sayin'. . . You know, I went to the OFS the other day and the candy bars were, like, four dollars each or somethin'. What a bummer. Gosh, when all of these punk rockers are in town and they're goin' around panhandlin' for change, they're never gonna get four dollars for a candy bar. We should try to get some candy that isn't four dollars at the theater. So, we got in touch with the manager here, Patty Kovax, who's been a perfect angel in every way, and we went down to the supply store and picked up some of these Ferrara Pan, vegan candy. They're selling them in the lobby for a quarter."

Calvin then picked up a bag of candy and proceeded to throw the small boxes out into the audience, the crowd cheering, screaming, and laughing through it all. Mr. Melon, Johnny Apple Treats, Jawbusters, Alexander the Grape, Fruit Cocktail Imperials, Lemonheads, Jelly Beans. Sales picked up immediately.

Then Beat Happening played. The crowd of several hundred bounced along to Heather's drumming, which over the years had become sharp, intricate, and more complex without losing its primal, dance-friendly core. Bret, dressed in a dark mock turtle-neck and jeans, laconically strummed through the band's jangly chord progressions as Calvin washed the audience in his deep baritone drawl. The singer swiveled his hips, rubbing his stomach and snaking his arms around his head, contorting his body into awkward poses that still managed to cast the front man as the very personification of cool.

The band played songs from throughout its history, including an incendiary rendition of "Cast a Shadow" off of *Jamboree* and "Look Around," from the first volume of the International Pop Underground singles series that served as the inspiration for the convention. The band also played songs from its latest, *Dreamy*, an album that had once again taken the band into a deeper shade of dark while never losing its pop hue. "Nancy Sin," the latest single, was a prime example, its beat undeniable, its minimal lyr-ics spiked with taboo sexual overtones, and its chorus a mantra of "Good girl, bad girl." "Revolution Come and Gone," though, was the darkest of Beat Happening's songs. As Bret played an unchar-acteristic atonal growl, Calvin dropped to his knees and sang to his friends and acolytes, "I love watching your face redden as we near Armageddon. I've got a lantern and I've got a cane, a secret in the cottage at the end of the lane, a safe haven for committing our crimes. We'll make love till the end of time."

By the time of Saturday night's headlining show, which packed nine hundred concertgoers into the theater, the convention was already a success. The Pastels, the Nation of Ulysses, and Kicking Giant were just a couple highlights, as was Mecca Normal, which ended its set with Jean standing on her guitar, playing it with her feet, slits she had cut into the soles of her shoes strumming out a tremendous racket. The band would later receive praise in the pages of *Rolling Stone*: reporter Ira Robbins wrote that "guitar-ist David Lester erected a complex one-man wall of sound, while singer-poet Jean Smith dramatically demonstrated her superb range and control, finishing off with a feedback dance (literally) on guitar."

With no security, the community managed to police itself. Even as a seemingly endless string of conventioneers climbed onto the stage and launched themselves into the crowd during L7's early set, there was little concern that anything was out of hand. Even when problems arose, members of the community stepped up, including Ian MacKaye, who at one point filled in for an ailing ticket taker.

The convention had sold 420 full-access passes, and most shows were well attended. Between five and nine hundred saw each of the Capitol Theater shows, while the North Shore Surf Club drew crowds of two to three hundred. The unexpectedly large crowds resulted in the bands getting paid more than Candice had planned.

"If not quite Woodstock West, the IPU was no less than a rousing success," Robbins concluded in the *Rolling Stone* article. "The week's biggest calamity occurred when the Capitol Theater's cat mistook a cache of T-shirts for a litter box."

The cat pee didn't stop money from flowing through the merchandising area upstairs in the theater, where fans could buy albums from a K Records booth, as well as T-shirts, zines, and cassettes from other vendors. The most sought-after item of the week was a twelve-inch record compilation of Olympia bands called *Kill Rock Stars*.

Since starting the Kill Rock Stars label earlier in the year, Slim Moon had continued his mission, putting out two more volumes of the *Wordcore* series. Then, one month before the convention, Slim saw the first performance by an Olympia band called Giant Henry and was inspired to put out a rock record. He pulled aside the band's lead singer, Justin Trosper, and told him that he wanted

Kill Rock Stars to release a seven-inch of the band in time for the convention. Trosper was honored but had bad news for Slim: the band didn't have any music recorded that he could release and Giant Henry was breaking up, though Trosper was putting together a new band. Slim's hope turned into discouragement. He would have put out a seven-inch by Trosper's new band, but there wasn't enough time. It was impossible.

The next day, Calvin called Slim. Trosper had run into the K head and told him about Slim's idea. Calvin convinced Slim that he should not only record and release a single by Trosper's new band, but that he should put together a full compilation of music for the convention. There was time, Calvin assured him, as long as Slim made the album covers by hand, sidestepping a slothlike printing process that was all too familiar to Calvin. Slim agreed and began forming a list of possible bands, but came up short. He called Calvin back.

"He said that he would help me line up bands," Slim says. "So the truth of the matter is, half of the bands on that compilation were suggested by Calvin. He knew of a Melvin's track that he had, he knew of a Jad Fair track, he called up Ulysses that day. The Nirvana track and the Bikini Kill track were both from me."

The next day, Calvin met Trosper and his new band at Yoyo Studios. There the band, which soon after adopted the name Unwound, recorded a song for the compilation. Three days after calling Slim, Calvin had helped him gather songs from fourteen bands. Calvin and Slim sequenced the track list together and sent the compilation off to be mastered. While the record was away, Slim ordered sleeves and enlisted an Olympia artist, Tenuviel, to silk-screen the covers with two different colors, a process that required lots of space to hang the prints and time to allow them to dry. At the start of the convention, there were a hundred copies of the *Kill Rock Stars* compilation ready for purchase.

Throughout the week, Tenuviel continued to print covers in her basement, missing most of the convention. Between spoken word performances, a Witchy Poo set, and a lot of schmoozing, Slim played courier from the artist's home to the merch area, restocking a supply that was constantly running out. The *Kill Rock Stars* compilation, which featured almost entirely artists playing the convention, had become the event's unofficial souvenir. By the end of the weekend, Tenuviel had printed covers for a thousand records. Slim had sold almost all of them.

The compilation wasn't the only album creating a buzz in the clubs of Olympia that week. Despite the fact that the band was half a world away playing a music festival in Belgium, Nirvana was the topic of many conversations. An unmastered tape of the band's second record was making the rounds, along with opinions on the fact that the band had signed to a major label, Geffen Records.

"People were still flabbergasted that Nirvana had signed to a major label," Slim recalls. "Nobody I knew was saying, 'Oh, they're going to be the next Guns N' Roses,' you know? Nobody was saying anything like that. They just thought it was going to be just another 'moderate punk rock band success on a major label' album, or whatever."

14

"THE INTERNATIONAL POP UNDERGROUND CONVENTION was the conceptual high point for the Northwest indie music scene," Bruce Pavitt says. "It was all about vibe, not about deals. There was a lot of heart, community, and resourcefulness. It was a revolutionary peak."

Two days after that peak, "Smells Like Teen Spirit" first aired on the radio. The song, DGC Records' first single from its upcoming Nirvana release, was born into an unsuspecting world with little fanfare, though it sounded like the beginning of a war.

Written in the traditional verse-chorus-verse style of pop music, the song is the musical manifestation of apathy and anger packaged in a Trojan horse of melody. "Smells Like Teen Spirit" kicks off with Kurt Cobain's quick, jangling electric guitar strum seesawing through a chord progression before exploding into a muscular riff, interrupted only by a few perfectly placed bits of feedback and undergirded by double-time drumming by Dave Grohl, a former member of the Washington, D.C., punk band Scream, who had joined the band since the release of *Bleach*. When the meaty guitar line drops out, Krist Novoselic's bass is left loping as Cobain plucks out two reverb-drenched notes and begins singing lines about lethargic youth in a laconic melody. After a swirling mantra of "Hellos," the song kicks back into high gear and Cobain's vocals become defiant as he growls through a melody that could linger for days: "With the lights out, it's less dangerous. Here we are now, entertain us."

"Smells Like Teen Spirit" did not explode immediately. The record label believed that the song was fit to be a hit on college radio stations, and that it would whet the appetite of the growing alternative rock market in advance of the band's major-label debut release on September 24. The plan was that the second single off of *Nevermind*, "Come as You Are," would be the hit. No matter the intent, "Smells Like Teen Spirit" was destined for a mass audience, thanks in large part to the production work of a Midwestern engineer named Butch Vig, who had convinced the reluctant lead singer to overdub his guitar and vocal tracks, giving both a heft that never appeared on the band's *Bleach* release. "Smells Like Teen Spirit" spent the autumn consuming hours of college radio airtime before the release of *Nevermind* garnered the band near-unanimous raves from the mainstream music press. On December 7, the song entered the Billboard Hot 100 Chart at No. 40. A month later, on January 11, 1992, the song peaked at No. 6 on the chart, the top rock song behind a long list of R & B songs by Michael Jackson, Color Me Badd, Mariah Carey, and Boyz II Men, as well as a rap song by MC Hammer. That week *Nevermind* topped the Billboard 200, a chart that the album would remain on for almost five years. The success was shocking.

"Prior to the explosion of grunge, *Nevermind* did not sound like a commercial record to our ears," Slim Moon recalls. "Before grunge was big, it sounded too grunge to be big. That's what we thought. We were surprised at its success."

Though both Dave and Krist were living in Seattle and the ensuing media maelstrom had labeled Nirvana as a Seattle band, Kurt's home address was still in Olympia, where he had written all of the songs that appeared on *Nevermind*. Still, due to incessant touring and media appearances, Kurt and his band were essentially gone from the scene. A party that the band played in a tiny dorm room at Evergreen in early June was the last Nirvana performance that Olympia would ever see.

"I was pretty happy for them, and not surprised," Candice recalls. "I always thought that everyone should love the music I loved. It was more difficult to see them, to have them in my world. Yeah, one, they were very, very busy, but also, it was just different. There was a distance."

Kurt eventually left Olympia, moving first to California and then, in March 1993, to Seattle, but the city, and in particular K Records, remained with him. In a list of his top fifty albums, written in his journal, Kurt listed Beat Happening's *Jamboree* and the *Burning Farm* cassette by Shonen Knife. In a few of the hundreds of photo shoots that the band did for numerous publications throughout the next few years, a small homemade tattoo appeared on his left forearm. It was a small "K" with a shield around it, not a perfect replica of the K Records logo that had since become standardized on the label's releases, but a homemade variation, in keeping with Calvin's original intention for the symbol. Though less tangible, Kurt also carried with him a wealth of bands that he had discovered in an Olympia scene that was teeming with new musical finds.

"Kurt was voracious about discovering new music," Slim recalls. "He wasn't very social, but if you could sit down with him and play him awesome shit that he'd never heard, that was the best way to have quality time with Kurt. So he learned about Leadbelly from me, and he learned about the Young Marble Giants from Tobi. He really connected with that part of what Olympia was all about, the sort of minimalism, simplicity, a lot of English bands that I don't think he'd heard before he moved to Olympia. And certainly Nirvana played a lot of shows with a lot of Olympia bands that were much more stereotypical Olympia bands than Nirvana was. But I feel like Kurt connected with that in a way that Krist or Dave didn't connect with. I mean, Dave is a very sweet guy, but he would ruthlessly make fun of the Olympia ethos. He thought it was hilarious and silly. He's a rock dude, you know?"

The influence of those relatively obscure musical acts on Nirvana was not immediately clear to the casual radio listener, and neither was the influence of the music that Kurt had heard from Beat Happening. Nirvana was definitely more of a rock band, but it was also infinitely more studied and talented than Beat Happening, and Kurt's lyricism more opaque and disquieting. But the restrained musicianship and memorable melodies that Kurt wove into even the most angry songs—the melodies that set the band apart from its grunge peers—carried a lineage from the more primitive Beat Happening material.

"We are Beat Happening, and we don't do Nirvana covers," Calvin was reported to have said at a show after Kurt's band broke. "They do Beat Happening covers, so let's get that straight."

Kurt also gave a world stage to the Vaselines, a band he likely first heard on a K cassette, when Nirvana released its own version of "Molly's Lips" on a split seven-inch single on Sub Pop in late 1991 and then performed the song during a live show on MTV the following year.

The success of the band changed Sub Pop's fortunes. *Bleach*, Nirvana's debut full-length on the label, was the first of a multialbum deal the record label had arranged with the band. In order for DGC to release *Nevermind*, it had to buy the contract, a move that gave Sub Pop a royalty on future Nirvana releases.

K Records, though, went largely unchanged. One impact that the band's rising popularity had on the label was actually incurred by Lois Maffeo. In 1991 Kurt began dating Lois's former roommate, Courtney Michelle Harrison. Like Lois, Harrison had used the name Courtney Love, adopting it for her acting debut in the 1986 punk biopic *Sid and Nancy*. Then she took it on stage with her band, Hole. When the band's debut album, *Pretty on the*

Inside, was released in August of 1991 on the major-label-affiliated Caroline Records with a production credit from Sonic Youth bassist Kim Gordon, Hole had surpassed Lois and Pat Maley's musical project in renown. For another year, Lois and Pat continued to release music as Courtney Love, including a final seven-inch for the International Pop Underground series, another seven-inch for a Chicago label called Feel Good All Over, and a song on a collection of recordings from the International Pop Underground Convention that K released the next year. After that, Lois's Courtney Love disappeared completely as the other Courtney Love became increasingly famous.

The owners of K Records watched with the rest of Olympia as Nirvana introduced the mainstream to alternative music, but they had little time to contemplate what it all meant. The record label was moving into a new phase, and both Candice and Calvin were focused on the business at hand.

In late 1991, following the disastrous implosion of the Rough Trade independent empire, Calvin received a phone call from the man who had introduced Beat Happening to Rough Trade eight years earlier, Phil Hertz. Hertz had since left Rough Trade and ambled about the independent music world in Britain and the United States. When he called Calvin, he had just started a Chicago outpost of Cargo, a manufacturing and distribution company aimed at servicing independent labels like K. He had an offer for the label: Cargo would manufacture all three formats for K and handle the distribution. K agreed to the deal, and the label's long-standing problem with multiple formats, a major hurdle to its ability to release full-length records, was gone. All Calvin and Candice had to do was get the recordings to Cargo, and they had plenty of them. Calvin had already recorded the next Mecca Normal album, as well as a new one by Some Velvet Sidewalk, and had a slew of others in the works, including the debut album by Heavenly, the International Pop Underground Convention compilation, the debut record from Rose Melberg's band Tiger Trap, and *International Hip Swing*, a compilation of all of the International Pop Underground singles the label had released in the last four years.

K was also readying a full-length album from Lois, who had made more changes to her musical identity than dropping the Courtney Love name. Pat Maley had split from the group to concentrate on production and his own upstart label, Yoyo Recordings, and in his place sat Bratmobile's Molly Neuman. That first album also featured the talents of Stuart Moxham, a former member of the Welsh underground band Young Marble Giants, an early Rough Trade band and K crowd favorite. In the spring of 1992 Moxham was releasing an album with the Feel Good All Over label, whose owner was putting together a tour. The owner called Calvin, who gladly set up a Northwest tour where Beat Happening could play with the artist, bringing along the newly minted Heavens to Betsy. Being on a shoestring budget, the Chicago label owner was also looking for a way that his artist could make some money.

"Lois and I were trying to maybe make a record, and I was like, 'Wouldn't it be cool if Stuart Moxham produced Lois's record?'" Calvin recalls. "We worked it out so he would come over to the Northwest. He did some shows, and then he did a week in the studio recording Lois, and then he had one short tour—we played Longview and Olympia or something like that."

Moxham would not only produce Lois's debut album, he also played bass on it. When it came time to decide on a name for the musical project, Lois decided to keep it simple and join the lineage of pop stars releasing music under their first names only. Lois's first full-length debut, *Butterfly Kiss*, was released in 1992 and quickly became a K favorite. The album's spare instrumentation and deft production placed the focus on Lois's clever lyricism, transcendent timbre, and acoustic guitar strum, all of which allowed her pop sensibility to shine. Courtney Love was quickly forgotten.

Powered by Cargo, K Records was in high gear. Though it had released only seven full-length records in the six preceding years, the label issued six full-length albums in 1992, ten in 1993, and seven in 1994. The single was still a high priority as well, with the International Pop Underground adding twenty-one titles in that same period. None of the band's records would receive much mainstream attention but, relative to the cassette days, the label was flush. K expanded its footprint in the China Town offices and began hiring employees to handle an increasing workload.

"I feel like '94 was my favorite year," Candice recalls. "It felt like we were putting out a fun, amazing record every moment. More than every month sometimes, we were so busy. And the bands would often record in Olympia, so people were coming in and out of the offices, and it was just very vibrant. It was just a really great environment. I would say that Calvin and I both worked very hard, but you didn't notice it. And we grew. I think we grew smartly. We never went nuts, you know? We were never, 'Oh, we got a lot of money!' Calvin and I were both very frugal people, and very conscientious of the money side."

The business style of K wasn't appealing to everyone involved in the label, at least in the early days of the boom. With the rise in Nirvana's popularity came demand for any record that featured the band. K possessed one such recording in its distribution inventory, Slim Moon's *Kill Rock Stars* compilation. The song the band contributed to that collection, "Beeswax," would later be made available on *Incesticide*, a compilation of rare recordings and outtakes released by DGC at the end of 1992. Until then, fans could only find it on the *Kill Rock Stars* release. Many of them did, and the orders came in by the thousands. In order to meet the demand, Kill Rock Stars did away with the silk-screen work and had the covers mass produced. Calvin connected Slim with Cargo to manufacture the CDs and LPs, and soon thousands of copies of *Kill Rock Stars* were being sent to Olympia. Unlike in its dealings with K, Cargo did not provide distribution for Kill Rock Stars; that role and the commission that came with it, stayed with K.

"It got so that by a year later, they owed me a lot of money," Slim says. "And I started pressing them, like, 'Dudes, what's up?' Candice scheduled a very solemn meeting with me about getting paid and basically laid out a payment plan. They had clearly spent the money on their own shit, and couldn't pay me. And she made this payment plan that would've taken three years to pay me off for the records they had sold."

While working out the financials with K, Slim continued to build on the success of the compilation, lassoing Steve Fisk to produce the first Unwound full-length and prepping a Witchy Poo album for release. Then Kathleen Hanna called. Hanna had since moved to Washington, D.C., where she and the rest of Bikini Kill were plotting the band's next move. In addition to the Bikini Kill song that was included on the *Kill Rock Stars* compilation, the band had self-released its debut EP, *Revolution Girl Style Now!*, a cassette that was produced and distributed by K. For its first full-length record, though, the band wanted to do something different. The members decided that they would ask Slim if Kill Rock Stars would handle the release.

"They were living in D.C., so I thought they were going to end up on Dischord," Slim says. "I just had figured that. So when they called and said, 'We want you to put out our record,' I was really floored. I kind of thought they were going to change their minds, so I immediately booked a ticket to D.C. I flew there and had a meeting with them to sort of cement the deal and talk it over, and schedule it, and figure out what songs would be on the album and talk about the artwork."

The band members didn't change their minds, though they did have one requirement. They didn't want to be distributed by K. Unsatisfied with his own dealings with the distribution side of K, and fearing that he would see a slow return on the records he continued to provide them with, Slim got to work.

When he released his first spoken word seven-inch the year before, Slim sent a copy to Mordam Records, another independent distributor based in Sacramento, inquiring whether they would be interested in helping his fledgling label. Started by Ruth Schwartz, one of the original editors of *Maximum RockNRoll*, Mordam worked with record labels that had a decidedly punk slant. Without an inventory of releases, though, Kill Rock Stars didn't have a chance. A rejection letter from Mordam soon followed, handwritten by Karin Gembus, an employee of the company and a member of the all-female anarcho punk band Spitboy. Gembus kindly informed Slim that Mordam only worked with established labels and that Kill Rock Stars was not that. Now with a fast-moving compilation, albums in the pipeline, and Bikini Kill waiting in the wings, Slim contacted Gembus. This time he was connected directly to Schwartz. Soon Mordam was distributing Kill Rock Stars, and though his office was right across from the K offices in the China Town building, Slim would never work with K again.

In June of 1992 Bikini Kill released its first EP on Kill Rock Stars, a self-titled release that featured "Suck My Left One," a dizzying, hard-hitting punk anthem that opens with Hanna making the titular request before singing, "Sister, sister where did we go wrong? Tell me what the fuck we're doing here?"

Bikini Kill's album was released into a D.C. scene that, like Olympia, was home to a growing number of women empowered by the punk ethos. The Girls Rock Night at the International Pop Underground Convention the year before had served as the first mass gathering of women from both scenes, but it was neither the beginning nor the end of a movement built around female empowerment.

Even after the dissolution of her Girl City store in 1983, Stella Marrs continued to provide women with a place to be creative and subversive while embracing their gender. In 1986, she organized her boldest project yet, 50 Girls, 50 States: Women for World Peace. A six-week affair, 50 Girls, 50 States culminated in a debutante ball during Olympia's annual Capital Lakefair. During the summer festival's official parade, fifty women recruited by Stella each marched in a gown that represented a state and promoted the idea of world peace. At midnight, there was a ball benefiting a shelter for victims of domestic violence that featured a performance of an original composition, in which K artist Tim Brock wove portions of each of the United States' fifty state songs.

"I think of the parade and the dance as the outcome," recalls Candice, who wore a gown representing Florida. "But the building up to it was about fifty girls who barely knew each other getting to know each other. I'm still connected to some of them."

Women in the Olympia and D.C. underground music scenes— and countless women in other cities who were inspired by their zines and music—continued what Stella started, celebrating their femininity by embracing the trappings of womanhood and then turning them on their heads. It was an approach best illustrated by a postcard Stella created pairing the image of a contemplative schoolgirl with the statement, "If you can bake a cake, you can make a bomb."

The spring before the Olympia gathering, Lois and one of her roommates at the Dischord house, Jen Smith, had begun talking about starting a girl riot. Girls Rock Night proved they had the numbers, and as Olympia artists, including Bikini Kill and Bratmobile, moved to the nation's capital, it became clear that they had a staging ground. From there, the member of those bands, along with Jen Smith, added some ferocity to the idea and started a zine called *Riot Grrrl*. In the second issue Hanna wrote the "Riot Grrrl Manifesto," listing a litany of reasons why the movement was needed.

"BECAUSE us girls crave records and books and fanzines that speak to US that WE feel included in and can understand in our own ways," she wrote. "BECAUSE we wanna make it easier for girls to see/hear each other's work so that we can share strategies and criticize/applaud each other. BECAUSE we must take over the means of production in order to create our own moanings." She continued with twelve more reasons, before concluding: "BECAUSE I believe with my wholeheartmindbody that girls constitute a revolutionary soul force that can, and will change the world for real."

At the end of July, the riot grrrls staged their own convention in Washington, D.C. The organizers invited zine editors, musicians, activists, and pen pals from across the country to the nation's capital to commiserate in an attempt to explode the movement out into the world. Also in attendance was Corin Tucker, the singer from Heavens to Betsy who played her first show at the Girls Rock Night.

After the band's performance at the convention, Calvin approached Tucker about releasing a seven-inch as part of the International Pop Underground series. A few months later, K released the single, a split record featuring both Heavens to Betsy and Bratmobile. Emboldened by the release, the bands sent the seven-inch to clubs everywhere and booked a grueling five-week tour down the West Coast and then east across the country.

Traveling in two station wagons, the women encountered a number of uncomfortable situations, including a night in Salt Lake City when their host was sent to the hospital after her boyfriend broke her wrist. During it all, K was there for the band.

"Everyone went swimming while I talked on the phone for like an hour with Calvin," Molly Neuman later wrote about a night early in the trip. "In the days before e-mail and cell phones the phone was so crucial and we were so new to being in the tour experience we were obsessed with staying connected. . . . The next day we stopped by the post office as Natalie had said there was a package waiting for us there and it was a cool present for me from Calvin. Some tapes and stuff that got us through the trip. I remember being happy to be thought of."

The bands played to small, enthusiastic crowds of young punks who were more inclined to like Fugazi, and maybe Beat Happening, but were excited to see the band. Those crowds consisted mostly of boys throughout the Midwest, but as the bands neared D.C., the final destination of their tour, more and more girls showed up. They arrived in D.C., surprised to discover that the riot grrrl convention was set to take place a few days later. Both bands decided to stay the extra days. When the weekend came, they gathered with like-minded women for workshops, concerts, spoken word performances, and an "All-Girl All-Night Dance Party." When it was over, the women returned to their hometowns on a mission.

Heavens to Betsy's music would carry the torch of the riot grrrl movement, its lyrics moving in a more political direction while its sound became even more fierce and urgent. That music, and the music being made by Bratmobile, was never again released on K Records. In the year following the riot grrrl convention, Kill Rock Stars released the first Bratmobile full-length as well as Heavens to Betsy's first EP. Years later, Tucker started Sleater-Kinney, the most enduring and successful band in the history of riot grrrl, and released a series of records that would become the cornerstone of the Kill Rock Stars catalog.

"Bikini Kill was just the coolest band ever, so that probably had something to do with it," Corin says, explaining her band's move away from K. "But Slim had started this record label and it was the new, hip, cool thing. It was a more rock 'n' roll label. Our bands were a lot grungier sounding and a lot dirtier sounding, and people were really excited about it. It was a little bit of a different direction. It wasn't that we didn't love Calvin and love K; it's just that this new thing that was starting was going to be so exciting."

Heavens to Betsy and Bikini Kill weren't the only bands jumping ship from K. Soon after the band received national attention for its IPUC performance, Mecca Normal was approached by Matador Records to release its next three studio albums. Calvin told Jean that she should take the deal.

"Calvin thought that maybe we could create something elsewhere that might work out to be somehow better," Jean says. "It was a big decision that we discussed together. There was certainly no animosity, or nobody stomping off, or nobody kicking anybody off, or severing any business relations or friendships."

15

AFTER THE SUCCESS OF NIRVANA and subsequent hit records from Seattle bands Pearl Jam and Soundgarden, the culture of independent music in the Northwest changed dramatically.

"The difference between the '90s and the '80s is like night and day," Calvin says. "In the '80s there was a very incoherent underground scene that was happening in lots of different places. Lots of people were interested in music on a local level or a homemade level, but there was no network of it. But the one thing was, there were underground bands and then there was the mainstream. In the '80s, if you were in an underground band, the mainstream was just this other universe. Huey Lewis and the News, they were a mainstream band. You don't know them. You don't hang out with them. You might've heard them on the radio or MTV or something, but you have no connection with them at all. It's completely two different worlds. And any band that tries to go from one to the other, it's like the kiss of death. No one ever thought, 'I want to be in a band and sell my records.' They thought, 'I want to be in a band. Maybe I'll put out a single. I'll play some shows with my friends.' And that was it, that was fine, that was what you did. And you never thought that anything else could happen."

After Nirvana bands knew that a lot more could happen. Representatives from the major labels descended on Seattle and began signing bands to multi-album contracts for large amounts of money. The money fed the local economy and also fed the egos of local musicians. The introduction of six-figure deals to the scene also infected the minds of the people who supported those musicians.

"There was a point in time where you would pick up a fanzine and read about the artists' art," recalls Sub Pop head Jonathan Poneman. "Then, somewhere in the early '90s, it started becoming less about the art and more about the nature of the record deal that they had—how much money they were able to get out of the record label. It became a pissing match of sorts."

As a Sub Pop band, Beat Happening was privy to that pissing match even though they were not part of it. The sound that the major record labels were hunting for was grunge, a hybrid of hardcore punk and heavy metal delivered in a pop format with an oddly humorless devotion to addressing societal ills. That was far from the stripped-down and oblique pop music being created by Beat Happening. Even if Calvin, Heather, and Bret had been making music that appealed to record executives, the band was already on a different trajectory, away from the professionalism of its peers.

Shortly before Beat Happening released its Sub Pop debut, *Dreamy*, Bret Lunsford's wife, Denise, gave birth to the couple's first child, a daughter, in a small Anacortes apartment.* With a young family to tend to, Bret made a request of the band.

"Bret asked that we limit our tours to three weeks," Calvin says. "At the time, it was a big shift from the long tours that we had been going on. My perspective now, knowing a lot of people with kids, is that three weeks is a long time. I don't know how he did it."

The band went on only two three-week tours to support the album. Bret's family was yet another constraint for a band that was rarely in the same room together. Since Bret had moved to Anacortes and Heather had settled in Seattle, Beat Happening

---

*The same apartment also served as a makeshift studio for Beat Happening when the band recorded "Nancy Sin."

had been constructing its albums largely in absence of one another. For many of the songs that the band released on the *Black Candy* and *Dreamy* albums, Calvin and Heather would each generate basic ideas in isolation; record spare, embryonic versions of the songs to cassette; and then send them to the other members to flesh out in time for one of the group's increasingly seldom practice sessions in Olympia. Sometimes they would bring the ideas to those sessions cold and build upon them on the spot with little time for reflection. The results were in keeping with the band's aesthetic; a simple pop formula with a focus on vivid lyricism and simple instrumentals.

By 1992, though, Bret decided that the band should return to the songwriting process it had employed for the first few sessions that had became the band's debut full-length release. Young and unencumbered, the band members were able to hole up in the Young Pioneers' practice space and then in a vacant apartment building in Japan to build their first songs together. The band's primary guitarist invited his bandmates to Anacortes for a series of weekend practice sessions, hoping to re-create the dynamic of those early sessions. The band members gathered in a vacant house being used as a rehearsal space by a band called Gravel, the latest group from Bryan Elliott, the Anacortes musician who played in the Spoiled and had reluctantly entered the world of K years earlier with his band the Few before starting Pounding Serfs with Bret's brother Jonn. In the isolation of that rehearsal space, the band set to writing and rehearsing the songs that would appear on its next album.

"If we had all lived in the same city, we might have not been able to spend as much time together making the album, because we wouldn't have had to get together and camp out in that way," Bret says. "We spent hours and days together with songs, just letting them develop. And so that whole album had a unity and a concentration to the way it was composed."

It was at this time that Stuart Moxham was wrapping up his Northwest excursion after recording Lois's debut album and touring the region with Beat Happening. With a few days free before heading back over the Atlantic Ocean, Moxham decided that he wanted to record the band. Happy to oblige, and with a few fleshed-out songs it had constructed in Anacortes, the band entered the studio with Moxham and recorded four songs: "Sleepy Head," "Godsend," "Hey Day," and "Tiger Trap."*

For the remainder of the songs, the band went again to Steve Fisk, who produced "Noise," "Pinebox Derby," "Teenage Caveman," "Bury the Hammer," and "You Turn Me On." That last song was adopted as the album's title.

You Turn Me On was released in late 1992, completing a two-album deal that Beat Happening had made with Sub Pop. The album was a critical hit with the mainstream press, receiving the type of attention that had eluded the band for so much of its existence. In the alternative music boom, though, the praise was in ample supply.

"Even after 10 years and 5 albums, the trio recalls the unspoiled creative energy of kids picking up instruments for the first time," a review in *Rolling Stone* read. "The band's amateurism might sound like just that, but it's really a celebration." A reviewer for *Spin* wrote that it was filled with "disarmingly unadorned, ingeniously inane songs," while *Entertainment Weekly* gave an A-grade for a record that sounded like "a charming racket dressed up in childlike innocence."

You Turn Me On contained the sound of a band in prime form. While the simplicity of its songs remained, the sound was refined. With the additional time to work on the songs, the band was able

---

*Tiger Trap was also the name of Rose Melberg's nascent band when she played Girls Rock Night at the International Pop Underground Convention. Calvin says that he did not intend to steal the name. Melberg's Tiger Trap would go on to release a full-length album and an EP on K.

to introduce multiple guitar parts, something it had done few times before.

In the summer of 1992, the band went on the road for a short tour with Gravel. It headed east, playing shows in cities that it had been touring for the last six years. The tour ended with a performance in Lawrence, Kansas.

"The show was at some hall out in the middle of nowhere, way out of town in a cornfield or something," Heather recalls. "There was a bonfire out in the field and these people had found a *huge* tree stump and rolled it across the field in to the fire and we watched it burn."

Beat Happening never toured again.

"We never talked about stopping," Heather says. "It just stopped. I remember feeling like I didn't think I could do it anymore. I really didn't like being onstage and I always had a lot of confusion about what I should be focusing on personally. I think I felt like as long as I kept doing Beat Happening I'd never do other things."

"We didn't ever break up, we just went inactive," Bret says. "We've recorded and done songs and done shows; I've probably seen Calvin perform every year since 1992, probably multiple times. We stayed together as friends, and that was the primary thing; the band never became more important than our friendship. It was a project we did as a group of friends."

For almost a decade, Calvin had a musical outlet. Between Beat Happening and the Go Team, he was able to create music, collaborate, and tour the country performing while spreading word about his record label. The Go Team had ended unceremoniously at the close of the '80s, and after the final Beat Happening show in Lawrence, Kansas, Calvin was without a band.

From late 1992 through the spring of 1993, Calvin and Candice focused on their growing label, which was prepping releases from mainstays Mecca Normal, Some Velvet Sidewalk, Lois, and

Heavenly, as well as an album by Rose Melberg's band, Tiger Trap. In 1993 Calvin moved out of the Martin Apartments and into an old house with a small basement. With the additional space, he was able to host the many musicians who had made Olympia their second home. One of those musicians was the Nation of Ulysses guitarist Steve Kroner. The Nation of Ulysses broke up the fall before after failing to complete its third album. Ian Svenonius transitioned into a band called the Cupid Car Club in Washington, D.C., but Kroner was, like Calvin, a man without a band. With no creative outlet to take him out on the road that summer, Calvin started playing music with Steve and another musician from Hertford, England, named Will, whom Calvin had met while touring England in 1988. The two musicians brought a different set of influences than Calvin had ever experimented with before. He was eager to delve into it and acquired an eight-track recorder to both chronicle and manipulate their attempts. The trio spent days recording instrumental songs that explored different rhythms and melodies in Calvin's basement. With plenty of time to play with the recordings, Calvin was able to apply the dub approach he had first attempted with the Go Team, taking the songs he, Steve, and Will had created and remixing them into different configurations.

"I've always been into '60s garage music, and underground rock 'n' roll, and British rock 'n' roll from the early '60s. And those are all things that Steve and Will were into, so that's why we were making this sort of racket in the basement," Calvin says. "It was just the KAOS idea, or *OP Magazine*, of being interested in lots of different kinds of indigenous pop music."

After a few days of recording, Will and Steve headed back to their respective homes, both promising that they would return to continue the project. With the two musicians gone, Calvin hoped to continue filling his basement with musical collaboration. He named the space Dub Narcotic Studio and invited musicians to come over and record. The first band to officially christen the new studio was a hardcore Olympia act called the Mukilteo Fairies; the name was both a pun on one of the many ferry routes that traversed the Puget Sound and a nod to the queer subject matter the band addressed in its music. The group recorded two sessions, walking out of Calvin's house with a dozen tracks that the band would release on its own.

After being inactive for the remainder of the summer, in October, Dub Narcotic began its stint as the primary recording studio for K. Calvin had been in contact with Doug Martsch, the guitarist for Treepeople, having booked the band twice before for shows in Olympia. But it wasn't until a Beat Happening tour early in 1992 when their bands shared a bill at a club called Emo's in Austin, Texas, that the two musicians spent time together. Doug, who was not impressed when he first saw Beat Happening open for Fugazi in Seattle two years earlier, had a completely different experience when he saw the band in Austin.

"The Fugazi show, it was all light out for some reason," Doug recalls. "It seemed like they were playing in the afternoon almost. The Emo's show was dark and heavy and loud. They were way louder and sounded cooler because they weren't in a big cavern, they were in a club. And I was really blown away by it."

Calvin and Doug traded tapes of their bands. When Calvin was putting together a tour with Beat Happening and the Nation of Ulysses later that fall, he called Doug and asked if Treepeople would be interested in coming along. By that time, Doug had split from the band. He offered to put Calvin in touch with the remaining members but, without Doug, Calvin was no longer interested. Doug's and Calvin's interest in each other continued. The two started corresponding on a regular basis. At one point, Doug sent Calvin a tape of music he had just recorded with a new band he was fronting called Built to Spill. Despite the new venture, Doug was still uncomfortable being a lead singer. He wanted to start a new project and he wanted Calvin to be the lead singer. The two had tried to get together throughout early 1993 but were unable to come to an agreement on how to proceed. When Calvin discovered that he could record in his basement, he invited Doug to come to Olympia.

For a week, Calvin and Doug collaborated on a series of incomplete song ideas that Doug had been working on since high school but hadn't been able to come up with lyrics for. Calvin listened to Doug play his complex guitar parts and began transforming them into pop songs, introducing the same style of simple melodies from his Beat Happening days and inventing lyrics almost on the spot. While Calvin's primitive abilities were stylistically anathema to Doug's more studied approach to music, the two musicians worked together harmoniously.

"It was really fun to work with Doug because he seemed like he was really good at playing guitar," Calvin says. "He seemed like a real musician-type person, but he didn't hold it against me that I wasn't. I hadn't really encountered that before, where someone was a really good musician and I didn't feel worse working with him."

With the help of two drummers that Doug had invited to the studio, the duo recorded a dozen wildly inventive songs, intertwining Doug's intricate guitar work and airy tenor voice with Calvin's simplistic sense of melody and deep monotone vocals. It was unlike any music either had heard before. Calvin invited Steve Fisk to do the final mix of the tracks they had recorded. When Fisk arrived, Doug thought the creative process had ended, but Calvin wasn't done experimenting with his new studio.

The process of mixing down the recordings involved setting the levels for each of the tracks and then playing them together as another recorder consolidated them onto a single, final track. When it came to mixing down a song called "Don't Touch My Bikini," Calvin wanted to add a cartoonesque "boing" sound in the chorus.

"We recorded that album on eight-track, and all eight of our tracks were filled up," Doug recalls. "They were mixing it and he had a keyboard, and he found some boing sounds. So Calvin did those live during the mix. Those aren't on the master tapes, they're just along with the mix."

It is a clear moment of studio amateurism in an otherwise polished track.

Doug and Calvin called themselves the Halo Benders and quickly released the single, "Canned Oxygen," with a short-lived Olympia label called Atlas Records. Soon after, the band would release the complete collection of songs it had recorded as its debut full-length on K, *God Don't Make No Junk*.

Two days after Doug headed back to his Seattle home to continue working on music with Built to Spill, another artist Calvin had met on his tour with Beat Happening in early 1992 arrived in town.

At the time Beck Hansen went to see Beat Happening play the L.A. date of that tour, the musician had been busking on the city's street corners and playing in coffee shops. He had recorded a cassette but was not widely known or respected. He had learned about K Records through a friendship with Lois Maffeo, but didn't maintain any considerable contact with the label or its bands. After the Beat Happening show, Beck approached Heather, talked with her for a bit, and traded cassettes. For the rest of the Beat Happening tour, Beck's cassette rarely left the tape deck of the band's van. When Calvin returned to Olympia, he began correspondence with the songwriter.

By the summer of 1993, much had changed for the artist. Earlier in the year, Beck released a single through a small L.A. independent label called Bong Load Custom Records. The song, "Loser," was played on *Morning Becomes Eclectic*, the popular morning show on the L.A. public radio station KCRW. The song, a drawling, self-flagellating rap set to a looped guitar line, was an immediate hit with listeners and major-label scouts. A bidding war ensued for the young musician. Geffen Records signed Beck after agreeing to the artist's terms, which included the freedom for him to record with independent labels even while he was under contract to the major.

With Dub Narcotic open for business, Calvin invited Beck to Olympia to record. Since Beck was planning to release a full-length album for Geffen, Calvin proposed a modest session that would result in a single for the International Pop Underground series.

At Beck's request, Calvin drafted a number of local musicians to help on the recording: a bongo player named Mario Prietto, the Spinanes drummer Scott Plouf, and Sam Jayne and James Bertram, two members of a new band on the K roster, Lync. Beck invited one more artist to help out, an unknown musician named Chris Ballew.

Ballew had attended a show Beck played at the Crocodile Café in Seattle a few days earlier at the suggestion of a musician friend from Boston named Mary Lou Lord.* In the middle of Beck's set at the small rock club, a tape containing the backing track to "Loser" malfunctioned. In an attempt to help salvage the song, Ballew jumped on stage with a harmonica and continued to play the repetitive guitar track while Beck sang. The song ended with the two musicians rolling around the stage together, laughing

---

*Mary Lou Lord would later release a number of EPs on Kill Rock Stars. She would also forever endear herself to the independent music world with the strummy sing-song track "His Indie World," in which she name-drops Calvin.

wildly. Beck told Ballew that he was heading to Olympia the next day to record some songs and could use another instrumentalist. He asked if Ballew could play slide guitar. He couldn't, but Ballew wasn't about to pass up the opportunity. The next day he bought a secondhand guitar and a slide. After making some slight modifications to the guitar, he boarded a bus for Olympia and arrived at the studio not knowing what he was getting himself into.

"Beck wasn't looking for proficiency or artistic excellence," Ballew says. "He was looking for a feel and intuitiveness; he was looking for something kind of human and real."

The process at Dub Narcotic was set up more for feel than proficiency. With Calvin carefully manning the studio's meager equipment, Beck was allowed to do whatever he liked. Calvin rarely talked with the other musicians; he focused on what Beck was trying to do with his music and was willing to continue taping as long as the artist liked. Soon Calvin's proposed single was growing into something much greater.

"Music just flowed from him," Calvin explains. "You know, he'll do a song and he'll be like, 'Oh, let me do that again.' And he'll do it and it'll be completely different. He'll change the words around, or he'll change the rhythm. It was just natural. He didn't go, 'I want to change the rhythm on this, let me . . .' He just did it. It just happened. He had a notebook full of songs. He came to record a single, and then it became an EP, and then an album, and then suddenly it was two albums, and then two albums and a single."

When they weren't recording, Beck and the musicians explored Olympia, swam in Ken Lake, and ate dinner together. Jeff Smith, another musician friend of Calvin's, followed them around with a camera. At one point he took a photo of Beck and James Bertram standing at the front door of Calvin's house.

Beck returned to Dub Narcotic in January to wrap up a few of the recordings he had started with Calvin. It was the last time he would set foot in the studio. A month later, the record label arm of the *Flipside* punk zine released *Stereopathetic Soulmanure*, an experimental album filled with Beck's poetry and sound collage. The next month, Geffen Records released *Mellow Gold*. On the strength of the single "Loser," the album debuted at No. 15 on the Billboard 200. The next week it peaked at No. 13. Calvin and Candice watched as Beck became an international star while the songs the prolific artist had recorded at Dub Narcotic sat on the shelf. The label owners knew they were in possession of a record that would sell far more than any previous K release, but the label was not prepared to put it out.

"We definitely knew that it would sell more because he had such a machine behind him," Candice says. "We were not savvy businesspeople in the sense of watching markets or gauging sales. Looking back, we probably could have been more efficient. But we knew that we needed a very good distributor, we needed money up front to make the record, to meet whatever demand is. I think we thought demand would be in the low tens of thousands, like maybe ten thousand, twenty thousand. Who knew? That seemed like a lot to us. Our average sales were somewhere in the two- to three-thousand range."

K's partnership with Cargo had served it well for sales in that range, but the Beck record demanded a more powerful distribution engine. Candice and Calvin found that engine right in their backyard. After the success of Nirvana, Sub Pop had partnered with major label Warner Music to form a new production and distribution company aimed at independent labels called the Alternative Distribution Alliance. The move was part of an ongoing relationship between the major label and the indie, which also involved Warner purchasing 49 percent of Sub Pop. With few other options, K signed up for the services of the company, which provided K with the same distribution reach as the major labels.

On June 27, 1993, K released its Beck album, titled *One Foot in the Grave* and featuring the black-and-white photo of Beck and James Bertram standing at Calvin's front door. *Mellow Gold* had dropped to No. 82 on Billboard's chart by that time, but K would still feel the impact of Beck's major-label machine. The album would become the best-selling record in the history of the label, eventually selling 168,000 copies.*

Despite the fact that it was now the province of a rock star and counting on the corporate ogre, in part, for its distribution, the label did not abandon its punk rock ethos completely. Beck was party to the same handshake agreement that all K artists received. Because of that, he received half of *One Foot in the Grave*'s profits and was not expected to put out another release with the label, even though Calvin had recorded plenty for a second album.

"At that point Beck was beginning to change enough that I didn't know if he would want those records out," Candice says. "There was enough material left over for another album, and Calvin always said there would be another album, but Beck was already going to a different world where he was doing something different. I didn't think that he would want there to be another *One Foot in the Grave*. So I never believed there was going to be another record. And I certainly wouldn't have advocated banking on that."

The label would have made much more money had it modeled its artist agreement after major-label contracts, but it is unlikely that Beck would have ever walked into Calvin's basement if the label didn't allow its artists such freedom. Despite the economic disadvantage the punk rock split afforded K, the release of *One*

---

*As of July 18, 2008, *Mellow Gold* had sold 1.2 million while *Stereopathetic Soulmanure* sold 146,000.

Foot in the Grave changed the economics at the label. The money that came from the release gave the label more freedom to continue growing, but it also brought with it new responsibilities to protect the label's relationship with the artist.

"Beck certainly got us out of debt," Candice says. "But one fifty-thousand-dollar royalty check really affected you. And that's hard to pay back if you don't pay it up front. So, I would prepay Beck."

In 1995, a year before Beck would solidify his place in the firmament of the alternative nation with the release of another hit album, *Odelay*, K Records issued the single "It's All in Your Mind." Containing three songs from the artist's Dub Narcotic sessions, the single made good on Beck's original agreement with Calvin to add his work to the International Pop Underground series. It was the last time Beck and K worked together.

IN THE SUMMER OF 1994, Julie Butterfield decided to escape the trappings of Minneapolis. Her destination had only two requirements: a nearby ocean that she could swim in and an independent record label she could work for.

A native of Omaha, Nebraska, Julie had worked at Minneapolis record stores for the previous five years. There she learned about the underground in the vestiges of its last great explosion. In the early '80s, two bands born of the punk rock revolution emerged from Minneapolis clubs. The Replacements and Hüsker Dü both formed in 1979 and released records on small local independent labels, the Replacements with Twin/Tone Records and Hüsker Dü with Reflex Records. The Replacements stuck with Twin/Tone for three records, while Hüsker Dü left Reflex for Los Angeles's SST after one. After slugging it out with the independents for five years, both bands signed with major record labels. Unlike their fellow Minneapolitan Prince, who emerged from the city's equally fertile R & B scene, neither of the bands would exit the '80s intact.

Julie immersed herself in that scene, seeing bands like the Jayhawks, Soul Asylum, and Golden Smog, whose music was aimed at an audience found in the dark bars of a decade before when their heroes were still playing punk rock. Julie went to those shows, but she also found new music in the fanzines that came into the record store and through customers who were more aware than ever of the bands on independent record labels, thanks to increasingly sophisticated distribution and mainstream press attention. She played Bikini Kill and Bratmobile records, and though she felt that those artists' cause was not her own, she was empowered by it. She went to every show by Babes in Toyland, the city's most beloved female-powered punk group. She also launched her own label, Skinny Girl Records, releasing three seven-inch singles from a few of Minneapolis's lesser-known female-centric bands. There weren't many to choose from, as the city's music scene was dominated by men.

"I knew about riot grrrl," Julie says. "I was a little older than those girls, so I wasn't part of the movement. But I did identify with them and I was supportive of that and I knew that there was this place where really forward-thinking women had a platform and a place to speak what they were thinking about, what they felt to be true. That was really intriguing to me."

That place was Olympia, and though the soundtrack to the riot grrrl movement was being largely released on Kill Rock Stars, Julie chose to send a letter of interest to K Records, the label that had launched most of those bands and had gained a reputation through articles in *Puncture* and *Maximum RockNRoll* as being fiercely independent. Fully fluent in the lingua franca of the underground, Julie decided against submitting a cover letter and resume and instead created a zine that provided her prospective employer with the reasons why she would be a perfect addition to the team.

She made only two versions. One she sent to K and the other to the New York offices of Matador Records, an independent label that had started in 1989 and released records from college rock darlings including Superchunk, Pavement, and Teenage Fanclub.

"I didn't want to work for a corporation," Julie recalls. "I wanted to work for people who I respected and who I identified with their politics and their tastes."

Two weeks after sending her unorthodox query to both labels, she received a call from Calvin Johnson. K was fully staffed with five workers at the time, but he wondered if Julie would come to Olympia to work K's merch booth at an upcoming music festival called Yoyo A Go Go. The festival wasn't being produced by K, but rather by Pat Maley, who had started his own Yoyo Recordings label and had since moved Yoyo Studios out of the chicken coop and into the Capitol Theater. Still, many K artists were scheduled and, as it had done three years before at the International Pop Underground Convention, the label would be selling records and T-shirts on the second floor of the theater. K needed someone with sales experience, and Julie, who was manager of the Northern Lights record store in downtown Minneapolis, was a perfect fit. The label was willing to pay for her plane ticket, and she could stay in one of the guest rooms at Calvin's house.

Two weeks later, at the end of June, Julie arrived in Olympia and was put to work while also getting to know her temporary employers. Calvin hosted a barbecue for musicians, friends, and K employees and rented out the Capitol Theater the night before the festival officially began. There he debuted a new band that he had been practicing with for the past few months. While Calvin was receiving praise in the independent press for his work with Doug Martsch in the Halo Benders, he was also still inspired by his first musical experiments with dub in his basement studio. Calvin had continued the project's evolution, bringing in a new group of musicians who were interested in making dance music rooted in the sounds of black America that he had first heard in the library at KAOS. The music was so firmly tied to the beginnings of his Dub Narcotic Studio that he extended the studio's name to his band: Dub Narcotic Sound System. Calvin adopted a similar moniker, introducing himself that night at the Capitol Theater as Selector Dub Narcotic.

Once the festival started in earnest, Julie began working closely with Candice to keep the K Records booth stocked for the crowds, while also helping run records and cassettes from the Kill Rock Stars office to the makeshift record store in the Capitol Theater. At night she would enter all sales into the ledger and, with Candice's help, track inventory and sales. At the end of the five-day festival, Julie had proven herself a useful and talented addition to the K team.

Candice and Calvin had been entertaining the idea of hiring a full-time in-house publicist. While they continued to include handwritten notes with the mail orders that came into K's offices, the size of its roster and frequency of releases made it impossible for the pair to reach out to press and radio for every K release. For the previous two years, K had hired publicists to work individual titles in its increasingly voluminous catalog. When the label added the Beck and Halo Benders albums—two records with considerable national appeal—Candice and Calvin knew they needed a sustained effort to reach as many music fans as possible. Julie proved that she had the work ethic and savvy to handle the books, and her experience releasing albums through her Skinny Girl label showed that she was somewhat familiar with what it took to get people to take a record out of its sleeve and put it on the turntable. Calvin approached Julie and offered her a full-time job at K.

By the end of August, Julie had moved across the country and began settling into a new life in Olympia, living at the Martin Apartments and working in the K offices above the Chinese restaurant. There she shared a room with Candice and another K employee. Four additional workers crowded into various other spaces in a creative hive filled with artists and musicians, some of whom actually lived in the space.

"Mike Dees from Fitz of Depression was living up there," Julie recalls. "Pretty much squatting. There was a bathroom down the hall with no shower. Mike wasn't known for his hygiene, but he was a very sweet guy."

Across the hall from Julie's shared office was the room where Calvin conducted his correspondence, worked on various art projects with the label's bands, and screen-printed the sleeves to a new single series called Dub Narcotic Disco Plates. The series was the realization of Calvin's original dub-inspired idea for the Go Team, but with a twist. Instead of having artists add their own contributions to songs that Calvin and Tobi Vail recorded, Calvin employed a growing number of tools in his studio to remix songs, adding effects and reconfiguring the individual tracks to create an alternate version of the song. At the time Julie arrived, the series consisted only of early Dub Narcotic Sound System recordings on the A-side and a chopped-up and twisted remix on the opposite side. Adopting the nomenclature of reggae, Calvin titled these reworked B-side instrumentals "Version." In the ensuing years, Calvin would broaden the Disco Plate roster to include recordings by half a dozen K bands, all subject to Selector Dub Narcotic's experimentation.

Julie's first job at the K office was to promote Calvin's other band, the Halo Benders, along with the Beck release, to radio and press outlets across the nation. The releases were well received by college radio and various alternative publications. But as she settled into the role of publicist, her job became more difficult. In addition to its legacy artists, including the bright and delicate pop of Lois and Heavenly, K was working with a new batch of bands that played much heavier and darker music.

"When I came in most people only knew about K as Beat Happening, twee, kid pop," she says. "Part of my job was to just spread the word about Lync, Fitz of Depression, and Karp."

Karp was not unfamiliar with the pop tradition of K Records, though they were more drawn to the music released on its sister label, Dischord. It was during Beat Happening's second Sound Out Northwest tour in 1989 when the high school students from nearby Tumwater who would form the band were exposed to the label, seeing both the Nation of Ulysses and Beat Happening play. By the time of the International Pop Underground Convention in 1991, the future members of Karp were enough a part of the K community that they convinced Calvin and Candice to screen all the *Planet of the Apes* movies on the convention's final day. By that point the high school students were making music that was sinister and brutal, yet delivered with humor and a pop sensibility. Candice, always a bigger fan of heavier rock than Calvin, helped usher the band onto the label's roster in 1994, along with the chaotic Lync, the dark and experimental Fitz of Depression, and the caustic and raging Modest Mouse, which recorded its debut EP at Dub Narcotic Studio.

No matter the style of band that Julie was promoting, the process of publicity was arduous. Though alternative outlets like *Flipside, Puncture,* and *Maximum RockNRoll* kept the faithful informed of new underground bands, and a loose network of venues those bands could play had formed across the country, letting local audiences know about a show was still a chore.

"At that point, I had to call the venue—and sometimes it wasn't a venue, it was like a house party or a community center," Julie recalls. "I had to call and ask what newspapers everyone who might come to a show were reading. It was a lot of physical work, tracking everything down and then sending a package."

For years, the K offices had been using computers for word processing and maintaining inventory databases, but they couldn't help Julie reach out to radio programmers or newspaper editors. Then, in 1995, Margaret Doherty, who years before had helped organize the Girls Rock Night at IPUC, came to the offices at the invitation of Calvin and Candice and introduced the staff to the Internet.

"I remember her coming over and showing us all the things that we could do on the Internet," Julie says. "It was definitely something that was like, 'Wow, what is this?' You could go to this screen and click on this and you'd go to this. You could just be on this thing for hours."

The Internet did not immediately change K's business operations. The office had only one connected computer, and while the amount of information available was impressive, it was by no means extensive. E-mail was still the province of college students and early adopters. Julie could search for the colleges and local newspapers in and around Springfield, Illinois, say, but she would still have to call those institutions' general information lines to find out who exactly would need a promotional copy of the Halo Benders album in advance of the band's show.

No matter the obstacles, Julie was proving her worth. In 1995 Lois released her third full-length album on K, *Bet the Sky*. The album was designated a "dud" by Robert Christgau in the *Village Voice*, but received a glowing review in *Rolling Stone*, accompanied by a photo of the artist. Landing one of the beloved but lesser-known K artists ink in the nation's most popular music magazine was a coup for the label. Kicking Giant, the duo of Rachel Carns and Tae Won Yu that had moved to Olympia since its performance at the International Pop Underground Convention, returned from tour enthusiastic about the press it had received for its K debut, *Alien I.D.*

"They came back and said, 'Oh my gosh, thank you so much,'" Julie recalls. "We actually saw stuff in the newspapers in the towns we went to. It felt like word was out. People saw the positives of press and publicity."

Reading the press was not always a pleasant experience. K had continued to grow throughout the mid-'90s, and so did its exposure. As the more charismatic of the label's two leaders and a member of two of its most popular bands, Calvin was K's primary spokesperson. When the number of articles about K mounted, the relationship between the owners of the label started to deteriorate as Candice demanded recognition for her role.

"I started having a lot more confidence in admitting my role," Candice says. "And I started getting a lot more frustrated. I think a tipping point was—I can't remember this year, I can't remember the magazine, all I can remember is the phrase where I was referred to as 'Calvin's trusted sidekick.' And I was furious. I was furious at Calvin for not disputing that. I was like, 'I am nobody's trusted sidekick.'"

The journalist's reference to the popular *Calvin and Hobbes* comic strip might have been a lazy mistake, but it ignited a reaction from Candice that had been long brewing.

"Calvin was doing a great job in being a spokesperson for us," Candice says. "But oftentimes I would wonder if he mentioned my name at all. Oftentimes in interviews where he would talk about the label, he never talked about me. And that was a problem for me. I felt like it was unfair. I felt like it was sexist. It was really hard for people to see what I did if the person who was the spokesperson couldn't really share that. There was always tension for sure."

Frustrated with Calvin's reluctance to recognize her role in K, Candice asked her partner if they could revisit their business agreement and put it in writing.

Candice and Calvin had not talked about the agreement since Candice moved back from San Francisco in 1989. They both recalled very different terms. Candice remembered that the handshake deal meant a fifty-fifty split. Calvin remembered it as a ninety-ten split. No written evidence existed to reinforce either's claim. Candice forced the issue, and the two eventually agreed on a split. Before they signed a contract solidifying their partnership, K hired an auditor to assess the value of the company.

By the time of the audit, the label had moved into a new location downtown at the old Olympia Knitting Mills building on the corner of Jefferson Street and Legion Way. The new spot was a marked improvement over the increasingly cramped offices above the Chinese restaurant. In the daytime, light streamed in through large windows and lit the big room on the second floor, which was festooned with playful graffiti from Olympia High School students who had thrown a dance in the mill in the '40s. There, surrounded by those remnants of an idyllic teen culture, Calvin set up his recording equipment, added a sixteen-track tape machine, and made the revamped Dub Narcotic Studio the literal and spiritual center of a space that housed numerous artists, musicians, a tour booking agency run by Chad Queirolo, and 24 Promotions, the publicity business Julie started after breaking away from K in 1997 and started working with a few select bands, most notably Sleater-Kinney. Julie's departure was not viewed as a betrayal. Rather, like he had done with most of the businesses and people that had grown out of K, Calvin kept Julie close, inviting her to be a part of his underground hub of creativity.

"Calvin had this vision," Candice recalls. "It was sort of this all-artists space. So that's why we wanted to rent it to people like Chad and Julie. We were all very—I don't like the word *incestuous*, because that's gross—but we were very tied together. We had a lot of personal relationships, but also professional. But I think that the personal always came first."

The old knitting mill was a flurry of activity at that time, with music being recorded, album covers being silk-screened, and various art projects always in the works. Holiday parties were held there, as were community meetings and art openings for numerous Olympia artists.

The K offices were busy as well, issuing albums at a blistering pace. K added more than thirty titles to its catalog between

1996 and 1997, including another Halo Benders album, multiple releases from Dub Narcotic Sound System, and debut albums from Rose Melberg's new pop band, the Softies, Bret Lunsford's first band since Beat Happening, D+, and Jonn Lunsford's new project, the Crabs, with his wife, Lisa Jackson.

The label was also introducing a new sound to the K catalog. After dabbling in the world of hip-hop by booking High Performance for the International Pop Underground Convention, Calvin continued to bring hip-hop into the fold. In 1995, he released a twelve-inch single by Dead Presidents, a local hip-hop trio that also performed with Calvin live as Dub Narcotic Sound System. More hip-hop releases by artists including Black Anger and Silent Lambs Project popped up throughout the next few years.

Increased output did not translate into increased income, and the business, flush just a couple years before, was again stretched thin. By 1998 the economic outlook, as well as the tensions between Candice and Calvin, started to darken the mood at Calvin's creative complex.

"People seemed frustrated and a little unhappy," Julie says. "I knew that Candice was frustrated. I'm pretty sure it was just money and organizational things. Calvin is not the most communicative person, so sometimes getting information out of him was difficult; you couldn't even find him. Sometimes he would be at the studio or sometimes he was on tour. It was hard. The communication broke down and there wasn't a lot of money. They were putting out a lot of records still, but it just wasn't coming in."

The next year, the audit came back and Candice and Calvin signed an agreement that cemented the terms of their partnership. Among other things, the agreement stated that, in the event that either Calvin or Candice wanted to sell their share of the company, the other partner would have first dibs.

After they had finished signing the contract, Candice turned to Calvin and said, "I'm going to sell my share." Calvin was shocked but agreed to pay off her portion.

K had come a long way in the previous decade. It was continuing to produce more albums than Calvin could have ever dreamed it would have at the end of the '80s. His business had grown to fill a warehouse with a staff of paid employees, as well as his own recording studio. But the label had also lost most of its defining artists. Beat Happening was no more. Mecca Normal had continued, but was putting out records for Matador and, more recently, Kill Rock Stars. After many reiterations of Some Velvet Sidewalk, Al Larsen called it quits to focus on the family he had started with Stella Marrs. With the departure of Candice, the label had fully transformed. The decade that had started in the early days of the pair's partnership would end with Calvin as the sole owner of K Records.

PART III

GET IN

Got a pigeon-toed clubhouse in my backyard, only the emotionally crippled allowed. You're lookin' for ugly ducklings, we're well-endowed. Good at math? You have to ask? Get in."

—From "Get In," by the Hive Dwellers

WHEN BRET LUNSFORD moved back to Anacortes from Olympia in 1988, he needed a job. At Evergreen Bret had studied history, community development, and writing, an ideal set of skills, he thought, for a reporter at the local newspaper. After he and wife Denise Crowe had settled into their new home, an apartment in the back of an old, empty hotel, Bret drafted a resume and set out on foot for the offices of the *Anacortes American*. On his way, Bret stopped by a shop called the Business to say hello to an old friend, Glen Desjardins.

Desjardins had opened the Business in 1978, offering the residents of Anacortes a place to buy used books and camera equipment. While in high school, Bret was a frequent customer, perusing the used books, looking at the art and photos on the walls, and joking around with the owner. It was, "just a place to go and be a part of something," as Bret recalls. In 1987, before he made his move back, Bret spent time in his hometown working on a family history project he needed to complete in order to graduate from Evergreen. Desjardins allowed Bret full use of the store's darkroom to develop some old film, and the two became close friends. When Bret arrived on his way to the newspaper in 1988, Desjardins offered him a job instead at the Business.

The arrangement was perfect for Bret, allowing him to continue touring with Beat Happening, sometimes for as long as four months. When Beat Happening disbanded in 1993, Bret became more involved with the shop. He added a café and, because

Anacortes didn't have its own record store, started to stock records. The Business carried a large number of independent releases, including a healthy stock of K and cassette releases from his own fledgling label, Knw-Yr-Own, but Bret also stocked music from major-label bands, like Nirvana and the Red Hot Chili Peppers, that might lure curious customers with more mainstream tastes.

In 1995 Bret became partners with Desjardins and took on a more managerial role. He continued to build his record inventory, and soon teenagers from Anacortes High School started to frequent the shop. Most came in just to buy the latest releases, but a small group started to spend the majority of their hours after the final bell in the store. There they would lounge in the used-book section, reading worn copies of novels while listening to the music that Bret played over the store's PA. Though he was happy to provide the local teenagers with a place to hang out, as he had done himself years before, Bret wanted the Business to be more than a store.

"In Olympia, I got tainted by this vision that people could make their own cultural products, and that some people might be interested in consuming those things," Bret says. "I just sort of brought that gospel to Anacortes."

One teenager named Phil Elvrum had first come in to the Business to buy the latest Nirvana release. After reading about Sonic Youth in an article about Nirvana in *Rolling Stone*, Phil's curiosity of underground bands grew and he began exploring the independent records that the store had to offer. Sonic Youth led him to Sub Pop, and Sub Pop eventually led him to the K bands that Bret had in stock. It didn't take long for Phil and his friends discovered that Bret had been in Beat Happening. One even bought a Beat Happening CD and asked the store owner to sign it. Bret obliged, printing only his first name in all capital letters. Phil began digging deeper into the collection of records.

"They had the craziest seven-inches that Bret would stock in the store," Phil recalls. "I don't know what he was thinking: who in Anacortes would buy them? I didn't actually think it was that weird, I was just like, 'Oh, this is music. This is another kind of music that exists.' I didn't have enough of the frame of reference to be weirded out by it."

Bret was aware of Phil's interest in the underground and soon started encouraging him to publish a zine, offering Phil free use of the store's photocopier. Phil did just that, publishing a zine called *The Paintbrush* with one of his friends. Phil printed up thirty copies of the first two issues, which were filled with jokes and reviews of records that Bret would give him from the store. Eventually Phil split off and created his own zine called *The Blimp*, which featured his creative writing and black-and-white photos, reflecting what Phil calls his "older depressed teenager phase."

Bret then suggested that Phil and his friends start their own band. They did. With Phil on drums, Tugboat practiced for hours in the shed behind Phil's parents' house, playing punk rock songs about food. The band eventually started playing shows at the local Eagles Lodge with Gravel and Captain Fathom, a local band fronted by another young musician named Karl Blau.

After an ill-fated two-week stint at a call center in nearby La Conner, Phil was offered a job by Bret. While Phil was working for Bret, touching up photos in the Business's photo lab, a friend of his inherited an eight-track recorder and a bunch of microphones and didn't know what to do with them. Phil told Bret about his friend's windfall.

"Well, that's a big deal," Bret said. "We should set that up here at the back of the Business and you can use that space after hours."

Again, Phil took Bret's advice and was soon recording his band in the back room at the Business. Phil quickly became fascinated with the process of recording and was soon spending all of his evenings there, sometimes staying until 2 a.m.

"I was just doing music experiments," Phil recalls. "I didn't have songs; it was more like, 'I want to see how low of a sound I could make, and then I want to gradually transition it into the highest pitch, the most distorted sound I could make over two minutes.' I just recorded the weird things I wanted to try, and then it would become an album."

What Phil was creating could be called music only in the most liberal sense. Still, it became an obsession of his that he could work on when he wasn't recording other Anacortes bands, booking live shows at the Business, and breathing new life into Knw-Yr-Own Records, which Bret had mostly abandoned after starting D+, his first band since Beat Happening.

D+ began as a musical project with his wife, Denise Crowe, who had continued playing drums long after filling in for Heather on Beat Happening's first U.S. tour in 1984. With two children to care for, it was impossible for the couple to take the band on tour, or even to a recording studio for an extended amount of time. When Bret became more serious about D+, Denise bowed out and Bret invited Phil to play drums and Karl Blau to play bass.

Phil invested himself in his music, taking a year off after high school to experiment with his recordings, work at the Business, and write the first D+ album with Bret and Karl. The band went to Olympia to record its first record at the original Dub Narcotic Studio in Calvin's basement.

Bret saw Phil as more than another musician. When Phil started talking about going off to school, Bret encouraged him to consider the Evergreen State College. The young Anacortian had yet to be led astray by one of Bret's suggestions, so he applied to the school and was accepted. Bret was happy that his young protégé was heading to his alma mater, but the former Beat Happening guitarist did have another motive.

"I never saw anybody with that kind of work ethic," Bret says of Phil. "Just a lot of time spent figuring out what he wanted to do and teaching himself. So, by the time he finished school and was thinking of going off, I said to Calvin, 'You should open your doors to this guy. He'll be runnin' the place in no time.'"

Phil was eager to be part of the creative community in Olympia that Bret had told him stories about. The summer before he started school, there was an opportunity. Pat Maley was hosting his second Yoyo A Go Go festival with a lineup that included Dub Narcotic Sound System, Sleater-Kinney, Modest Mouse, Built to Spill, and Some Velvet Sidewalk. Phil got a pass from a musician named Sandman, who had played a show at the Business, lived in Olympia and was performing at the festival. Phil went alone, sleeping on Sandman's porch and taking in Olympia at its most idyllic.

"It was just an incredible paradise," Phil recalls. "Amazing music from all over the world and hundreds of people who had traveled from really far. People were just making things happen and it was totally working. Somebody was walking down the street selling food that they made, out of a bucket, and it was delicious, and everything was great. People were all working together on these projects that didn't have to exist in the preexisting framework of the real world. It was just a temporary illusion that happens during a festival, but I was won over, for sure."

The month after the festival, K Records released the first D+ record, filled with Bret's introspective lyricism delivered in a high and lonesome voice never heard on Beat Happening releases and off-kilter instrumentals from Karl and Phil. Within days of the release, the band went on its first tour, a three-week cross-country trip with Dub Narcotic Sound System. The tour served as a showcase for the artists on Knw-Yr-Own. Phil started each night's set with two of his songs, followed by a short set by Karl and then a brief set by D+.

Throughout the tour, Bret continued to talk to Calvin about what Phil had done in Anacortes and what he thought he could do at Dub Narcotic Studio. After three weeks, D+ headed home while Dub Narcotic Sound System continued onward for another three-week stretch. Before the two groups went their separate ways, Calvin handed Phil his key to Dub Narcotic Studio, which he had just moved from his basement into the old knitting mill on Jefferson Street and Legion Way. Calvin told Phil he could use it whenever he wanted to.

"That was the apprenticeship," Phil says. "He didn't really tell me anything. He just turned me loose in the Dub Narcotic Studio, which was amazing."

Phil returned from the tour one week after his classes had started. With savings from his year of work at the Business, Phil was able to spend all the time when he wasn't in class at Dub Narcotic, experimenting. After two quarters at Evergreen, Phil decided to devote his energies entirely to the studio. Since Dub Narcotic was largely dormant when Calvin wasn't recording, and was no longer housed in his basement, Phil had plenty of time to continue his audio experimentation.

"When I first started Dub Narcotic, I had this idea that it could be this studio where K artists could record if they wanted to," Calvin says. "Of course they didn't have to. A lot of them didn't really want to, because they wanted to go to a real studio to record an album. I also think that they thought that I didn't really know what I was doing, which was true. I didn't."

Phil had little concern for the advantages and trappings of a "real studio." The equipment at Dub Narcotic was modest and relatively primitive compared to what was housed in the Northwest studios that had emerged during the grunge boom of the previous ten years, but it was far beyond what was available to Phil in Anacortes. Phil began recording audio collages, crashing drum tracks, and delicate folk songs, with no larger plan than figuring out how to make the sounds that he heard in his head real. In 1998 Phil released his first solo album on the Knw-Yr-Own label, fittingly titled *Tests*. He named his project after what he viewed as his most important collaborators: the Microphones.

Phil had more than his studio equipment to keep him company. Shortly before he moved to Olympia, he had met a curious musician named Arrington de Dionyso when the Olympian's wildly experimental band Old Time Relijun played the Business. The two connected over their love for outsider music. When Phil told Arrington that he was moving to Olympia, his new friend found the Anacortes native a place to live and introduced him to a circle of downtown artists that Arrington had come to know since coming to Olympia to attend Evergreen in 1992.

The real reason Arrington chose Olympia for his college education was his love for K Records. This deep appreciation for the label and its leader had taken root when he was a confused teenager in Spokane, Washington.

Arrington was an outcast in Spokane, a transplant from Little Rock, Arkansas, whose worldview was formed by a progressive youth theater program and revolutionist anarchist literature. There were only three places where he felt comfortable in his unfamiliar Spokane home: at the library listening to its eclectic record collection, in the company of street musicians downtown, and at an all-ages space in town called 123 Arts. Every weekend, the venue hosted punk rock shows and Arrington rode his bike down to see whatever band was playing. One weekend, he walked into a Go Team show.

"I had never seen anything like it before," he says. "They would take just one guitar riff and just repeat it over and over and over again and the drumbeat was this bouncy drumbeat you could bounce to throughout the entire song. And Calvin's stage presence was so unusual. My friends and I were like, 'They must be on really crazy drugs.' It felt like this really intense shamanic ritual. There was this very vibratory energy that struck me as something completely new."

Arrington didn't have any money to buy one of the band's cassettes at the merch table, but he did walk away with the latest K newsletter. A few allowances later, he ordered twenty dollars worth of cassettes and singles, including the Beat Happening debut full-length. The music inspired him, as did the label's simple means of production. Within a few months, Arrington had written twenty songs on his acoustic guitar, recording each one to a cassette. He made twenty copies of the cassette and handcrafted his own album covers. He called his nascent record label Pine Cone Alley and started busking on the sidewalk in downtown Spokane, selling the cassettes for five dollars each.

Arrington continued the label after moving to Olympia, but didn't release anything but his own songs, strange compositions featuring guitar, saxophone, bass clarinet, and anything he could bang on, recorded to four-track. He and some friends hosted a show on KAOS where they would make studio collages with the assistance of callers. Calvin was still doing his *Boy Meets Girl* show on Tuesday nights, and though Arrington would see him in the library, he would rarely speak with the man who by then was a verifiable icon, much less hand him another tape.

"Everyone in a band in Olympia was giving Calvin demo tapes to listen to," Arrington recalls. "Even then I knew he was probably sick of it. People walking up to you and handing you tapes all the time gets kind of irritating."

Near the end of his college career, Arrington worked up the nerve to ask Calvin for an internship at K. The internship turned into a short-lived job at the record label. But even after working at K, Arrington had not figured out how to get Calvin to like his band, Old Time Relijun. He wasn't even able to get Calvin out to a show until a year after the band had been playing. Even then, Arrington's only place at K remained in the office.

The key to getting on K was not recording a great demo or even working in the office, Arrington learned. The key was proving that you were willing to work on your art. Phil also figured that out firsthand.

"I was recording so much in there without really any intention," Phil recalls. "I was just accumulating these songs because that's what I wanted to do. Maybe I'd put out a tape, who knows. But Calvin said, 'Well, why don't you put those out on K?' It was a weird way to sign a band. Not that they were really signing anything, but that was how I got invited. Crazy."

Calvin took D+ on another tour with Dub Narcotic Sound System in 1998. The band again played for three weeks, but when Bret and Karl went home, Phil stayed on the road, playing a short set before Dub Narcotic unleashed the dance party. During those performances, Calvin watched as Phil entranced the audience.

"You could see that people responded to him," Calvin says. "People were just rapt. He was clearly connecting with people. It was obvious."

In 1999 K released the Microphones *Don't Wake Me Up*, an album that intertwined Phil's sonic collages with tender, heartbreaking songs. The record set a new precedent for the label. The equipment Phil was working with was not much better than it had been for the records that Calvin recorded. But the young musician had managed to master those supposed limitations, creating an album that was praised for its production rather than accepted despite it.

"He didn't have the attitude that this wasn't a real studio," Calvin says. "He was more like, 'Hey, this is fun.' And he made really good records there because he didn't know any better than to make good records."

Full faith was bestowed upon Phil. When Dub Narcotic Sound System collaborated with the blistering electric soul outfit the Jon Spencer Blues Explosion, Calvin asked Phil to be the album's producer. Soon Phil was bringing the artists he wanted into the studio, and those recordings were increasingly being released on K. In 1999 Arrington finally made his way on to the label, moving Old Time Relijun from the Pine Cone Alley roster over to K, where it released its second album, *Uterus and Fire*.

Before Phil had moved to Olympia, Arrington had introduced the young producer to one of his old college friends, Mirah Yom Tov Zeitlyn. Once Phil was settled in to Dub Narcotic, Mirah asked if he could help her record a track for a performance. Mirah had only been performing for a short time, but she was known in the world of K. In 1996 she joined a number of K artists, including Calvin, on a touring variety show organized by Jen Smith called the Cha Cha Cabaret. She had subsequently released a short EP on Pat Maley's Yoyo Recordings, a twelve-inch record that featured art by Nikki McClure etched on its B-side.

Phil helped Mirah with her recording project, a backing track to a John and Yoko song she was performing. The two became fast friends and creative partners and soon started collaborating on each other's songs. After Phil left Evergreen, they went on a short tour together, riding in his station wagon down to Florida, where they met with Phil's girlfriend. On the way, they played shows at numerous coffee shops and all-ages clubs, including one in Searcy, Arkansas, that was being booked by a couple K devotees who would later move to Olympia and form the band the Gossip.*

---

*The Gossip would go on to record a volume for the International Pop Underground series. The band released three popular full-lengths with Kill Rock Stars before being signed by major label Sony Music Entertainment.

Mirah added her breezy coo to Phil's songs and Phil encouraged Mirah to record a full album. In 2000 they recorded that album, *You Think It's Like This But Really It's Like This*. It came out on K later that year.

Other artists began taking the controls at Dub Narcotic as well. A musician named Adam Forkner moved up from Portland and lived in Calvin's basement. Early on he would go to the studio and make a series of recordings he called "Guitar Solos," recording a simple 4/4 drumbeat for an hour, playing a basic bass line over it, and then playing long extended guitar solos. Those tapes were never released, but he did produce K albums by Wolf Colonel and his own band, Yume Bitsu, and engineered numerous recording sessions at the studio, including records by Dub Narcotic Sound System.

Khaela Maricich, another school friend of Arrington's and cousin to Bret, was a regular at Dub Narcotic Studio, though not as a producer, or even a musician, at first. She and two friends had rented out one of the studio spaces in the building and started the Ace Detective Agency, an art project disguised as an investigative firm. Khaela was a performer and, like Mirah, had toured with the Cha Cha Cabaret and played the Yoyo A Go Go festival. After seeing Phil record with her friends, she asked him to record her, resulting in a simple, short collection of songs called *Look For It in the Sky It Will Always Be There*.

"Phil helped me record my first tape, just me sitting on a chair playing ukulele and putting all the songs onto two tracks in the recording studio," she recalls. "We didn't really work that well together. It was a great song, but it wasn't that organic. So then Calvin let me set up a studio, a little area back in the back of the big room."

Phil lent Khaela his old eight-track and she began recording her own music. In 2002 she released *Bonus Album*, her K debut as the Blow.

Calvin continued to bring his own musicians into the studio, but he was producing fewer of their records. As the new millennium wore on, Phil and his fellow producer-musician hybrids would make up a considerable portion of the label's output. By moving Dub Narcotic Studio out of his basement, Calvin had created an environment where K artists could grow in ways they never had before. The result was a new normal for K: musicians who were as comfortable experimenting in the studio as they were playing on the stage.

18

IN THE SUMMER OF 1994, while K Records was busy promoting the first release by Calvin Johnson and Doug Martsch's Halo Benders, Doug and his other band, Built to Spill, entered a Seattle studio called John and Stu's Place with Phil Ek, an unproven apprentice of grunge producer Jack Endino. Ek recorded the band's second full-length album, *There's Nothing Wrong with Love*.

The album was released on a new Seattle independent called Up Records. Up, though, would be just a pit stop for the band. While it didn't break into the mainstream, *There's Nothing Wrong with Love* was a college radio hit and earned Built to Spill attention from major labels.

Though Built to Spill was taking more of Doug's time, Doug and Calvin managed to continue working on the Halo Benders.

"When we didn't have anything else going on, we'd get together and work on it," Doug says. "The second record, Calvin came to Boise, we worked on it together, and then we showed it to the band and recorded them."

In late 1995 Calvin invited Ek to Dub Narcotic to record another Halo Benders album, *Don't Tell Me Now*. The rehearsals resulted in a sound that was less clumsy and playful than the debut album. Though better woven together, the incongruity of Doug's ascendant tenor and Calvin's blunt baritone, as well as the artists' lyrical content and songwriting styles, were still the hallmark of the band.

"Sometimes he'd have an idea that didn't make sense or wasn't even physically possible," Doug says about Calvin. "Taking the song and changing the time signature but keeping some other aspect of it the same. Weird Captain Beefheart–type of ideas. He heard things in his head but didn't understand if you were doing this you'd lose this other thing. He's not a musically trained person."

While *Don't Tell Me Now* contained its fair share of disjointed songs, the album had moments when the songwriters' visions came together to create muscular, off-kilter pop songs, as in the band's theme song "Halo Bender." *Don't Tell Me Now* was remarkable in at least one other respect: it featured a political diatribe written and spoken by Calvin in the song "Bomb Shelter, Pt. 2." While Calvin was never shy about his rejection of corporate culture in interviews about his record label, he rarely spoke about issues outside the dissemination of culture and information. Even while surrounded by overtly political artists like Slim Moon, Jean Smith, and numerous riot grrrls, Calvin had never politicized his art to reveal his own beliefs in song. In "Bomb Shelter, Pt. 2," Calvin delivered a screed on the state of his nation, with particular heed paid to the militarism most recently on display in the U.S. invasion of Iraq in 1991.

"You know there in Washington, they've got a monument covered with names," Calvin spoke over the fluid and melodic backdrop of Doug's guitar. "Names of folks they say gave their lives for their country and we oughta honor them. The way I see it, they were just doing what they were told. Now, who I'd like to bestow my gratitude to is them free-thinkin' folks of independent mind. I'd like to say, 'Thank you,' to all of you Vietnam-era draft dodgers and 'Thank you' to all of you Gulf War military deserters. And I just want to give a big 'Thanks' to all those Americans out there who put their freedom on the line as conscientious objectors and military resisters. All you youngsters out there; all you young men age eighteen to twenty-two, you're probably wondering what you can do to follow in the footsteps of the American way and assert yourself as major individuals who can decide your own future. I'm not going to suggest you shouldn't register for the draft. That wouldn't be legal. But why not take a cue from my buddy Sam and register ten times, fifty times, a hundred times. There's no law against it. No law against a woman eighteen to twenty-two registering fifty or sixty times, or a man or a woman, fourteen or forty registering for the draft one hundred and fifty times, five hundred times. Just let them know what's on your mind. About all the bugaboo, concerning folks burnin' the flag, I'd always learned that burning was the proper, respectful way to dispose of a flag when it has become obsolete and worn out its usefulness. Hell, being an American is all about gettin' things off your chest, saying your piece. A visual aid can come in mighty handy for getting your point across. So, don't be usin' up all your matches and lighters, wavin' them at those big concerts. Save them for the streets where they can express your true feelings and those of our founding fathers. God bless all you flag-burning patriots, exercising your rights, as Americans."

The Halo Benders provided a tense listening experience, but one with melody and transcendent release, courtesy of Doug's increasingly dynamic musicianship. Ek's growing talents as a producer were also evident in the much cleaner and intentional production. Still, unlike the music being created by Built to Spill, which maintained the melody and musicianship without the politics and blurting baritone, the Halo Benders were unlikely contenders for major-label status.

In early 1996 K released *Don't Tell Me Now* to continued praise from the independent press and college radio. Later in the year, the label released a patchwork of songs that Built to Spill had recorded in Dub Narcotic Studio and live in concert, collected under the title *The Normal Years*.

By the time the Halo Benders reconvened in 1997, Built to Spill had released its major-label debut, *Perfect from Now On*, with Warner Bros. Records. While the record never appeared on the Billboard charts, the band was dominating college radio and playing to larger crowds than ever before. While the Halo Benders had gone on a couple small tours, the band was now becoming solely a studio project between the two musicians. A couple times, the band members would take the stage together when Doug invited Calvin up during Built to Spill shows to perform a Halo Benders song or two. In those moments, Calvin performed for his largest audiences and Doug, an understated artist in a live setting, witnessed Calvin's impact on audiences.

"People just lit up when he stepped up there," Doug recalls. "I've never seen anything like it since. People would enjoy our shows all right, but when he got on stage, they got super excited and couldn't hide it from their faces."

Between Doug's in-demand band and Calvin's duties at K Records, heavy Dub Narcotic Sound System touring schedule, and work producing K artists at his studio, the Halo Benders were becoming more difficult to keep together, even as a studio project. For the band's third record, Doug sought to use the musicians' time more wisely and bring the band closer together. In the summer of 1997, he invited Calvin to Boise to jam with the entire band and write the next record.

"I had been inspired by other bands like Modest Mouse and Lync and Karp, Unwound," Doug says. "A lot of bands that were interesting to me because of the fact that they were a band. You could tell that people were coming up with things jamming together instead of just coming up with ideas on their own. Everyone had a part in it."

After the jam session in Boise, the band reunited at the new Dub Narcotic Studios with Ek, who had continued working with

Built to Spill after producing the band's major-label debut. The resulting recordings were a revelation. Well crafted and swinging, with both musicians in lyrical harmony, the songs represented a perfect marriage of the two artists' spirits, best exemplified on the opening track, "Virginia Reel Around the Fountain." The song was a team effort.

"I remember distinctly that Calvin came up with the beat," Doug says. "Ralf [Youtz] was playing something different and Calvin told him what to play on the drums. And he didn't really do that very often. So, yeah, that was his drum part idea and I thought that brought it to life."

The recordings were released in early 1998 as *The Rebels Not In*, and "Virginia Reel Around the Fountain" became a minor hit on college radio. The song became better known to Built to Spill's growing fan base as a seven-minute live rendition performed by the band, without Calvin, and released on a live album that Warner issued in 2000. A few months after that release, the original Halo Benders' version of the song showed up at No. 188 on the list of the "Top 200 Tracks of the 1990s" published by Pitchfork, an online-only magazine that had replaced *Rolling Stone* as primary reading material for a generation of music fans raised on independent music. The site, started in 1995, featured music news and reviews of a wide array of bands on truly independent record labels and major labels alike. While there was no Green Line Policy, Pitchfork's content had come to resemble—in its devotion to independent releases, tolerance of major-label output, and eclectic array of styles—the playlist at KAOS. The stakes, though, were higher for the media company, which was working hard to shape an independent culture that had gone a decade and a half without a defining institution. K fit into that emerging definition, though Calvin's unsophisticated approach to music had clearly become a liability.

"That they're mostly forgotten now outside of International Pop Underground devotees makes some sense," wrote reviewer Mark Richardson about the Halo Benders. "Their three full-lengths were heavy on ramshackle indie charm and a little light on memorable songs. 'Virginia Reel Around the Fountain' from 1998's *The Rebels Not In* is the exception that proves the rule."

The song was the only K release on a list that included works by Bikini Kill, Sleater-Kinney, and Fugazi, along with Built to Spill's single "Car," which was recorded at Dub Narcotic Studio and released on the Olympia label Atlas. Nirvana's "Smells Like Teen Spirit" was No. 11. Beck's "Loser" was No. 8.

In 2000 Calvin and Doug met again to jam and work on yet another Halo Benders album. This time, the two approached the music from uncharacteristically common ground.

"Calvin and I both got into the blues and old folk music," Doug says. "I thought we could see what we could do with that sort of an approach. I learned to play some open guitar slide stuff. I had written some things. And he had written some songs along those lines. We worked on stuff together, and then I felt like I didn't have much to offer his thing, and I felt like he wasn't doing much to my stuff that I was liking."

The Halo Benders didn't break up, but they have yet to make another album. Some of the ideas that were generated in the abandoned session ended up on future Built to Spill releases, but most found a home on the artists' own releases. In 2002 both men released their first solo records. Doug recorded a collection of songs with blues and folk influences called *Now You Know*, while Calvin released *What Was Me* on K.

While Calvin had often taken command in his recordings, never before had he been in complete artistic control of an album. Given the opportunity, Calvin decided to keep it as simple as possible. With years of music-making experience behind him, able and willing musicians all around, and a studio of equipment at his disposal, Calvin featured only a single instrument on the album, a nylon-string guitar. Phil Elverum took on the role of producer, but restrained himself from tinkering. The only collaboration came in the form of two female voices, courtesy of Mirah and the Gossip's Beth Ditto. *What Was Me* was an album filled with unabashed love songs.

As if to announce the new work as wholly his own, the album opened with Calvin singing a regretful ballad a cappella. "I never should have gone," Calvin sang, his bold baritone getting slightly lost in the space of Dub Narcotic. "I know now I was wrong. Broke up without reason. Hearts committing treason. When it's you that I'm wanting, the past comes back to haunt me."

The rest of the songs followed with Calvin singing with full confidence. In complete control of his instrumental accompaniment, played in a deft yet spare manner, he was rarely off-key. Calvin had stripped away much of the clever lyricism, childish themes, and coy sexuality of his previous recordings. Gone were the sly, thinly veiled come-ons. In their place were laments and passes made clearly, but with endearment.

On "Can We Kiss?" he asked, crooning, "What would happen if we happened to kiss? Would the clouds curl up, would the earth still exist? Would the stars melt down to a waxen pool? Would the sky fall down like I'm falling for you?"

"Lightnin' Rod for Jesus" featured Calvin singing, again a cappella, to the snap of fingers, an earnest take on old gospel in a duet with Ditto's soulful, belting voice.

The title track was the only other song on the album that didn't touch on love, though it did involve another subject that Calvin had sung about at length in his Beat Happening days: death. Here, though, the specter of the end did not appear as a B-movie caricature. "When I die, there'll be a song and everyone will sing along," Calvin sang as he strummed his guitar. "And that will be me."

Unlike Beat Happening's music, this was not a record that a teenager could have written, no matter how passionate he might be.

In his solo recording, Calvin found a place for his ruminations on love, but he continued to exercise his love for dance music through Dub Narcotic Sound System. Since its first performance at the Capitol Theater in 1994, the band had released a number of Dub Narcotic Disco Plates, three EPs, two full-length albums, and the collaboration with the Jon Spencer Blues Explosion. Dub Narcotic Sound System never received much acclaim for its recorded output, but the band was an incessant touring machine, turning small clubs across the nation into sweaty dance halls with music steeped in funk and soul, fronted by a frantic, boogying Calvin.

In 2003 the band released its fourth EP, *Handclappin'*, and set out again on tour. The final destination was New York City, where Dub Narcotic Sound System would join a host of other K artists to perform a showcase at the CMJ Music Marathon. Calvin invited Old Time Relijun, which had just released its fifth full-length album, *Varieties of Religious Experience*, to go on a tour across the country and to the East Coast.

The first stop of that tour was in Moscow, Idaho, followed by a show in Spokane and then a two-day break to drive to Lincoln, North Dakota. At the last minute, Old Time Relijun was offered a show in Billings, Montana, on the off night at a bar. Since Calvin refused to play anything but all-ages shows, Dub Narcotic Sound System took the night off. Calvin and his bandmates got off to a slow, leisurely start from Spokane and arrived in Billings too late to catch the Old Time Relijun show. They had planned to stay in the city and waited for Arrington at another local bar from which he would take them to a house where the band members could rest up for the long seven-hour commute the next day. On his way to the bar, Arrington's van broke down. When 11 p.m. rolled around, the members of Dub Narcotic Sound System decided to cut their losses and make the drive overnight, something that they, like most other touring bands, had done before.

Bass player Chris Sutton drove east on Interstate 94 as Calvin and drummer Heather Dunn slept in the back. Four hours after departing, outside the city of Glendive, Montana, Sutton swerved to miss a deer, sending the van crashing into a ditch. Calvin and Heather were thrown through the side window of the rolling van.

At nine in the morning, Arrington received a phone call from the K offices with the news that his tourmates had been in an accident. All three band members survived the crash and had been transported to the hospital in Billings. Arrington and his bandmates, still in Billings, arrived at the emergency room to find Heather pacing in the waiting room and clearly in shock. As Arrington comforted her, she told him scraps of what she remembered from the night before and the condition of her bandmates. Chris had broken his jaw. Calvin had separated his shoulder, broken three ribs, and suffered a traumatic brain injury. While Chris was still in surgery, having his jaw wired shut, Arrington went to Calvin's bedside.

"He was on some other planet," Arrington recalls. "His brain was obviously not allowing him to organize his perceptions. He was half awake, half in some kind of hallucination. He was speaking this kind of automatic speech. There were some words, but not really any fully formed words. He would be laying on the hospital bed for a bit and then he would sit up and start waving his arms around and not know where he was. It was a very shocking state to find someone in, especially someone who has shaped the direction of your life."

Even though Calvin couldn't communicate with him, Arrington reassured his friend and informed him that his mother was already on a flight to Billings. Before leaving, Arrington spoke with Calvin's doctor.

"You never know with concussions," the doctor cautioned. "He could be normal in a couple weeks, or it could take years. You never know. But he'll probably be fine."

After a week in the Billings hospital, Calvin returned to Olympia. A couple weeks later, he was back in the K offices, trying to continue his work.

"I just wanted to get back to normal as quickly as possible," Calvin says. "It was very slow at first."

Calvin's injuries were evident. Never before at a loss for words, Calvin would stop a conversation in midsentence, searching for a word that he couldn't find. He had also developed a severe stutter. Despite the difficulties, he continued to work, engaging his coworkers in sometimes-halting conversations not only because the survival of the label depended on it, but also because he knew that, in order to regain his ability to speak and think clearly, he had to continue talking.

Calvin had also forgotten how to play his songs. In the months following the accident he retaught himself the compositions he had written just a few years before for *What Was Me*. Progress was slow, but Calvin was confident that he would be back in performance shape shortly. When the Museum of Modern Art in Oxford, England, requested his presence at a festival of arts and music that it was hosting in February, he agreed to play and organized a tour around the country.

"I figured, well, I'd be ready by then," Calvin says. "It was four months later, so it gave me something to work towards."

By the time he arrived in Bristol for his first show since the accident, Calvin had managed to reteach himself all of the songs off of *What Was Me* and could perform them as if he had never forgotten, but in his banter between songs, his stutter remained.

While relearning his material, Calvin had developed a new perspective on his work. In particular, the title track from his solo debut, a song that explored the possibility of his own demise, resonated with new meaning. During the performances, he would tell the story of the accident between the song's verses.

Calvin continued to play the songs off his new album, but he decided that the rest of the music he had created was best left behind.

"I had spent all that time relearning those old songs," Calvin says. "I started thinking, 'Why not just write new ones?'"

IT'S AN EARLY SATURDAY EVENING in late July of 2011 and the sun is setting over the small fishing town of Anacortes. As the wide blue skies of a pristine Pacific Northwestern summer day turn purple, Bret Lunsford, Karl Blau, and Phil Elverum are playing a set of D+ songs in the basement of the Croation Club of America hall as a roomful of old friends and curious fans break bread together. This is the Dinner Show, the spiritual center of an annual gathering of musicians called What the Heck Fest.

A few blocks away, on Commercial Avenue, forty-eight-year-old Calvin Johnson is setting up for another of the festival's shows in an art gallery located downstairs from the apartment where he and Bret and Heather Lewis recorded the song "Nancy Sin" in their Beat Happening days, the same space where Bret's daughter was born twenty years before. Heather Lewis is there sitting in the corner of the room next to Bret's wife, Denise Crowe. Arrington de Dionyso is there as well. The next night he will be singing Indonesian translations of William Blake's poetry to the backdrop of a propulsive punk soundtrack in his latest band, Malaikat dan Singa. Right now he is sitting on the floor with thirty strangers, all squeezed in to watch Calvin play a set of songs with his newest band.

Calvin's hair is gray, but it is still as short as it was when he got his first punk haircut before moving to Washington, D.C., for his senior year of high school. His eyes are still brilliantly blue. His nylon-string acoustic guitar is painted pink. Along the edge of the instrument's body a single sentence is written in marker, surrounded by two hearts: "Calvin, You're Kind of Amazing."

The Hive Dwellers is the eighth band that Calvin has formed since he performed his first show with the Beachheads in a near-empty studio space on the Evergreen State College campus. It is also the only band that Calvin is currently a member of. After his accident in 2003, Dub Narcotic Sound System released one more record that they had already recorded by the time they headed off for the CMJ Music Marathon with Old Time Relijun. They never played another show.

Calvin continued to write. In 2006 he released another solo album filled with songs about lust and death. Titled *Before the Dream Faded*, the album features a photo of Calvin hanging precariously off the side of a pay phone, holding the receiver up to his ear. Two years later he released an album of reworked post–Beat Happening material with a backing band, Sons of the Soil, consisting of K artists Kyle Field (Little Wings), Jason Anderson (Wolf Colonel), and Adam Forkner.

After a five-year interruption, Calvin continued to put out Dub Narcotic Disco Plates in 2008 with a new group of K artists, including Joey Casio, Mahjongg, and Bobby Birdman. K continued releasing records uninterrupted, thanks entirely to Mariella Luz, whom Calvin had hired as a general manager shortly after the departure of Candice Pederson. While the label still makes little money, the fact that it weathered the near death of its founder without radically shifting course is a testament to both its nimbleness and the continued affordability of Olympia.

There are some changes, though, that K has absolutely no control over. The Internet as an unregulated source for information and entertainment has turned the music industry on its head, leaving major and independent labels alike struggling for profit. The flow of records being produced by K is far below the label's late-'90s output and, thanks to a lack of record buyers, will likely never reach that level of production again.

It's not all bad, though. The Internet has provided K with new avenues to reach its audience through online music outlets, and the label has turned the idea of a singles series digital with a K Singles Zip-Pak subscription. And then there is the cultural impact of the new technologies. His label is suffering like all the rest, but Calvin has viewed the rise of the digital network as a natural extension of the movement he first joined thirty-five years ago.

"People now are sidestepping that whole process of production and they are almost directly singing to each other," Calvin said during an interview on Ian Svenonius's online interview series, *Soft Focus*. "They don't need the record store or a record label. They can just do their song on their laptop or their ukulele, and then it's available instantly, all around the world. It's really the most basic form of the punk rock revolution. It's a very exciting time."

It's also a time when the idea of the corporate ogre might have passed. With the dawn of digital music, file sharing, and plummeting record sales, major labels are no longer the source of money or resentment from independent artists that they once were. Instead of major-label contracts, commercial licensing has become the avenue through which money is funneled to artists, sometimes from small regional companies, but more often from large multinational corporations.

K artists have benefitted from this new world of music. Kimya Dawson, who released three albums of simple and subversive childlike folk songs on K in the mid-'00s, was drafted to provide the soundtrack to the independently produced, but widely distributed, Oscar-winning film *Juno*, giving a sales bump to her back catalog. YACHT, an experimental Portland music group started by Jona Bechtolt, an early collaborator in the Blow with Khaela Maricich, released a song called "Psychic City" that soon appeared in a slick commercial for the Cadillac car company. The song features words written by Rich Jensen and first performed, a cappella, as "Voodoo City" on *Two Million Years*, a cassette released by K in 1987.

The landscape in and around K continues to change, in the same way it always has. Clubs have come and gone with a space called Northern, started by Mariella, serving the all-ages community. Kill Rock Stars moved from Olympia to Portland, which has been transformed into a sort of Olympia on steroids, filled with more young, enthusiastic musicians and a similarly relaxed demeanor. The K offices moved out of the knitting mill space and into an old synagogue. The studios filled with artists are gone, but Dub Narcotic Studio is still on site and active. Phil is not. After returning from a yearlong stay in Norway in 2002, he returned to the Pacific Northwest and, after recording one more album at Dub Narcotic, moved back home to Anacortes, added a "u" to his last name and started his own record label, P.W. Elverum & Sun.

Artists' agreements are still done with a handshake, and the punk rock split is still the terms of the agreement, meaning that the revolving door of artists at K continues. After releasing a few more records with the label, Mirah and Khaela both moved on, taking their respective projects to other labels, other cities, and larger audiences. In their place is a new crop of bands: Tender Forever, LAKE, the Curious Mystery, City Center, and the latest from Ian Svenonius, Chain & the Gang.

The new generation of artists that Calvin is working with is different. Having grown up with independent music as readily available as radio-ready pop hits, the artists have stopped drawing an impenetrable line between the underground and the mainstream. Calvin's punk rock mantras hold less sway in a world where everything seems equal. When Jean Smith and David Lester visited Dub Narcotic Studio to record Mecca Normal's sixth contribution to the International Pop Underground series and its first K release in more than fifteen years, Smith brought a camera to capture the proceedings. She was relentless in her questioning of Calvin about the nature of performance and punk. The conversation sounds like it could have come from one of their first recording sessions together until Calvin shares a candid moment with his old friend.

"Last week LAKE was in here recording, and they are just a different generation than us, Jean," Calvin said. "They can, completely without irony, reference Steely Dan, and Daryl Hall and John Oates, and Fleetwood Mac as if those bands had some merit in this world. And they can admit to listening to them and enjoying it, and I'm like, 'Wow, that's just not the way we did it back then, in the '70s and '80s.'

"But that's what's great about this younger generation is that they are able to understand and appreciate a Jean Smith next to a Stevie Nicks," he continued. "They can see equal merit in both and not have to judge one against the other in any way."

It is mostly members of that younger generation that are sitting on the floor of the art gallery in Anacortes, waiting for the Hive Dwellers to perform. Whether or not they can differentiate between the man who started K Records and Bruce Springsteen is difficult to say. What matters is that they are there.

The reason they are there goes back to 1980. That year, the city of Anacortes hosted its first ever Shipwreck Day, an annual community garage sale where anyone who lived in or around the small island town could clean the unused, ill-fitting, and junky items out their garage and set up a table on Commercial Avenue where one neighbor could peruse and, perhaps, buy another one's junk. Always held in the summer months, when the skies were almost guaranteed to be sunny and the neighbors neighborly, the event was as much about community as it was commerce.

By 2002 Shipwreck Day was an annual highlight for Bret. That year, the owner of the Business and the Knw-Yr-Own record label started to make plans to set up a separate table for all of his label's releases. Knw-Yr-Own's roster was modest, consisting largely of Anacortes artists that also had releases on K, including D+, the Microphones, Bret's cousin Khaela Maricich, and his brother's husband-wife duo the Crabs. Bret has described it as "just like the minor league team to K's major league ball club."

Bret's Shipwreck Day plan grew as the weeks wore on. By the time the rains had cleared, Bret had booked a roster of music for the weekend that included Dub Narcotic Sound System, Mecca Normal, Lois, and the Pounding Serfs. Mining the spirit behind its carefree origins, he called his gathering What the Heck Fest.

The festival has happened every year since, never growing much larger than that first weekend. Like so many other things that Bret has created in his life, it has been passed on to Phil. If the chatter between those in attendance is to be believed, this edition, the tenth, will be the last. Calvin has heard this chatter. After the first song from the Hive Dwellers, he quickly gets to the point.

"They say this is the last What the Heck Fest," he says, staring into a corner of the room, his hip cocked. "But they always say it's the last What the Heck Fest. But this year, they say they really mean it. They've been saying that for a couple years now. Well, if it is, in fact, the last What the Heck Fest, just let me say . . . wow."

Then, as his bandmates play a clumsy shuffle, he sings.

Got a pigeon-toed clubhouse in my backyard, only the emotionally crippled allowed. You're lookin' for ugly ducklings, we're well-endowed. Good at math? You have to ask? Get in. Biker chick, lemming, panic attacks. Visible scars on arms or neck. Compulsive, pinko, birth defect. Tubby, urine-stained, neurotic, cross-eyed, homeless. Looking for a fat lip, negroid, listless, porn addict. Hysterical, abusive, turkey neck. Autistic, topless, sociopath, lezbo, kleptomaniac. Worthless, wear no underpants. Missing teeth, shoeless, smoker's hack.

The litany of misfits continues, until the final verse:

I got internal bleeding and bad breath, an obsessive misfit with
a sunken chest. Would you sell your soul for unrequited love?
Then do what Jesus does. Get in. Get in. Get in, get in, get in.

It's Calvin's latest song, but it reaches back to the very beginnings of his musical awakening. It was then, in the Northwest
corner of the United States, in the capital city of a far-flung state,
that a few young visionaries were in the right place at the right
time to make something extraordinary happen for all the musical
misfits of the world. Inspired by the punk movement that preceded them and bolstered by emergent technologies and a radical
school, Calvin and his coconspirators took to the airwaves, created their own publications, and recorded their own music on cassette tapes. They shared ideas, punch lines, heartache, and, most
importantly, music.

DISCOGRAPHY

k RECORDS RELEASES

(International Pop Underground singles and Dub Narcotic Disco Plates not included)

KLP 001 Beat Happening *Beat Happening*

KLP 002 Beat Happening *Jamboree*

KLP 003 Beat Happening *Dreamy*

KLP 004 Mecca Normal *Calico Kills the Cat*

KLP 005 Pounding Serfs *Pounding Serfs*

KLP 006 Beat Happening *Black Candy*

KLP 007 Beat Happening *You Turn Me On*

KLP 008 Mecca Normal *Water Cuts My Hands*

KLP 009 Thee Headcoats *Cavern by the Sea*

KLP 010 Some Velvet Sidewalk *Avalanche*

KLP 011 Various Artists *International Pop Underground Convention Compilation*

KLP 012 Snuff *Reach*

KLP 013 Heavenly *Le Jardin de Heavenly*

KLP 014 Mecca Normal *Dovetail*

KLP 015 Lois *Butterfly Kiss*

KLP 016 Various Artists *International Hip Swing Compilation*

KLP 017 Tiger Trap *Tiger Trap*

KLP 018 Mecca Normal *Jarred Up*

KLP 019 Some Velvet Sidewalk *I Scream*

KLP 020 Steve Fisk *Over and Thru the Night*

KLP 021 Lois *Strumpet*

KLP 022 Mecca Normal *Flood Plain*

KLP 023 Tiger Trap *Sour Grass EP*

KLP 024 Some Velvet Sidewalk *Whirlpool*

KLP 025 Heavenly *P.U.N.K Girl* Maxi Single

KLP 026 Fifth Column *36C*

KLP 027 Karp *Mustaches Wild*

KLP 028 Beck *One Foot in the Grave*

KLP 029 The Halo Benders *God Don't Make No Junk*

KLP 030 Lync *These Are Not Fall Colors*

KLP 031 Fitz Of Depression *Let's Give It a Twist*

KLP 032 Some Velvet Sidewalk *Shipwreck*

KLP 033 Heavenly *The Decline and Fall of Heavenly*

KLP 034 Kicking Giant *Alien I.D.*

KLP 035 Dead Presidents *Spread Butter/(Into) Somethin' (Else)* 12"

KLP 036 Lois *Bet the Sky*

KLP 037 Lois *Shy Town* Maxi Single

KLP 038 Mecca Normal *The First LP*

KLP 039 Dub Narcotic Sound System *Industrial Breakdown* Maxi Single

KLP 040 Dub Narcotic Sound System *Boot Party*

KLP 041 Fitz of Depression *Swing*

KLP 042 The Crabs *Jackpot*

KLP 043 The Softies *It's Love*

KLP 044 Talulah Gosh *Backwash*

KLP 045 Dub Narcotic Sound System *Rhythm Record Volume One—Echoes From The Scene Control Room*

KLP 046 The Halo Benders *Don't Tell Me Now*

KLP 047 Black Anger *Feel What I Feel/No Commercial* 12"

KLP 048 Karp *Suplex*

KLP 049 Sandy Dirt *Self Titled EP*

KLP 050 Dub Narcotic Sound System *Ridin Shotgun* Maxi Single

KLP 051 Love As Laughter *The Greks Bring Gifts*

KLP 052 Built To Spill *The Normal Years*

KLP 053 Wandering Lucy *Leap Year*

KLP 054 Glo-worm *Glimmer*

KLP 055 Various Artists *Project: Echo Compilation*

KLP 056 The Crabs *Brainwashed*

KLP 057 Lois *Snapshot Radio* Maxi Single

KLP 058 Lois *Infinity Plus*

KLP 059 Heavenly *Operation Heavenly*

KLP 060 Dub Narcotic Sound System Featuring Lois *Ship to Shore*

KLP 061 The Softies *Winter Pageant*

KLP 062 Some Velvet Sidewalk *Generate!*

KLP 063 Modest Mouse *The Fruit That Ate Itself* EP

KLP 064 The Make-Up *Sound Verite*

KLP 065 Satisfact *Satisfact*

KLP 066 Various *Cha Cha Cha Cabaret—Chez Vous*

KLP 067 Karp *Self Titled LP*

KLP 068 Dub Narcotic Sound System *Bone Dry* Maxi Single

KLP 069 Treepeople *Guilt Regret Embarrassment*

KLP 070 Mocket *Fanfare*

KLP 071 Black Anger *206 Mix Tapes (Worldwide)* 12"

KLP 071 Black Anger *Maxed Out Singles*

KLP 072 D+ *D+*

KLP 073 Lync *Remembering the Fireballs (Part 8)*

KLP 074 The Crabs *What Were Flames Now Smolder*

KLP 075 Selector Dub Narcotic *Drop the Needle* (unreleased)

KLP 076 Love As Laughter *#1 USA*

KLP 077 Some Velvet Sidewalk/ Heavy Friends *The Lowdown*

KLP 078 Various Artists *Classic Elements Compilation* EP

KLP 079 Various Artists *Classic Elements Compilation*

KLP 080 Gaze *Mitsumeru*

KLP 081 The Halo Benders *The Rebels Not In*

KLP 082 Various Aritsts *Selector Dub Narcotic Compilation*

KLP 083 Dub Narcotic Sound System *Out of Your Mind*

KLP 084 D+ *Dandelion Seeds*

KLP 085 ICU *Chotto Matte A Moment!*

KLP 086 Cadallaca *Introducing*

KLP 087 Gaze *Shake the Pounce*

KLP 088 Satisfact *The Third Meeting at the Third Counter*

KLP 089 Take One *Emergency Breaks*

KLP 090 Silent Lambs Project *Comrade* 12"

KLP 091 Bedroom Produksionz *S.E.L.F./I Know Ways* 12"

KLP 092 The Make-Up *I Want Some*

KLP 093 Enemymine *Enemymine* EP

KLP 094 IQU with Miranda July *Girls on Dates* EP

KLP 095 The Crabs *Sand and Sea*

KLP 096 Sarah Dougher *Day One*

KLP 097 Old Time Relijun *Uterus and Fire*

KLP 098 Jason Traeger *My Religion is Love*

KLP 099 The Microphones *Don't Wake Me Up*

KLP 100 Marine Research *Sounds from the Gulf Stream*

KLP 101 Sub Debs *She's So Control*

KLP 102 Tilson *Action*

KLP 103 Dub Narcotic Sound System & the Jon Spencer Blues Explosion *Sideways Soul: Dub Narcotic Sound System Meets the Jon Spencer Blues Explosion in a Dancehall Style!*

KLP 104 Marine Research *Parallel Horizontal* 12"

KLP 105 Make Up *Save Yourself*

KLP 106 Internal/External *Featuring . . .*

KLP 107 Wolf Colonel *Vikings of Mint*

KLP 108 IQU *Teenage Dream*

KLP 109 Beat Happening *Music to Climb the Apple Tree By*

KLP 110 Old Time Relijun *La Sirena de Pecera*

KLP 111 The Shinin' *Director's Cut* EP

KLP 112 Mirah *You Think It's Like This But Really It's Like This*

KLP 113 Gene Defcon *Come Party With Me 2000*

KLP 114 Wolf Colonel *The Castle*

KLP 115 Beat Happening *Crashing Through* Box Set

KLP 116 The Microphones *It Was Hot, We Stayed in the Water*

KLP 117 Calvin Johnson *What Was Me*

KLP 118 C.O.C.O. *C.O.C.O.*

KLP 119 The Softies *Holiday in Rhode Island*

KLP 120 Chicks on Speed *The Re-Releases of the Un-Releases*

KLP 121 Yume Bitsu *Auspicious Winds*

KLP 122 Bedroom Produksionz *Non-Fiction/Temple No. 8* 12"

KLP 123 Internal/External *Inside Out* EP

KLP 124 Chicks on Speed/Mäuse *Euro Trash Girl* 12"

KLP 125 The Microphones *Song Islands*

KLP 126 Tender Trap *Film Molecules*

KLP 127 The Rondelles *Shined Nickels and Loose Change*

KLP 128 Old Time Relijun *Witchcraft Rebellion*

KLP 129 Heavenly *Heavenly vs. Satan*

KLP 130 All Girl Summer Fun Band *All Girl Summer Fun Band*

KLP 131 Modest Mouse *Sad Sappy Sucker*

KLP 166 Jason Anderson *The Wreath*

KLP 167 The Blow *Poor Aim: Love Songs*

KLP 168 The Blow *Everyday Examples of Humans Facing Straight into the Blow*

KLP 169 Little Wings *Grow*

KLP 170 Calvin Johnson *Before The Dream Faded . . .*

KLP 171 Old Time Relijun *2012*

KLP 172 Woelv *Tout Seul Dans La Forêt En Plein Jour, Avez-Vous Peur?*

KLP 173 Tender Forever *The Soft and the Hardcore*

KLP 174 Karl Blau *Beneath Waves*

KLP 175 Kimya Dawson *Remember That I Love You*

KLP 176 Arrington de Dionyso *Breath of Fire*

KLP 177 Mirah *Joyride: Remixes*

KLP 178 The Blow *Paper Television*

KLP 179 Maher Shalal Hash Baz *L'Autre Cap*

KLP 180 Calvin Johnson & The Sons Of The Soil *Calvin Johnson & the Sons of the Soil*

KLP 181 Mirah and Spectratone International *Share This Place: Stories and Observations*

KLP 182 Saturday Looks Good to Me *Fill Up the Room*

KLP 183 C.O.C.O. *Play Drums + Bass*

KLP 184 Old Time Relijun *Catharsis in Crisis*

KLP 185 Adrian Orange & Her Band *Adrian Orange & Her Band*

KLP 186 The Pine Hill Haints *Ghost Dance*

KLP 187 Jeremy Jay *A Place Where We Could Go*

KLP 188 Tender Forever *Wider*

KLP 189 Jason Anderson *The Hopeful and the Unafraid*

KLP 190 The Microphones *"The Glow" Pt. 2*

KLP 191 Mahjongg *Kontpab*

KLP 192 Karl Blau *Nature's Got Away*

KLP 193 Kimya Dawson And Friends *Alphabutt*

KLP 194 Wallpaper *On The Chewing Gum Ground*

KLP 195 Mirah *(a)spera*

KLP 196 LAKE *Oh, the Places We'll Go*

KLP 197 Jeremy Jay *Slow Dance*

KLP 198 Desolation Wilderness *White Light Strobing*

KLP 199 Calvin Johnson solo album (unreleased)

KLP 200 Arrington De Dionyso *I See Beyond the Black Sun*

KLP 201 Britta Johnson *Share This Place* DVD

KLP 202 Jeremy Jay *Love Everlasting* 12"

KLP 203 Chain And The Gang *Down with Liberty . . . Up with Chains!*

KLP 204 Desolation Wilderness *New Universe*

KLP 205 Karl Blau *Zebra*

KLP 206 The Curious Mystery *Rotting Slowly*

KLP 207 Tara Jane O'Neil *A Ways Away*

KLP 208 The Pine Hill Haints *To Win or to Lose*

KLP 209 Hornet Leg *Ribbon of Fear*

KLP 210 Maher Shalal Hash Baz *C'est La Dernière Chanson*

KLP 211 Rose Melberg *Homemade Ship*

KLP 212 Jeremy Jay *Dream Diary*

KLP 213 LAKE *Let's Build A Roof*

KLP 214 The Bundles *The Bundles*

KLP 215 Arrington De Dionyso *Malaikat Dan Singa*

KLP 216 Angelo Spencer et Les Hauts *Sommets Angelo Spencer et Les Hauts Sommets*

KLP 217 Tender Forever *No Snare*

KLP 218 Jeremy Jay *Splash*

KLP 219 Mahjongg *The Long Shadow of the Paper Tiger*

KLP 220 Chain & the Gang *Music's Not for Everyone*

KLP 221 Electric Sunset *Electric Sunset*

KLP 222 Mirah *Gone Are All the Days Remixes* Maxi Single

KLP 223 The Hive Dwellers *Get In* 12"

KLP 224 Kendl Winter *Apple Core*

KLP 225 The Curious Mystery *We Creeling*

KLP 226 Arrington De Dionyso's Malaikat Dan Singa *Suara Naga*

KLP 227 Karl Blau *Max*

KLP 228 LAKE *Giving & Receiving*

KLP 230 Eprhyme *Dopestylevsky*

KLP 231 City Center *Redeemer*

KLP 232 Joey Casio *Daybreak*

KLP 233 Nucular Aminals *Nucular Aminals*

KLP 234 Tara Jane O'Neil *Tara Jane O'Neil and Nikaido Kazumi*

KLP 235 Angelo Spencer *World Garage*

KLP 236 Pine Hill Haints *Welcome to the Midnight Opry*

KLP 237 Tender Forever *Where We Are From*

KLP 238 Kendl Winter *The Mechanics of Hovering Flight*

KLP 239 Ruby Fray *Pith*

KLP 240 Chain and the Gang *In Cool Blood*

KLP 241 The Hive Dwellers *Hewn From the Wilderness*

SOURCES

BOOKS

Andersen, Mark, and Mark Jenkins. *Dance of Days: Two Decades of Punk in the Nation's Capital.* New York: Akashic Books, 2009.

Azerrad, Michael. *Our Band Could Be Your Life: Scenes from the American Indie Underground 1981–1991.* New York: Back Bay Books/Little, Brown and Company, 2001.

Cobain, Kurt. *Kurt Cobain Journals.* New York: Riverhead Books, 2002.

Cross, Charles R. *Heavier Than Heaven: A Biography of Kurt Cobain.* New York: Hyperion, 2001.

Gray, Marcus. *The Clash: Return of the Last Gang in Town.* Milwaukee, Wisconsin: Hal Leonard, 2004.

Maffeo, Lois. *Crashing Through.* Olympia, Washington: K Records, 2002.

Meltzer, Marisa. *Girl Power: The Nineties Revolution in Music.* New York: Faber and Faber, Inc., 2010.

Oakes, Kaya. *Slanted and Enchanted: The Evolution of Indie Culture.* New York: Holt Paperbacks, 2009.

Sandford, Christopher. *Kurt Cobain.* Cambridge, Massachusetts: Da Capo Press, 1995.

True, Everett. *Nirvana: The Biography.* Cambridge, Massachusetts: Da Capo Press, 2007.

MULTIMEDIA

Clark, Tex. *Radical Act.* DVD. Directed by Tex Clark. Portland, Oregon: A Million Movies a Minute, 2010.

Dominic, Heather Rose. *The Shield Around the K.* DVD. Directed by Heather Rose Dominic. Bloomington, Indiana: Blank Stare Films, 2006.

Jensen, Rich. "Episode 1: This Time Let's Do It Right." Produced by Rich Jensen and Amber Cortes. Seattle, WA: Hollow Earth Radio, 2011.

Mitchell, Justin. *Songs for Cassavetes: An All-Ages Film*. DVD. Directed by Justin Mitchell. The Breadcrumb Trail, 2001.

Svenonious, Ian. *Calvin Johnson*. Streaming. Directed by Ian Svenonious. New York: VBS IPTV, 2008.

Wilson, Chris. *Do It Yourself: The Story of Rough Trade*. Broadcast. Directed by Chris Wilson. London: Prospect Pictures, March 13, 2009.

ARTICLES

Abebe, Nitsuh. "Twee as Fuck." *Pitchfork*, October 24, 2005.

Kanner, Bernice. "Up From Down Under." *New York*, March 21, 1988.

Maffeo, Lois. "Fascist Bully: Henry Rollins." *The Stranger,* April 1, 1999.

Nelson, Chris. "The Day the Music Didn't Die." *Seattle Weekly*, August 8, 2001.

Neuman, Molly. "Bratmobile/Heavens To Betsy U.S. tour June 1992 Pt. 1 Olympia-SF." *Punk Tour Blog*, October 2, 2008.

Neuman, Molly. "Bratmobile/Heavens To Betsy U.S. tour June 1992 Pt. 2 Sacramento/SLC." *Punk Tour Blog*, October 3, 2008.

Nichols, Travis. "A punk-rock legend is back from serious injury with a new intensity." *Seattle Post-Intelligencer*, February 18, 2008.

Ragland, Cathy. "Pop Underground Acts Convene for the Fun of It." *The Seattle Times*, August 16, 1991.

Robbins, Ira. "The Alternative Underground." *Rolling Stone*, October 17, 1991.

Roberts, Roxanne. "Here's One Too Cool Total Babe." *Washington Post*, September 22, 1990.

Staff, "Music Without Borders: KAOS and KXXO make local radio history." *Olympia Power & Light*, April 7, 2010.

Vail, Tobi. "Go Team West Coast Tour: November 87." *Punk Tour Blog*, October 4, 2008.

West, Phil. "Olympia's Original Riot Grrrl: Lois' New Album Benefits From Electric Sound." *The Seattle Times*, December 24, 1993.

White, Emily. "Revolution Girl-style Now!" *The Chicago Reader*, September 25, 1992.

WEBSITES

10 Things Zine (http://10thingszine.blogspot.com)

Beat Happening (http://ohnobeathappening.tumblr.com)

Billboard (www.billboard.com)

Discogs (www.discogs.com/label/K)

Ear Candy (http://earcandy_mag.tripod.com)

Gig Posters (www.gigposters.com)

Girl Trouble official website (www.wig-out.com)

K Staff Tumblr (http://krecs.tumblr.com)

Mecca Normal (http://meccanormal.wordpress.com)

Nirvana Live Guide (www.nirvanaguide.com)

Zinebook (www.zinebook.com)

ZINES

Bikini Kill

Chainsaw

Flipside

Girl Germs

jigsaw

K Newsletter

New York Rocker

OP Magazine

Paranoid

Puncture

The Rocket

sand

Subterranean Pop

Writer's Block

ACKNOWLEDGMENTS

WHEN I FIRST CALLED Calvin Johnson and told him I wanted to write a book about K Records, he considered the prospect silently for a few moments before responding, "That sounds like a really boring book." When I assured him that I was certain it wouldn't be, he replied that he didn't "know anyone who would read that book." So, first, I would like to thank you for proving him wrong. And, second, I would like to thank Calvin for helping me overcome my doubts by forcing me to focus on my hopes. I think it worked out.

The many other people I interviewed also deserve thanks, both for living adventurously creative lives and for sharing them with me. In particular I am grateful to Candice Pedersen and Bret Lunsford for always providing me with a little bit more information when I needed it. To those with whom I spoke but did not quote in these pages, know that our time was not wasted. Your recollections and thoughts were essential to my understanding of this story, even if your words do not appear in it.

Thanks also to the entire editing and production team at Sasquatch Books, especially Whitney Ricketts for her faith in my abilities, and Kurt Stephan for his irrepressible enthusiasm and his deep knowledge of indie rock. My assistant Diana Le deserves unyielding praise (and deep sympathies) for transcribing the endless hours of interviews that made this book possible while restraining herself from throwing heavy things at me.

I would have never been able to write this story if not for my family raising me to recognize and respect the power, beauty, and fun of storytelling. I know that some of you might not make it all the way through this book, but I appreciate you trying.

And finally I would like to thank Paige Richmond for standing by me even when I was an unbearable crank. I love you, I love you, I love you . . .

INDEX

Photo by Hayley Young

ABOUT THE AUTHOR

MARK BAUMGARTEN is a Seattle-based writer who has covered music in the Pacific Northwest for the past decade. His work has appeared in *Willamette Week*, *The Village Voice*, *Seattle Weekly*, *Lost Cause*, and *City Arts* magazine, where he currently serves as editor at large. Read his past and future work at MarkSBaumgarten.com.